PHILOSOPHY FOR AS

Philosophy for AS is the core textbook for the new 2014 AQA Advanced Subsidiary Philosophy syllabus. Structured closely around the AQA specification this textbook covers the two units, Epistemology and Philosophy of Religion, in an engaging and student-friendly way. With chapters on 'How to do philosophy', exam preparation providing students with t' e b r   ls they need to succeed, and an extensive glossa y o support understanding, this book is the definitive textbook for students.

Each chapter includes

- explanation and commentary of the AQA anthology texts
- comprehension questions to test understanding
- discussion questions to generate evaluative argument
- 'going further' sections for advanced study
- cross-references to help students make connections
- bullet-point summaries of each topic.

The companion website hosts a wealth of further resources, including PowerPoint slides, flashcards, further reading, weblinks and handouts, all structured to accompany the textbook. It can be found at www.routledge.com/cw/alevelphilosophy.

Michael Lacewing is Senior Lecturer in Philosophy at Heythrop College, University of London. He is the founder of the company A Level Philosophy and a consultant on philosophy at A Level for the British Philosophical Association.

'*Philosophy for AS* maintains a sharp focus on the syllabus content, imbibing teachers with the confidence to know they are covering the required material at the appropriate depth. Michael Lacewing is adept at breaking down complex philosophical arguments and his approach directly embraces the spirit and ethos of the new specification. This new textbook will be a godsend to teachers and will provide inestimable help to students.'

Jane Ball, *Head of Philosophy, Peter Symonds College, UK*

'*Philosophy for AS* is an outstanding philosophy textbook that successfully manages to make the subject accessible without dumbing it down. The student will be left with a synoptic understanding of the issues along with an insight into how to do philosophy and how to write philosophically.'

Dr J.S. Green, *Head of Philosophy and Senior Sixth Form Tutor, Haberdashers' Aske's Boys' School, UK*

PHILOSOPHY FOR AS

Epistemology and Philosophy
of Religion

Michael Lacewing

Routledge
Taylor & Francis Group

LONDON AND NEW YORK

First published 2014
by Routledge
2 Park Square, Milton Park, Abingdon, Oxon OX14 4RN

Simultaneously published in the USA and Canada
by Routledge
711 Third Avenue, New York, NY 10017

Routledge is an imprint of the Taylor & Francis Group, an informa business

British Library Cataloguing in Publication Data
A catalogue record for this book is available from the British Library

Library of Congress Cataloging in Publication Data
Library of Congress data has been applied for

ISBN: 978-1-138-79393-4 (pbk)
ISBN: 978-1-135-75832-9 (ebk)

Typeset in Mixage
by Saxon Graphics Ltd, Derby

Printed and bound in Great Britain by
CPI Group (UK) Ltd, Croydon, CR0 4YY

CONTENTS

PERMISSIONS

Heythrop College

The Specialist Philosophy and Theology College
of the University of London

Heythrop is a specialist college of the University of London with one of the largest faculties in philosophy and theology in Britain. It offers a wide range of undergraduate and postgraduate degrees, and Heythrop students can choose to focus in areas such as ethics, politics and comparative religions, alongside philosophy and theology.

Since its foundation in 1614, Heythrop College has continued to attract some of the leading thinkers in their fields. With its small size of around 1,000 students, the College offers a high level of personal supervision, along with small group seminars and interactive lectures facilitated by a highly engaged student body.

Heythrop students have the advantage of belonging both to a friendly campus community and to the largest student body in the country through the University of London.

Visit www.heythrop.ac.uk to learn more about the college and the courses it offers.

INTRODUCTION

The AQA AS Level Philosophy aims to introduce you, as a student, to some key concepts and methods in philosophy, studied as an academic discipline. It raises two big philosophical questions: 'What can we know?' and 'Can the existence of God be proved?' It introduces you to philosophy by considering some of the very best attempts to answer these questions, the arguments of some of the very best philosophers in history as well as recent discussions.

One aim of this textbook is, of course, to cover the ideas and arguments that are on the syllabus. But it aims at more than that. First, it aims to show you *how* to do philosophy – not just to tell you, but to show you, what philosophical thinking and philosophical writing is like. This is important because the AS level aims to introduce the methods of philosophy, as well as the ideas. Second, it aims to get you *engaging* in the argument. The discussion is provocative and leaves many lines of thought hanging. So, for instance, you might come up with new objections or replies that haven't yet been discussed, or argue that a particular point is convincing or implausible. That's the idea. This textbook doesn't try to tell you what *should* be said, only (some of) what *could* be said. That leads to one important difference between this book and your essays. The book tries to be even-handed, and doesn't often draw firm conclusions. In your evaluative essays, you'll be expected to defend a particular point of view.

How to use this book

How to do philosophy

If you haven't done any philosophy before, you'll soon find that it involves reading and thinking in ways that can be quite different from how you normally read and think. In Chapter 1, I talk about what is involved in doing philosophy – how to reason, read, and write philosophically. Philosophy is all about reasoning and argument. So it is probably worth at least skimming the section on PHILOSOPHICAL ARGUMENT (p. 7) before going on to study Chapter 2. And it is worth having a look at the section on ENGAGING WITH THE TEXT (p. 15) to help you read this textbook. But Chapter 1 is intended as a resource to which you can return again and again, as and when you need to.

Each paragraph of Chapters 2 and 3 is intended to be taken as a thought to be considered, reread, and reflected on. *Philosophy needs to be read slowly, and more than once, to be understood*. You will probably find, in addition, that you are not able to completely understand a particular theory until you also understand rival theories that oppose it. And so, at the end of each major section (e.g. 'Perception'), you may feel that you need to return to earlier discussions, to think about them again in the light of what you learned later.

Following the syllabus

Epistemology is covered in Chapter 2 and philosophy of religion in Chapter 3. Each chapter opens with a brief synopsis of what the chapter covers and what you should be able to do by the end of it. This is followed by the AQA syllabus, which I have structured by topic and subtopic. The bullet points from the syllabus are used to structure the discussion, with each section further divided by the main ideas, arguments and objections. The table of contents, with its many headings and subheadings, shows how each part relates to the others. There is also an INDEX BY SYLLABUS CONTENT on p. 306, which provides the page numbers on which each bullet point of the syllabus is discussed.

Additional features

Alongside the text, there are a number of features in the margin. Most commonly, there are questions that test your understanding and cross-references to other relevant discussions and ideas. To get the most out of the book, stop and answer the questions – in your own words – as you go along. The questions are the kinds that you'll find on the exam, so it is good practice for that. It is also worth following up cross-references, especially when you have read, but forgotten, the sections referred to. Understanding philosophy is often about being able to make connections. Also in the margin are occasional illustrations; definitions of technical terms; and references to philosophical texts where the argument being discussed can be found.

You'll frequently come across sections called 'Going Further'. These discuss more difficult ideas or take the arguments further. So they will broaden and deepen your knowledge, and help you 'go further' in your evaluation of the theories and arguments.

At the end of each main section covering a theory or debate, there is a list of 'Key Points', summarising clearly the main issues the section has covered. And at the end of each topic, there is a 'Summary' in the form of a list of questions, to show what issues have been addressed. Both the Key Points and the Summary should help with exam revision and testing your knowledge.

Using the anthology

The syllabus includes a list of texts. Many of the arguments identified in the syllabus content come from these texts. You aren't expected to read all the texts (though it would be good to try to read some of them), but you are expected to understand and be able to evaluate the arguments they discuss. To help with this, you'll find these texts and the arguments they present discussed in 'Anthology' boxes. All the texts listed in the syllabus are discussed at some point, and they are included in the index by syllabus content, so you can look up the discussion of any text in order of author.

Where the syllabus identifies a particular edition of a text, in print or online, I have used that edition for page numbers and quotations. Where the syllabus doesn't specify a particular edition, then I have indicated the edition or online source that I have used.

Glossary

The glossary provides brief definitions for an extensive list of terms. We have included terms that have a technical philosophical use, that identify an important philosophical concept, or that name a theory, argument or objection. While such terms are explained in the text, if you can't understand or remember the explanation, use the glossary to help you. It should also prove a useful resource for revision.

Companion website and further resources

You can find further resources supporting the study of AQA Philosophy on the Routledge companion website, www.routledge.com/cw/alevelphilosophy. The resources include

1. handouts based on this text, including material on philosophical skills, revision and exam technique
2. PowerPoint presentations
3. further-reading lists
4. helpful weblinks
5. flashcards, for revising and testing your knowledge of philosophical terms and the names of theories and objections
6. the AQA list of texts with links where provided, and
7. an additional chapter providing commentary on Descartes' *Meditations*, which the syllabus identifies as a key text for the A Level as a whole.

Acknowledgements

Thanks to Rebecca Shillabeer, Tony Bruce and Emma Hudson at Routledge for supporting this textbook and producing it in record time, and to my colleagues at Heythrop College for supporting my work with A Level philosophy. Thanks also to the AQA subject team for answering a number of queries on the interpretation of the syllabus. And a special thanks goes to Joanne Lovesey for her stellar work on compiling the glossary.

HOW TO DO PHILOSOPHY

1

Philosophy is thinking in slow motion.

(John Campbell)

This chapter covers three skills that you need to do philosophy well: reasoning (or argument), reading and writing. You may want to skim through at the least the first section on argument before beginning Chapter 2, but without actually *doing* some philosophy, this chapter may be a little too abstract to understand completely. So perhaps come back to it when you need to.

Philosophical argument

At the heart of philosophy is philosophical argument. Arguments are different from assertions. Assertions are simply stated; arguments always involve giving reasons. An argument is a reasoned inference from one set of claims – the premises – to another claim, the conclusion. The premises provide reasons to believe that the conclusion is true. If the premises are true, the conclusion is more likely to be true. Arguments seek to 'preserve truth' – true premises will lead to a true conclusion. It is worth knowing a little bit more about arguments straightaway.

Deductive argument

Philosophers distinguish between two types of argument – deductive and inductive. Successful deductive arguments are *valid* – if the premises are true, then the conclusion *must* be true. In this case, we say that the conclusion is entailed by the premises. Here is a famous example:

- Premise 1: Socrates is a man.
- Premise 2: All men are mortal.
- Conclusion: Socrates is mortal.

A valid deductive argument with true premises is called *sound*. But a valid deductive argument doesn't have to have true premises. Here is an example:

- Premise 1: There are gnomes in my house.
- Premise 2: My house is in Oxford.
- Conclusion: Therefore, there are gnomes in Oxford.

If the premises are true, then the conclusion must be true – so the argument is valid. But the premises aren't both true.

There are two ways that a deductive argument can 'go wrong'. First, it could be *invalid*: even if the premises are true, it is possible that the conclusion might be false. Second, it could be *unsound*: even though the conclusion is entailed by the premises, at least one of the premises is false.

> Give an example of a) an invalid argument; b) a valid argument with false premises; and c) a sound argument.

Inductive argument

A successful inductive argument is an argument whose conclusion is supported by its premises. If the premises are true, the conclusion is *likely* to be true, but it is still possible that the conclusion is false. So inductive arguments are not described as 'valid' or 'sound'.

But they can also go wrong in just two ways. First, the premises might not make the conclusion more likely – they don't offer good reasons for believing the conclusion is true. Second, one of the premises may be false.

> Explain and illustrate the difference between inductive and deductive arguments.

One type of induction is induction through enumeration, as in this famous example:

- Premise 1: This swan is white.
- Premise 2: This other swan is white.
- Premise 3: That third swan is white.
- …
- Premise 500: That swan is white as well.
- Conclusion: All swans are white.

The example shows that an inductive argument can be a good argument, but the conclusion can still be false!

Hypothetical reasoning

There are other types of inductive argument, e.g. hypothetical reasoning. In hypothetical reasoning, we try to work out the best hypothesis that would explain or account for some experience or fact.

> A hypothesis is a proposal that needs to be confirmed or rejected by reasoning or experience.

Medical diagnosis provides an example – what would explain exactly *this* set of symptoms? This isn't a matter of comparing this case with other cases which all have exactly the same symptoms. There may only be some overlap or the case might involve some complication, such as more than one disease being involved. We use hypothetical reasoning – if such-and-such were true (e.g. the patient has disease *x*), would that explain the evidence we have? The evidence supplies the premises of the argument, and the conclusion is that some hypothesis is true because it accounts for the evidence.

When we are using hypothetical reasoning, it is not usually enough to find some hypothesis that can explain the evidence. We want to find the *best* hypothesis. What makes a hypothesis a *good* hypothesis? Philosophers have argued for several criteria.

1. Simplicity: the best-known is probably Ockham's razor, which says 'Don't multiply entities beyond necessity'. Don't put forward a hypothesis that says many different things exist when a simpler explanation will do as well. A simpler explanation is a

better explanation, as long as it is just as successful. For example, the explanation that plants flower in the spring in response to an increase in light and temperature is a better explanation than saying that they flower in the spring because that's when the fairies wake them up. The second explanation is committed to the existence of fairies – and we shouldn't think that fairies exist unless there is something we cannot explain without thinking they exist.

2. Accuracy: a good hypothesis fits the evidence that we are trying to explain.
3. Plausibility: a good hypothesis fits with what else we already know.
4. Scope: a good hypothesis explains a wide range of evidence.
5. Coherence: a good hypothesis draws and explains connections between different parts of the evidence.

What makes a good hypothesis?

The best hypothesis will be the hypothesis that demonstrates all these virtues to a higher degree than alternative hypotheses. A lot of philosophy involves arguing about which theory provides the best hypothesis to account for our experience.

Understanding arguments

See UNDERSTANDING THE QUESTION, p. 272.

Understanding arguments is central to doing philosophy well. That is why throughout this book, you will be asked to outline and explain arguments. You'll be asked to do so in the exam, in 5- and 9-mark questions.

Understanding an argument involves identifying the conclusion, identifying the premises, and understanding how the premises are supposed to provide reasons for believing the conclusion. Use linguistic clues, like 'since', 'because', 'if ... then ... ' and many others, to help you do this. It is also important to distinguish between what someone supposes for the purposes of argument, and what they actually want to assert.

Many arguments involve quite a complex structure, with some premises establishing an initial conclusion, which is then used as a premise to establish a second conclusion. In coming to understand an argument, it can be very helpful to create an *argument map*. This is a visual diagram of how the argument works. For example,

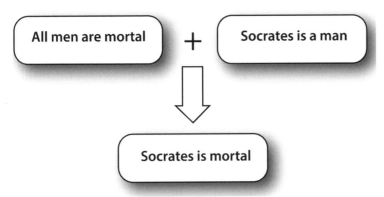

Figure 1.1 An argument map

Evaluating arguments

When you evaluate an argument, you are yourself *making* an argument. You are arguing that the argument evaluated is either a good or bad argument. In other words, the conclusion of your evaluation is that the argument evaluated is a good/bad argument, and you have to provide reasons to support this claim. There are three types of reason you can give, three different ways of evaluating arguments:

1. As already stated above, you can argue that one or more of the premises is false. If you are right, then the argument does not give you a reason to believe the conclusion, because it rests on a false premise.
2. As also already stated above, you can argue that the conclusion does not follow from the premises. If you are evaluating a deductive argument, you are claiming that the argument is not valid. If you are evaluating an inductive argument, you are claiming that the premises do not provide a (good or strong) reason to believe the conclusion. For example, with inferring the best hypothesis, you could argue that the conclusion is not the best explanation for the premises, e.g. that it isn't plausible

or simple, or at least that the argument doesn't show that it is, e.g. there may be other explanations that haven't been considered.

3. You can also evaluate the formal features of an argument. Without worrying about whether it is true, you can ask whether it is clear, whether the premises are relevant to the conclusion, whether the support offered by the premises has been demonstrated, and so on. You may want to offer an improvement on the argument, e.g. rephrasing it to be clearer, supplying missing premises, identifying assumptions, and so on.

Evaluating claims

In addition to evaluating arguments, you can evaluate claims on their own. In evaluating a claim, you provide an argument for thinking that it is true or false.

For any claim C (e.g. 'God exists'), there are four related ways of discussing it, as shown in this diagram:

C is true: God exists	C is false: God does not exist
1 Arguments for C being true	2 Arguments for C being false
3 Objections to arguments for C being false	4 Objections to arguments for C being true

When you are arguing for or against a claim, don't overstate your case. Your claim is only as strong as the reasons that you can provide for it.

In 15-mark questions, you are typically asked to evaluate a claim. You need to break this down into a series of arguments and their evaluation (discussed below in WRITING PHILOSOPHY, p. 17). After you've explained the claim, for each section of the answer, you should consider an argument for or against the claim, objections to that argument, and possible responses. You'll also need to indicate how *strong* you think the argument is, and weigh up the strengths of the arguments for the claim against the strengths of the arguments against. This isn't a matter of 'comparing strengths and weaknesses' on the page, but identifying what you think the *really important and critical* arguments or objections are. This is, of course, something that you need to argue for!

See UNDERSTANDING THE QUESTION, p. 272.

An aside: why reason?

Why, you may wonder, should we place so much importance on reasoning in this way? Is it worth it? Here are four quick reasons in favour of reasoning:

1. To discover the truth
2. To uncover poor reasoning, e.g. fallacies (see below) and sophistry
3. To recognise when, where, and how a dialogue ceases to be reasonable or instructive
4. To probe both sides of a controversial issue in a sensitive and intelligent way.

Can I justify these claims? If I present an argument in favour of reasoning, then I'm using reasoning to justify reasoning, which is circular. Then again, if you object to reasoning for this reason, you are using reasoning to make your objection! An alternative justification of reason is to check the results of reasoning by a different method. Science does this all the time by hypothesis and observation. In many cases, we can confirm, by observation, that the conclusion of a piece of reasoning is correct. Some people are sceptical about reasoning or claim, for example, that all beliefs are equally 'reasonable'. For an excellent discussion dismantling this view, see Stephen Law's *Believing Bullshit*, Ch. 4.

To criticise an argument or claim is not necessarily to reject it. You can be concerned to reject bad reasons because you want to find stronger ones! To show respect to someone does not require that you agree with them. Taking someone else's thought seriously – so seriously that you test it rigorously in your mind – is to pay them a compliment.

It is important to remember that the *point* of philosophical argument is not personal victory.

Fallacies

A fallacy, as philosophers use the word, is not a mistake of fact or truth. A fallacy is an error in reasoning. More exactly, it is an argument in which the premises do not offer rational support to the conclusion. If the argument is deductive, then it is fallacious if it is not valid. If the argument is inductive, it is fallacious if the premises do not make the conclusion more likely to be true.

There are many types of fallacy; the *Nizkor Project* lists 42, *Changing Minds* 53, and *Wikipedia* over 100. It's good to become familiar with some of the main types. If you do, it is really important to understand *why* the fallacy is a fallacy.

Spotting fallacies has two purposes: 1) evaluating the strength of an argument and 2) improving it. When learning how to spot fallacies, try to develop the skill of how you would reformulate the argument to avoid it. It is not always clear-cut whether a fallacy is being committed or not, and the answer depends on just how the premises are being deployed or further assumptions being made. The question is always ultimately about the strength of support the premises offer.

To learn how to avoid fallacies in your own work, it can be helpful to learn first how to spot them! Fallacies are always easier to spot in someone else's work, so start with people you don't know, then look at the work of other students, then try to spot them in your own work.

See 'Fallacies', at www. nizkor.org/features/ fallacies/; 'Fallacies: alphabetic list (unique)', at http:// changingminds.org/ disciplines/argument/ fallacies/fallacies_ unique.htm; and 'List of fallacies', at http://en. wikipedia.org/wiki/ List_of_fallacies

Reading philosophy

The syllabus includes a list of books and articles to read and think about. Reading philosophical texts is challenging, especially if you haven't read any philosophy before. You may not know much about the background of the text – when was it written and why? The form of the text is difficult – there can be long and complicated arguments, unfamiliar words, an unusual style of language from hundreds of years ago, and abstract ideas. It is unclear just how the text should be interpreted, and commentaries on the texts often disagree. The first thing to remember, then, is that it is *normal* to feel confused and challenged.

What can help? Here are some suggestions.

Approaching the text

For these first three points, you'll need to use a commentary on the text, or an introduction:

1. Contextualise: it can help to set the scene, but this shouldn't be restricted to a historical understanding. An awareness of central ideas is useful.
2. Identify what philosophical *problems* the text addresses.
3. Get an overview: look at the title, introductory and concluding paragraphs, and the chapter and section headings. Knowing the conclusion does not ruin the text (it isn't a detective story). Understanding the structure can help fit different arguments and claims together.

These next three points are about how to interact with the text:

4. For long texts, don't feel the need to start at the beginning. Start with what will best get you into the thinking of the author, e.g. connections to previous topics, points of interest, etc.
5. Don't get bogged down in details: reading the text more than once is helpful and often necessary. Read it quickly first, noting the main points, skimming what is most unclear; then read it again more closely.
6. Distinguish the text from secondary interpretation: for example, knowing what other people said Descartes said is not knowing what Descartes said.

Engaging with the text

1. Read slowly and actively: philosophy should not be read like fiction or even most non-fiction. Go slowly, take notes, and constantly question not only whether you've understood what the author is trying to say, but also whether what s/he says is true, and whether the arguments support the conclusions.
2. Look for signposts: sentences that indicate what the text is about, what has been, is being, or will be argued.

3. Ask what the passage of text offers: a new concept, a framework for understanding an issue, an argument for a conclusion?
4. Argument mapping: find the arguments. Identify premises, inferences, and conclusions. Break arguments down into steps (there can be many interim conclusions).
5. Don't be afraid to challenge: try to find inconsistencies in the text, but also try to find ways to interpret the text to remove the inconsistencies.
6. Ask what interpretation best fits the purpose of the author. Does an interpretation presuppose ideas that were not available to the author?
7. Know the point of any example used: examples can seize the imagination and memory, but knowing its purpose and what it is supposed to show is central to understanding the text.
8. Look up key words in a dictionary of philosophy: don't be lazy, and don't use a normal dictionary (for philosophical words) as they won't capture or explain the relevant sense.

Beyond the text

1. Visualise: if you put the text, or the arguments within it, into some other visual form, that can help generate understanding.
2. Use secondary sources carefully: always question the authority of secondary sources, and always go back to the text.
3. Find different ways to think about and interact with the text. These will help you understand more than if you simply read it. For example, you might want to
   a. practise precis (either rewrite a passage more briefly in your own words or, if you have the text electronically, try deleting words while retaining the argument);
   b. rewrite a passage of the text in a different genre (e.g. a detective story);
   c. select quotations that make important points (good for revision);
   d. mark up the text for premises, conclusions, linguistic clues, etc.;
   e. do some argument mapping.

Writing philosophy

What you need to know

Different types of knowledge are needed to do well in philosophy. Each is tested by different types of question on the exam. The 2-mark questions ask you to define a term. The 5-mark questions ask you to outline and explain an argument for an important philosophical idea. The 9-mark questions ask you to explain a longer or more complex argument. The 15-mark questions ask you to evaluate a claim.

See UNDERSTANDING THE QUESTION, p. 272.

1. *Understanding what the question is asking*: For each type of question, you need to understand what the question is asking you to *do*. So you need to know the difference between a definition, an outline, an explanation, and what is needed for an evaluative essay.
2. *Knowledge of the issue*: You need to understand the relevant concept, argument or claim. Evaluating claims is most complex. You'll need to know what the options are, the key arguments defending and attacking the claim, the theories that philosophers have defended that pull different arguments and claims together into a coherent whole.
3. *Structure of arguments*: Knowing how an argument works (or doesn't) is more than knowing the conclusion and the premises used; it is understanding *how* the premises are supposed to connect together to support the conclusion. With your own arguments, you equally need to understand how they work, and you should present them with a clear structure.
4. *Relevance*: A good part of philosophical skill is a matter of selecting ideas, concepts, examples and arguments that you encountered in the material you studied that are relevant to the question. Knowing what is relevant is a special kind of knowledge, which involves thinking carefully about what you know about arguments and theories in relation to the question asked.

5. *Critical discussion*: When you evaluate a claim (15-mark questions), it is important to know that *presenting* ideas is distinct from *critically discussing* those ideas. You need to understand whether an argument succeeds or fails and why, and be able to present and compare arguments and counter-arguments to argue towards the most plausible position. You will usually need to draw on more than one source or author, and above all *think*.

Planning an essay

When you are answering a 2-, 5- or 9-mark question, what you need to do is straightforward. You don't need to make any choices about *what* concepts or arguments to talk about, since that is specified by the question. You should still organise your thoughts before writing. But essays – both coursework essays and answers to 15-mark exam questions – need to be planned in more detail.

1. Take time to understand the question in detail. This includes understanding what *kind* of question it is. Exam questions tend to be straightforward, but teachers ask all kinds of questions (explain and critically discuss, compare two positions, apply a theory to an example). Most weak essays are weak because they fail to answer the actual question.
2. Keep the question in mind throughout writing, to ensure that your thought and planning stay relevant. Someone should be able to tell from the essay itself what question it is answering.
3. If it is appropriate, think about challenging the question. Does it make assumptions that can be questioned?
4. Brainstorm to generate ideas of what you might discuss. (In an exam, recall the relevant revision plan.) One way is through 'successive elaboration' – take a single-sentence statement of a position, and then make it more detailed, e.g. by providing some premises, then think what would be necessary to establish the premises, etc. Another is 'conceptual note-taking', simply writing what comes to mind: even starting from 'I don't know anything about *x*' suggests and leads to others, such as 'I don't

know what *x* means' and 'So and so defines *x* as … '. Half-formed thoughts are better developed when out on the page.

5. If you are researching the essay, start by making the relevant ideas familiar, but make decisions on what to concentrate on, and narrow your research to achieve depth in a few central areas.

6. An essay needs shape, it is always directed towards a conclusion, so you'll need to decide what to include and what to leave out.

7. Don't aim to cover too much; three main arguments is usually enough. Even fewer can be fine if you go into real depth.

8. Plan an essay that argues for a particular position. You will often want to argue for or against a specific claim (as in a debate). But you don't have to. For example, you can argue that we can't know either way. Whatever your conclusion (your position), you'll need to defend it. Have it in mind throughout the plan and writing. The essay should read like one long argument (taking in various smaller arguments, objections and replies) for your conclusion.

9. The evaluative discussion is the most important part of the essay, so only introduce and explain material that you will use in discussion. You can think of this as two halves: the arguments in favour of your conclusion; and the objections to your arguments, or separate arguments against your conclusion, and replies to them. Make sure you consider the objections and counter-arguments – avoid being one-sided!

10. In light of all of the above points, write a plan which includes key points (definitions, arguments, objections, etc.) and the paragraph structure.

11. Each paragraph presents an idea. Paragraphs should not be divided on *length*, but as 'units of thought'. If you made a one-sentence summary of each paragraph, would the resulting account of the essay read logically?

Writing an essay

Once again, I'll just provide some advice on the most difficult writing task, the essay:

1. Plan the essay. It is very rare that good philosophical essays are written 'off the cuff', taking each thought as it occurs to you in turn. An essay is not (just) a test of memory, but of intelligence, which includes organisation and clarity.

2. However, new ideas will probably occur as you write. It is fine to deviate from the plan, but think through new ideas before incorporating them to make sure they are good and to structure them.

3. The usual starting point for constructing an argument is explaining other people's ideas. The idea here is to be *accurate* and *sympathetic*. An argument works best when the ideas are presented as strongly as possible – otherwise the opponent can simply rephrase the idea, and your counter-argument falls apart.

4. In general, aim to be concise. Present the kernel of the idea clearly and relevantly. Stick to what you need to present in order to properly discuss the question. This can involve surrounding detail, since you need to show an awareness of the situation of the topic in the subject. But be selective and relevant.

5. Never just *report* or *allude to* the arguments you have read – *make* the argument. To use a metaphor from war, you are not a reporter at the front line, but a combatant engaged for one side or the other.

6. Use the three-part structure: make a point, back it up, show its relevance.

7. In critical discussion, reflect on what a particular argument actually demonstrates, and whether there are counter-arguments that are better. You should be able to argue both for and against a particular view. Relate these arguments to each other, evaluating which is stronger and why. You need to work at shaping the material and 'generating a discussion'.

8. Alternatively, you may want to relate a particular argument to a broader context, e.g. a philosopher's overall theory, other philosophers' ideas on the same issue, etc. – in general, work to understand the relation between the parts and the whole.

9. Understand and be careful about the strength of your assertions. It is important to know whether your arguments indicate that all, some, most, or typically ... (e.g. beliefs are unjustified,

design arguments are flawed, etc.) and to distinguish between whether this *is* so or simply *may be* so.

10. Never introduce new material in the conclusion. The conclusion should reflect the argument of the essay. Don't feel you have to personally agree with your conclusion! Essays are not confessions of belief.

11. In an exam setting, you also need to keep note of the time, and leave time to review and correct what you've written.

A standard essay structure

1. Introduction: how you understand the question, what you'll argue for (and perhaps some indication of how you will discuss the question)

2. An explanation of the claim to be evaluated, perhaps including some of the relevant background theory, and either including or followed by …

3. The arguments in favour of the claim (give the arguments, and if you think they work, argue that the reasoning is valid and the premises are true)

4. Objections to these arguments and replies to the objections

5. Arguments against the claim

6. Objections to these arguments

7. Conclusion: a clear statement showing how the claim is supported/defeated by the arguments discussed. This will require you to make some points, either as you go along or in the conclusion, about which arguments or objections are strongest and why.

> **Alternatively, you may consider objections to each argument (in 3) in turn as you consider the argument.**

General advice

When doing coursework essays:

1. Do not wait until you have finished your research to start writing the essay. If you find, as your research continues, that someone else has written what you've written, then reference it; if you

find an objection, then explain it and explain why it is wrong, or, if the objection persuades you, rewrite what you've written as 'one might think …' and use the objection to show why it is wrong.

2. Rewrite the essay – almost no one does themselves justice in one draft.

3. Quotations do not substitute for understanding. Use them when you want to illustrate the precise wording of an idea or back up an interpretation.

4. Don't plagiarise.

In both coursework and exam essays:

5. Be precise, especially with words that have a philosophical meaning, like 'valid', 'assume', 'infer'.

6. Be clear. Being vague gives the reader the sense that you don't really know what you are talking about. Don't hide behind long words or technical terms – it rarely impresses people who understand them. Define technical terms and ordinary words that have a non-standard, philosophical meaning.

7. Don't use long and involved sentences. Use active, not passive, constructions, e.g. 'Plato argued …' not 'It was argued by Plato …'.

8. Include signposts. Generally speaking, the first sentence of a paragraph should give some indication to a reader as to where you are in the argument (e.g. 'A second criticism of the argument that …).

9. While it is acceptable to use the first person ('I'), this should not be to say 'I feel …' or 'I think …' or 'In my opinion …' as though such an assertion adds any weight to the plausibility of the conclusion. The whole essay is what you think, however it is phrased.

EPISTEMOLOGY

2

What can we know? And how do we know what we know? These questions are central to the branch of philosophy called epistemology. At its heart are two very important, very interesting questions about being human: how are human beings 'hooked up' to the world? And what 'faculties' do we have that enable us to gain knowledge?

In this chapter, we will look at three issues. The first is perception. A quick, common-sense answer of how we are 'hooked up' to the world is this: the world is made up of physical objects that exist outside, and independently of, our minds. We discover this physical world and gain knowledge about it through our senses (vision, hearing, touch, etc.). In other words, we perceive it. But is this right? What is the best account of perception? Does it, in fact, give us knowledge of a physical world that exists independent of our minds? We will see that the common-sense picture gets complicated very quickly.

The second part of the chapter steps back from the question of how we know, to ask what knowledge is. We will look at a famous definition of knowledge that was widely accepted from almost the beginnings of philosophy in Plato until 1963, when Edmund Gettier published a paper that showed that the definition was wrong. We will discuss some of the different responses to Gettier's argument.

In the third part of chapter, we return to the question of what and how we know. We start again from the

Epistemology is the study (-*ology*) of knowledge (*episteme*) and related concepts, including belief, justification, certainty. It looks at the possibility and sources of knowledge.

common-sense idea that we gain our knowledge through our senses. We then ask whether there are any *other* ways by which we acquire knowledge. This will lead us to talk about different kinds of knowledge (a priori/a posteriori) and different kinds of truth claim (analytic/synthetic, necessary/contingent). We end with a related discussion about how we acquire our concepts.

By the end of the chapter, you should be able to analyse, explain, and evaluate a number of arguments for and objections to theories about perception, about what knowledge is, and whether we gain concepts and knowledge only through sense experience or in other ways as well.

SYLLABUS CHECKLIST

The AQA AS syllabus for this chapter is:

I. Perception: *what are the immediate objects of perception?*

A. Direct realism:
✔ the immediate objects of perception are mind-independent objects and their properties.

Issues, including:
✔ the argument from illusion
✔ the argument from perceptual variation (Russell's table example)
✔ the argument from hallucinations (the possibility of experiences that are subjectively indistinguishable from a veridical perception)
✔ the time-lag argument.

B. Indirect realism:

✔ the immediate objects of perception are mind-dependent objects that are caused by and represent mind-independent objects.

Issues, including:

✔ it leads to scepticism about the existence of the external world (attacking 'realism')
- ● responses:
  - ○ external world is the 'best hypothesis' (Russell)
  - ○ coherence of the various senses (Locke)
  - ○ lack of choice over our experiences (Locke)
✔ it leads to scepticism about the nature of the external world (attacking 'representative')
- ● responses:
  - ○ sense-data tell us of 'relations' between objects (Russell)
  - ○ the distinction between primary and secondary qualities (Locke)
- ● problems arising from the view that mind-dependent objects represent mind-independent objects and are caused by mind-independent objects.

C. Berkeley's idealism:

✔ the immediate objects of perception (i.e. ordinary objects such as tables, chairs, etc.) are mind-dependent objects
- ● Berkeley's attack on the primary/secondary property distinction
- ● Berkeley's 'master' argument.

Issues, including:

✔ it leads to solipsism
✔ it does not give an adequate account of illusions and hallucinations
✔ it cannot secure objective space and time
✔ whether God can be used to play the role He does.

II. The definition of knowledge: *what is propositional knowledge?*

A. Terminology:

✔ distinction between: acquaintance knowledge, ability knowledge and propositional knowledge (knowing 'of', knowing 'how' and knowing 'that').

B. The tripartite view:

✔ justified, true belief is necessary and sufficient for propositional knowledge

- S knows that p only if S is justified in believing that p, p is true and S believes that p

✔ necessary and sufficient conditions.

Issues, including:

✔ the conditions are not individually necessary:

- justification is not a necessary condition of knowledge
- truth is not a necessary condition of knowledge
- belief is not a necessary condition of knowledge

✔ cases of lucky true beliefs show that the justification condition should be either strengthened, added to, or replaced (i.e. Gettier-style problems).

C. Responses:

✔ strengthen the justification condition: infallibilism and the requirement for an impossibility of doubt (Descartes)

✔ add a 'no false lemmas' condition (J+T+B+N)

✔ replace 'justified' with 'reliably formed' (R+T+B) (reliabilism)

✔ replace 'justified' with an account of epistemic virtue (V+T+B).

III. The origin of concepts and the nature of knowledge: *where do ideas/concepts and knowledge come from?*

A. Knowledge empiricism:

✔ all synthetic knowledge is a posteriori; all a priori knowledge is (merely) analytic (Hume's 'fork').

Issues, including:

✔ knowledge innatism (rationalism):
  ● there is at least some innate a priori knowledge (arguments from Plato and Leibniz)
  ● knowledge empiricist arguments against knowledge innatism:
    ○ alternative explanations (no such knowledge, in fact based on experiences or merely analytic)
    ○ Locke's arguments against innatism
    ○ its reliance on the non-natural
✔ intuition and deduction thesis (rationalism):
  ● we can gain synthetic a priori knowledge through intuition and deduction (Descartes on the existence of self, God and the external world)
  ● knowledge empiricist arguments against intuition and deduction:
    ○ the failure of the deductions or the analytically true (tautological) nature of the conclusions
✔ arguments against knowledge empiricism: the limits of empirical knowledge (Descartes' sceptical arguments).

B. Concept empiricism:

✔ all concepts are derived from experience
  ● *tabula rasa*
  ● impressions and ideas
  ● simple and complex concepts.

I have reversed the order of concept empiricism and knowledge empiricism for reasons that will become clear when we discuss CONCEPT EMPIRICISM, p. 132.

Issues, including:

✔ concept innatism (rationalism): there are at least some innate concepts

- Descartes' 'trademark' argument
- other proposed examples such as universals, causation, infinity, numbers etc.

✔ concept empiricist arguments against concept innatism:

- alternative explanations (no such concept or concept redefined as based on experiences)
- Locke's arguments against innatism
- its reliance on the non-natural.

I. PERCEPTION: what are the immediate objects of perception?

In this section, we will look at three theories of perception: direct realism, indirect realism, and idealism. By the end of the section, you should be able to demonstrate not just knowledge, but a good *understanding*, of each of the three theories, and be able to analyse, explain, and evaluate several arguments for and against each one.

The most obvious and immediate answer to the question 'how do we gain knowledge of what is outside our minds?' is 'sense experience'. Sense experiences are those given to us by our senses – sight, hearing, smell, taste, touch and bodily sensations. What can perception by sense experience tell us about the world? To answer this question, we will need to think carefully about what this kind of perception involves.

(We are not asking how we can know what is *inside* our minds. How do you know that you are thinking what you are thinking? How do you know that you are feeling pain when you are? These are interesting questions, but the answers, whatever they are, are not our concern here. We are asking about how we know what is outside our minds.)

We return to talking about sources of knowledge in KNOWLEDGE EMPIRICISM, p. 96.

Philosophers of perception divide into realists and idealists. Realists claim that what we perceive are physical objects, which exist independent of our minds and of our perceptions. Idealists argue that physical objects, at least in the sense that realists think of them, don't exist. What we perceive, they argue, are mental things – ideas of some kind (p. 58).

What does realism about perception claim?

The question of whether physical objects exist is actually a question in metaphysics, not epistemology. Metaphysics is the branch of philosophy that asks questions about the fundamental nature of reality. *Meta-* means above, beyond, or after; physics enquires into the physical structure of reality – but there may be more to understanding reality than what physics can explain. One question in metaphysics is 'what exists?' So the debate over perception deals with both epistemology (how do we know?) and some metaphysics (what exists?).

The study of what exists is called ontology (the study of (*-ology*) of what exists or 'being' (*ont-*)).

A. Direct realism

Direct realism is the natural starting point for theories of perception. It is common sense to say that we perceive physical objects, and these exist independently of our minds. 'Physical objects' include tables, books, our own bodies, plants, mountains. Cosmology and the theory of evolution suggest that physical objects, such as stars and planets, existed for billions of years before minds existed to experience them. It is part of our idea of physical objects that they exist objectively in space and time. They continue to exist when we don't perceive them. When I leave my study, all the physical objects – the desk, the chairs, the books, and so on – remain just as they are.

We could also call them 'material' objects. But physics shows that matter and energy are interchangeable. So 'physical objects' is better, because physics is the science that studies what such things are, ultimately, made of.

According to direct realism, what we perceive through our senses are just these very things, physical objects, together with their various properties. When I perceive my desk, for example, I perceive its size, shape, colour, smell and texture (I've never experienced its taste, but I could, I suppose!). So, direct realism claims that what we perceive are mind-independent physical objects and their properties.

What is direct realism?

The argument from perceptual variation

RUSSELL, *THE PROBLEMS OF PHILOSOPHY*, CH. 1

A little reflection suggests that what we perceive isn't quite the same as what is 'out there'. Russell uses the example of looking at a shiny, brown desk. We say it is brown, but it doesn't actually look an even colour all over: depending how the light falls, some parts are lighter than others, and some are even white from the shininess. So Russell objects that saying the table is brown means no more than that it looks brown 'to a normal spectator from an ordinary point of view under usual conditions of light' – but why think that this colour is more real, more *a property of the table*, than any of the other colours that you experience? Just what colour any part of the desk looks to you depends on where you stand. If you and someone else look at the table together, you will see different patterns of colour. Suppose a shiny spot on the table looks light brown to you but white to the other person. The table can't *be* both brown and white in the same spot at one time.

Russell then runs the same argument, appealing to variations in our perceptual experience, for the properties of texture and shape. The table might be smooth to touch, but at a microscopic level, there are all kinds of bumps and dips – so should we say that when we touch the table, the smoothness we feel is a property of the table? And the shape that something appears to have, like its colour, varies with the angle from which you view it. A rectangular table, from every angle except 90 degrees, does not *look* perfectly rectangular.

These examples draw our attention to a distinction between appearance and reality. Obviously, much of the time, we talk as though things are just as they seem. But, clearly, we also distinguish between appearance and reality – and Russell remarks that having any skill as a painter requires that one does.

All this perceptual variation causes a real problem for the direct realist. The direct realist says I perceive physical objects and their properties, in this case the desk, 'directly', as they are. Another way of putting this is to say that the *immediate object*

Locke makes a similar point, and explains why we don't normally notice this, in *An Essay concerning Human Understanding*, Bk 2, Ch. 9, §§8, 9

of perception is the physical object itself. The argument from perceptual variation runs like this:

1. There are variations in perception.
2. Our perception varies without corresponding changes in the physical object we perceive. (For instance, the desk remains rectangular, even as the way it looks to me changes as I look at it from different angles.)
3. Therefore, the properties physical objects have and the properties they appear to have are not identical.
4. Therefore, what we are immediately aware of in perception is *not* exactly the same as what exists independently of our minds.
5. Therefore, we do not perceive physical objects directly.

We now need a name for talking about what we are immediately aware of in perception, e.g. the colour and shape of the desk as I see it now. Russell calls these 'sense-data' (singular: 'sense-datum'). When I look at the desk, I have a (visual) sensation – I am immediately aware of something. The 'content' of my sensation – what I am immediately aware of – is sense-data (on Russell's view). We can also think of sense-data as appearances (how things appear to us to be).

Sense-data are distinct from the table. The table exists independently of my perception of it, while sense-data are defined as what it is that I perceive – so they depend on my perception. If I close my eyes, the colour and shape of the table *as seen by me*, cease to exist. And the colour and shape of the table *as seen by me* varies from where I look at it, while we don't want to say that the table itself varies in this way. We can summarise the argument so far by saying that perceptual variation shows that what we directly perceive are not physical objects, but sense-data.

Give your own example that supports the view that what we 'see' is not what is 'out there'.

For further discussion, see WHAT ARE SENSE-DATA?, p. 39.

Outline and explain the argument from perceptual variation as an objection to direct realism.

OBJECTIONS

We can challenge Russell's claim that there is no good reason to say that one of the colours we experience the table as having is more real than the others. As he notes, what we *mean* by the colour of an object is the colour that it appears to have when seen by normal observers under normal conditions. That we don't *always* see this colour – that our perception of its colour varies – doesn't show that direct realism is false: we can still say that we see the table, and its colour, under normal conditions. After all, we do all see it as some shade of *brown* (shading to white), rather than some of us seeing it as brown, others as red, others as blue. So, in seeing its colour (as some variant of brown), we see the desk and its properties.

With shape, we have an even better reason to privilege the claim that the desk is rectangular, rather than obtuse – we can use its shape to perform various actions, like getting it through a narrow doorway, which will only succeed if it *is* rectangular and not obtuse.

But direct realism does need a more sophisticated account of what it is to see the desk and its properties. In perception, we can be aware of a range of properties, some of which the object has independent of our minds, and some of which it has in relation to being perceived. For instance, a rectangular desk has the property of 'looking obtuse'. The property of 'looking obtuse' is a distinct property from 'being obtuse' – so a desk can *be* rectangular and *look* obtuse. The property of 'looking obtuse' is a *relational* property, in this case, a property the desk has in relation to being *seen*. (Another relational property is 'being to the north of' – the desk has this property in relation to me when it is to the north of me.) 'Looking obtuse' is a property *the desk* has, claims direct realism, not the property of a sense-datum. And we can even explain why the desk has the property of looking obtuse (to us) in terms of its being rectangular plus facts about light and vision.

Direct realism claims that *what* we perceive are physical objects (not sense-data), but it doesn't have to claim that *all* their properties, as we perceive them, are mind-independent. This response challenges the inference from (4) to (5) above.

See THE DISTINCTION BETWEEN PRIMARY AND SECONDARY QUALITIES, **p. 44.**

What is a relational property?

See EVALUATING ARGUMENTS, **p. 11.** on the ways arguments can be challenged. This response from direct realism challenges the inference from premises to conclusion.

The argument from illusion

The appearance/reality distinction challenges direct realism in cases of illusions and hallucinations. Illusions first: if you half-submerge a straight stick in a glass of water, it looks crooked; but it isn't. We see a crooked stick, but the stick isn't crooked. However, *just* from what you experience, you can't tell whether you are seeing an illusion or not. Someone who doesn't know about the crooked stick illusion thinks they are seeing a crooked stick. It *looks* just like a crooked stick in water. Illusions can be 'subjectively indistinguishable' from veridical perception.

Figure 2.1
Pencil in liquid.

1. We perceive something having some property *F* (e.g. a stick that is crooked).
2. When we perceive something having some property *F*, then there is something that has this property.
3. In an illusion, the physical object does not have the property *F* (the stick is not crooked).
4. Therefore, what has the property *F* is something mental, a sense-datum.
5. Therefore, in illusions, we see sense-data, and not physical objects, immediately.
6. Illusions can be 'subjectively indistinguishable' from veridical perception.
7. Therefore, we see the same thing, namely sense-data, in both illusions and veridical perception.
8. Therefore, in all cases, we see sense-data, and not physical objects, immediately.
9. Therefore, direct realism is false.

Direct realism can give the same reply as before. When the stick in water looks crooked, there is nothing that *is* crooked; (2) is wrong. Instead, the stick has the property of *looking crooked* when half-submerged in water. There is a difference between the property 'being straight' and the property 'looking straight'. Usually, of course, something looks straight when it is straight. But the two properties can come apart, and something can look crooked when

> **An experience is veridical if it represents the world as it actually is.**

> **Outline and explain the argument from illusion.**

Outline and explain direct realism's response to the arguments from perceptual variation and illusion.

it is straight. So, sometimes we perceive the 'looks' properties of physical objects, sometimes we experience the properties they have that don't relate to how they are perceived. In both cases, we directly perceive physical objects and their properties.

Going further: the argument from hallucination

We can experience perceptual hallucinations – not just visual ones, but auditory and olfactory hallucinations as well.

1. In a hallucination, we perceive something having some property *F*.
2. When we perceive something having some property *F*, then there is something that has this property.
3. We don't perceive a physical object at all (unlike the case of illusion).
4. Therefore, what we perceive must be mental – sense-data.
5. Hallucinations can be experiences that are 'subjectively indistinguishable' from veridical perceptions.
6. Therefore, we see the same thing, namely sense-data, in both hallucinations and veridical perception.
7. Therefore, in all cases, we see sense-data, and not physical objects, immediately.
8. Therefore, direct realism is false.

Outline and explain the argument from hallucination.

The disjunctive theory of perception

Direct realism's reply to the argument from illusion won't work here. We can't say that what is seen is how some physical object looks, because no physical object is seen at all! But there is a different way of challenging premise (2). According to the disjunctive theory of perception, if something looks a certain way, then one of *two quite different things* is going on: *either* I directly perceive a mind-independent physical object that is *F or* as in the case of hallucination, it appears to me just *as if* there is something that is *F*, but there is nothing that *is F*. Hallucinations and veridical perception are two completely different kinds of mental state, because in hallucination, the person isn't connected up to the world. They can *seem* exactly the same, but that doesn't prove that they *are* the same. We can use this to challenge (6). The fact that hallucinations are subjectively indistinguishable from veridical perception tells us nothing significant about what *perception* is. In hallucination, we don't *perceive* anything, we *imagine* it. To imagine something is not to perceive something mental, such as sense-data, but not to perceive anything at all. So the argument from hallucination doesn't show that in veridical perception, we perceive sense-data instead of physical objects.

> An either/or claim is called a disjunction.

> Outline and explain the disjunctivist theory of perception.

The time-lag argument

As Russell notes, it takes time for light waves, or sound waves, or smells, to get from physical objects to our sense organs. For example, it takes 8 minutes for light from the sun to reach the earth. If you look at the sun (not a good idea!), you are actually seeing it as it was 8 minutes ago. If it blew up, you would see it normally for 8 minutes after it had blown up – it wouldn't even exist anymore, and you'd still see it! Therefore, we could argue, you aren't seeing it directly.

> Russell, *The Problems of Philosophy*, Ch. 3.

But this doesn't show that what you perceive is actually a sense-datum of the sun. The 'image' you see is *physical*, carried in light waves. The light waves exist during those 8 minutes. So *if* you see the sun indirectly, then it is because you see light waves directly. But then what we perceive immediately is not the sun, but the light from the sun. We can generalise: what we perceive is the physical medium by which we detect physical objects (light waves, sound waves, chemicals for smell and taste). So, we don't perceive (ordinary) physical objects directly.

Direct realism can reply that this is a confusion between *how* we perceive and *what* we perceive. Compare these two pairs of questions:

1.   'Can you see the lake?' and 'Can you see the light reflecting off the lake?'
2.   'Can you see the paper?' and 'Can you see the light reflecting from the paper?'

In (1), we can turn our attention from the lake to the light reflecting off it. So we can talk, literally, about seeing the light. But in (2) there is no difference in *what* one is supposed to see. To 'see' the light that the paper reflects is just to see the paper. In fact, you cannot *see* the light itself – only the paper. So, direct realism can argue, except in special conditions, we don't perceive light waves directly and physical objects indirectly. Light waves are part of the story of how we see physical objects.

The time lag means we see the physical object as it was a moment before, not as it is now. This means that we see into the past. We always experience the world as it was a moment ago, or in astronomy, when we look at distant stars and galaxies, we look into the distant past.

> Outline and explain the time-lag argument. Does it succeed as an objection to direct realism?

Going further: direct realism and common sense

Describe what you see. You would usually do so by referring to physical objects: 'I see a desk, covered with pens and paper, and a plant'. If you perceive the world via sense-data, the immediate 'content' of what you perceive is mental. So try to describe your experience in terms of sense-data, without referring to any physical objects. You could talk about 'coloured patches' standing in spatial relations (above, below, left, right, etc.) to each other. But this is very awkward, and it is virtually impossible for any normal scene. What shape is that coloured patch on the left? – well, 'plant-shaped'! But 'plant' refers to a physical object. So our way of describing sense-data is dependent on concepts of physical objects. We can't give an account of what we experience without referring to physical objects, even if we try.

What this shows is that our perceptual experience presents what we perceive as mind-independent objects. That doesn't

Figure 2.2
A giraffe and buildings. Can you describe this scene without referring to physical objects?

prove that we perceive mind-independent objects, but it does make such a claim highly intuitive. Only direct realism holds onto this basic intuition. It is very counter-intuitive to think, then, that what we perceive are sense-data. Any theory that claims that we perceive sense-data has to say that perception is not what it seems to be. It has to say that it *seems* that we perceive mind-independent objects, but we don't. We need very strong reasons to accept that perception is misleading in this way.

Do we perceive physical objects directly?

Key points: direct realism

- Direct realism claims that physical objects exist independently of our minds and of our perceptions of them.
- Direct realism claims that when we perceive physical objects, we perceive them 'directly'.
- The argument from perceptual variation points out that different people perceive the same physical object differently. Therefore, what each person perceives is how the object appears to them. This appearance is mind-dependent sense-data. Physical objects are therefore not perceived directly.
- The arguments from illusion and hallucination claim that in illusions and hallucinations, we see something, but we do not see the physical world as it is. What we see are sense-data. The arguments depend on the assumption that when we have a sensation of something having some quality *F*, then there must be something that is *F*.
- Direct realism rejects this assumption. To the arguments from perceptual variation and illusion, direct realism can reply that the physical object has the property of *looking* a certain way. What you perceive is how the physical object looks.
- Disjunctivists argue that hallucinations are a completely different type of mental state to perception. So we cannot generalise from cases of hallucination to claim that in perception, we see sense-data.

- The time lag argument points out that what you see is not how the physical world is, because light and sound take time to travel from the physical object to your senses.
- Direct realists reply that this only shows that, when we reflect on *how* we perceive physical objects, we should conclude that we perceive them in the past.
- Direct realists note that when we describe what we perceive, we use physical object concepts. This shows that perception seems to be perception of physical objects. To deny this is therefore very counter-intuitive.

B. Indirect realism

Indirect realism claims that we perceive physical objects which are mind-independent, but we do so via, or in virtue of, perceiving mind-dependent sense-data that are caused by and represent physical objects. We perceive sense-data immediately, and physical objects indirectly.

Arguments in favour of indirect realism often begin as objections to direct realism.

See THE ARGUMENT FROM PERCEPTUAL VARIATION (p. 30), THE ARGUMENT FROM ILLUSION (p. 33) and GOING FURTHER: THE ARGUMENT FROM HALLUCINATION (p. 34).

1. There are many perceptual experiences in which what we experience are not the properties of physical objects.
2. When we perceive something having some property F, then there is something that has this property.
3. In such cases, given that what we perceive is not the way the world is, what we perceive are sense-data.
4. Such cases are subjectively indistinguishable from veridical perception.
5. When two perceptual experiences are subjectively indistin-guishable, they are perceptual experiences of the same thing. (This claim is the best hypothesis, given (4).)

See HYPOTHETICAL REASONING, p. 9.

6. Therefore, we *always* perceive sense-data (not just in cases in which what we perceive is not the way the world is).
7. Nevertheless, except in hallucinations, it still makes sense to say we perceive *the world*. In cases of both veridical perception and illusion, the sense-data we perceive are caused by and represent

physical objects. This representation can be accurate or inaccurate in certain ways – physical objects may be as they appear to us, or they may differ in certain ways.

8. Therefore, we perceive physical objects indirectly, via sense-data.

Outline and explain the argument from non-veridical perception to indirect realism.

What are sense-data?

When we first introduced the term 'sense-data' (p. 31), we used Russell's definition of them as the 'content' of my perceptual experience. The arguments from non-veridical perception show that, whatever sense-data are, they cannot be physical objects. Sense-data exist as part of the mind.

Assuming realism about physical objects, we can draw the following contrasts:

When Russell was writing, in the early twentieth century, some philosophers thought that sense-data were nevertheless still mind-*independent*. But this understanding quickly gave way to other theories that treated sense-data as mind-*dependent*, and this is how we shall understand them.

1. Sense-data are mental things which are the way we perceive them to be. They are appearances, and so are exactly as they seem. There is no further reality to an appearance than how it appears. Physical objects can appear differently from how they really are.

2. Sense-data only exist while they are being experienced. An experience must be experienced by someone to exist at all. Physical objects can exist when no one experiences them.

3. Sense-data are 'private'. No one else can experience *your* sense-data. They are the particular sense-data they are, by definition, as part of your consciousness. Physical objects are 'public'. One and the same object can be experienced by different people.

What are sense-data?

Scepticism about the existence of the external world

RUSSELL, *THE PROBLEMS OF PHILOSOPHY*, CH. 2

The specification refers separately to 'Problems arising from the view that mind-dependent objects are caused by mind-independent objects', but I discuss both together here.

Russell ends his argument in favour of sense-data in Chapter 1 with a puzzle. If what we perceive directly are sense-data, then all we *know* about are sense-data. We believe that 'behind' the sense-data there are real physical objects, that physical objects cause our sense-data. But how can we know this? To know that physical objects cause sense-data, we first have to know that physical objects *exist*. But the only access we have to physical objects is through our sense-data.

Although Russell doesn't comment on this, his line of thought forms an objection to indirect realism. Because we directly perceive sense-data, we cannot know that a world of physical objects – a world external to and independent of our minds – exists. Scepticism is the view that we cannot know, or cannot show that we know, a particular claim, in this case the claim that physical objects exist. Indirect realism leads to scepticism about the existence of the external world.

Outline and explain the argument that indirect realism leads to scepticism about the external world.

The existence of the external world is the best hypothesis

On this type of argument, see HYPOTHETICAL REASONING, p. 9. For a completely different argument for the existence of physical objects, see GOING FURTHER: DESCARTES ON THE EXISTENCE OF THE EXTERNAL WORLD, p. 111.

Russell offers two responses, both appealing to how we should *explain* what we do know. The first is this: the fact that sense-data are private means that no two people actually ever perceive the same thing, unless we can say that there are physical objects that they both perceive (indirectly). People perceive the same thing. They have very similar sense-data if they are at the same place and time. The best explanation of this is that there are physical objects causing their sense-data.

Russell rejects this argument because it assumes something that we can't know: that there are other people, and that they have sense-data, and that their sense-data is similar to mine. To assume that there are other people is to to assume that there are physical objects, since people are physical objects. But the question was how, from my sense-data, do I know that there are physical objects? In answering that question, I can't *assume* that there are physical objects (such as other people) – that's begging the question!

So Russell offers a second argument.

1. Either physical objects exist and cause my sense-data or physical objects do not exist nor cause my sense-data.
2. I can't *prove* either claim is true or false.
3. Therefore, I have to treat them as hypotheses. (A hypothesis is a proposal that needs to be confirmed or rejected by reasoning or experience.)
4. The hypothesis that physical objects exist and cause my sense-data is better.
5. Therefore, physical objects exist and cause my sense-data.

What is Russell's argument for (4)? One way to test a hypothesis is to see whether it explains why my experience is the way it is. If I see a cat first in a corner of the room and then later on the sofa, then if the cat is a physical object, it travelled from the corner to the sofa when I wasn't looking. If there is no cat apart from what I see in my sense-data, then the cat does not exist when I don't see it. It springs into existence first in the corner, and then later on the sofa. Nothing connects my two perceptions. But that's incredibly puzzling – indeed, it is *no explanation at all* of why my sense-data are the way they are! So the hypothesis that there is a physical object, the cat, that causes what I see is the best explanation of my sense-data.

Russell runs the same argument for supposing that other people have minds. When I perceive how people behave, e.g. when talking to me, the best explanation of my experience is that it is caused by what they say (a physical event) and this is caused by their thoughts.

> Outline and explain the argument that the best explanation of sense-data is that sense-data are caused by mind-independent physical objects.

> This issue is discussed further in THE PROBLEM OF OTHER MINDS in *Philosophy for A2: Ethics and Philosophy of Mind*.

LOCKE, *AN ESSAY CONCERNING HUMAN UNDERSTANDING*, BK. 4, CH. 11
The lack of choice over our experiences and the coherence of the various senses

The syllabus mentions two further responses to scepticism about the existence of the external world from John Locke. First, in perception, I cannot avoid having certain sense-data 'produced' in my mind. By contrast, if I turn from perception to memory or imagination, e.g. by shutting my eyes, I find that I can choose what I experience. Perceptual experiences – which 'I have whether I want them or not – must be produced in my mind by some exterior cause' §5. Second, our different senses 'confirm' the information that each supplies. If I see a fire and doubt whether it is real, I can confirm its reality by touching it §7.

Locke brings the two responses together in an extended example. I know from experience that I can change how a piece of paper looks by writing on it. (This connects sight and proprioception – my sense of my hand moving.) I can plan what to write, and I know in advance what the paper will look like. But I cannot bring about the sense-data of seeing the paper with words on it just by imagination; I have to actually write. And once I have written something, I can't change the words I see. This shows that sense-data aren't 'merely playthings of my imagination'. Finally, if someone else reads those words aloud, what I hear corresponds to what I intended to write. And this 'leaves little reason for doubt' that the words exist outside my mind.

> Outline and explain why, according to Locke, we should think that physical objects exist.

OBJECTIONS

We can object that Locke hasn't *shown* that physical objects exist. Although he says that there 'must' be some external cause of sense-data, this is overstating the case. Locke doesn't add new *reasons* to Russell's argument; he just makes that (same) argument stronger by adding further features of our experience that need explaining. If physical objects don't exist, we can't explain

1. why sense-data aren't under our control but imagination and memory are;
2. why we should get the same information from different senses;
3. the very complex interaction between our actions and our perceptions.

If indirect realism is correct, then it seems the existence of physical objects remains a *hypothesis*, something we have to *infer*. Direct realism can argue that this is a significant weakness. First, perhaps some other hypothesis that explains our sense-data is just as good, but we just don't know it. Scepticism still threatens. Second, it is very counterintuitive to think that perception doesn't put us in direct touch with physical objects.

> These points return in ARGUMENTS AGAINST KNOWLEDGE EMPIRICISM: THE LIMITS OF EMPIRICAL KNOWLEDGE, p. 101.

Going further: the external world is not a hypothesis

Some indirect realists have responded to these objections by rejecting the theories of Russell and Locke. Russell and Locke seem to think that sense-data 'come between' us and the world, so that in perceiving sense-data, we *aren't* also perceiving physical objects. But instead, we should say that we perceive physical objects via sense-data. Sense-data don't get in the way of perceiving physical objects. They are *how* we perceive physical objects. They don't block our access to the external world, they mediate it. The existence of the external world is *not a hypothesis*. It is something that we experience in perception.

But what of the fact that sense-data differ from the physical objects they represent, e.g. in perceptual variation and illusions? Doesn't this show that sense-data come between us and the world? No, this is all explicable in terms of physical objects and their effects on us, and *only* in these terms. The best explanation of illusions and perceptual variation needs *both* sense-data and physical objects.

> Compare: we describe the world using words. But words don't get in the way of describing the world. We couldn't describe the world without them!

> If indirect realism is true, can we know that there is an external world that causes our sense-data?

Scepticism about the nature of the external world

We have assumed so far that in talking about the external world, we are talking about physical objects. But even if we can show that our sense-data are caused by *something* that exists independent of our minds, can we establish *what kind of thing* that cause is? We can't tell what a cause is like just from its effects. Consider: if all you knew was smoke, would you be able to work out that its cause was fire? Fire is very different from smoke; and experience shows that the world is full of surprising causal relationships. So, if all we experience are sense-data, how can we know whether the world is similar to how it appears to us in sense-data, or whether it is very different?

Indirect realism maintains that sense-data are not only caused by the external world, but they also *represent* it. There are at least some *systematic correlations* between what we experience and the nature of the world. But is what we experience an accurate representation? Is appearance a good guide to reality?

Perhaps the most famous distinction between the appearance of physical objects and their reality is Locke's distinction between 'primary' and 'secondary' qualities. It is worth understanding the distinction before returning to the question of the nature of the external world and how we know it.

> Explain the difference between scepticism about the existence of the external world and scepticism about the nature of the external world.

The distinction between primary and secondary qualities

> ### LOCKE, *AN ESSAY CONCERNING HUMAN UNDERSTANDING*, BK 2, CH. 8
>
> The distinction between 'primary' and 'secondary' qualities is most famously associated with John Locke, but many other philosophers and scientists working at the same time (the seventeenth century) also made the distinction in some form. Locke's argument begins in Bk 2, Ch. 8, §8. A 'quality' is a 'power' that a physical object has 'to produce an idea in our mind'. So a snowball has the powers – the qualities – to produce in us the ideas of 'white', 'cold' and 'round'.

See DESCARTES ON THE CONCEPT OF A PHYSICAL OBJECT (p. 142) for another account of the distinction.

Locke then argues that qualities are of two different kinds. *Primary* qualities are qualities that are 'utterly inseparable' from the object whatever changes it goes through, even if it is divided into smaller and smaller pieces. The object has these properties 'in and of itself'. The primary qualities are extension (Locke also talks of size), shape, motion, number and solidity. *Secondary* qualities are qualities that physical objects have that are 'nothing but powers to produce various sensations in us'. Locke lists 'colours, sounds, tastes, and so on', later adding smells and temperature.

The important phrase here is 'nothing but'. Primary qualities, of course, also produce sensations in us – both the roundness (primary quality) and the whiteness (secondary quality) of the snowball cause sensations in us. But shape is a quality that the snowball has irrespective of whether we perceive it or not. Colour, by contrast, has to be understood in terms of how the snowball affects us. By definition, colour is something that is *experienced in vision*. So it is a quality that an object can have only in relation to its being *seen* by someone. And similarly for sound, taste and the other secondary qualities. By contrast, primary qualities are those properties of an object that are not related by definition to perceivers.

The distinction between primary and secondary qualities is a distinction between qualities that physical objects have 'in themselves', and qualities they have that are related to how they are perceived.

Explain and illustrate the difference between primary and secondary qualities.

Locke on primary qualities

Why does Locke pick out extension, shape, motion, number and solidity as primary qualities? He says that these qualities cannot be separated from a physical object. For example, physical objects must always have *some* size and shape, they must always be at rest or in motion of some kind, they can be counted. By contrast, physical objects don't have to have the secondary qualities of colour or smell, e.g. odourless, transparent glass.

Is Locke's list right? He believed that when you break up physical objects, you get smaller objects which have all these same qualities. But physics has moved on, and sub-atomic particles aren't like physical objects that we know in lots of ways. Many of them have some form of electrical charge and many of them can behave as much like packets of energy as like small bits of matter. We may want to change Locke's definition of primary qualities to those qualities that physics tells us physical objects have 'in and of themselves'.

In Bk 2, Ch. 4, Locke explains what he means by 'solidity'. He does *not* mean to contrast being 'solid' with being liquid or gas. Rather, solidity is the quality of a physical object whereby it takes up space and excludes other physical objects from occupying exactly the same space. This is just as true of liquids and gases – I can put my hand into water or move it around in the air, but my hand and the water or air can't occupy exactly the same space. The water or air move out of the way. Just as anything physical has to have some size and shape, thinks Locke, it must also take up space.

> Explain why, for Locke, solidity is a primary quality.

> Explain and illustrate what Locke means by 'resemblance'.

Locke on resemblance

In Bk 2 Ch. 8, §15, Locke adds a further distinction. Our perceptual experiences of primary qualities 'resemble' the primary qualities that the object we are perceiving has. Physical objects have shape, extension and so on just as we perceive them. By contrast, our perceptual experiences of secondary qualities don't resemble the object at all. Or again, secondary qualities as we perceive them are nothing like what they are in the object, viz. macroscopic effects of the primary properties of atoms and molecules.

Going further: do secondary qualities exist outside the mind?

In trying to explain exactly what secondary qualities are, and how they differ from primary qualities, Locke makes a number of points that are not entirely consistent.

He first defines a secondary quality as a quality *of the object.* It is a quality, or power, that the object has to produce certain sensations when perceived. This power is the result of the primary qualities of the object's 'imperceptible parts' (§15) – or as we would now put it, in terms of its atomic and molecular structure. Light, by which we perceive colour, can be explained in terms of the effects and activity of subatomic particles, smell in terms of chemical compounds, and so on. Physics and chemistry deal only with primary qualities – the size, shape, motion and so on of tiny bits of matter. Because an object has primary qualities, and its secondary qualities are the effect of its primary qualities, then we can say that objects have secondary qualities. Defined like this, secondary qualities are relational properties of objects.

On the other hand, Locke emphasises the fact that secondary qualities don't 'really exist in' physical objects in the same way that primary qualities do (§§16–19). If we 'take away the sensation of them', then secondary qualities 'vanish and cease, and are reduced to their causes' (§17). If you prevent light from reaching a red and white stone, 'its colours vanish' (§18). So it loses its colour, but not, for example, its size or solidity. Furthermore, we shouldn't identify the cause of what we experience with what we experience. Suppose you eat something that is white and makes you ill (Locke gives the example of 'manna'). The food has two effects on you in virtue of its primary qualities: it affects your eyes, so you experience it as white, and it affects your stomach, which causes you to experience pain. But just as we don't think of the pain you experience as 'in' the food itself, we shouldn't think of the colour as 'existing in' the food either. This way of speaking inclines us to say that secondary qualities are *effects* on us, and so exist in the mind, not in physical objects themselves.

On relational properties, see THE ARGUMENT FROM PERCEPTUAL VARIATION (p. 30). See also DIRECT AND INDIRECT REALISM ON SECONDARY QUALITIES (p. 49).

Explain the difference between the two accounts of secondary qualities as relational properties and as mind-dependent properties.

But this second account confuses (qualities and ideas) (§8). Qualities are powers in the object, and the causes of ideas; ideas are the effects of these powers on our minds. If colour is a secondary *quality*, then it is what *causes* our experience of colour – and this exists outside the mind. If colour is an *idea*, a type of sensation we experience, then it is the *effect* of the object (its primary qualities) on our minds – and this does not exist outside the mind. Locke is not consistent about which definition of colour he wants. So, when talking about the red and white stone, he says that it 'has at every time [even in the dark] a configuration of particles that is apt to produce in us the idea of redness when rays of light rebound from some parts of that hard stone, and to produce the idea of whiteness when the rays rebound from some other parts; but at no time are whiteness or redness in the stone' (§19). But if the stone's colour just *is* its power to produce certain sensations of colour in us, and this power is the result of its 'configuration of particles', then it has its colour 'at every time', even in the dark! Its colours 'vanish' in that they are no longer perceived; but that doesn't mean that its colours *cease to exist* – because the stone's atomic structure has not ceased to exist.

Which definition of secondary qualities – as causes in the object or effects on our minds – is better? In §21, Locke invokes THE ARGUMENT FROM PERCEPTUAL VARIATION (p. 30). If you have one warm hand and one cold hand, and put both in a bowl of tepid water, the water will feel hot to the cold hand, and cold to the hot hand. The temperature of water can be explained in terms its average molecular kinetic energy (roughly, how much its molecules are vibrating or bouncing around). The water has just one level of average molecular kinetic energy (primary quality), so it can't *be* both hot and cold. Yet it seems to be both hot and cold, i.e. it seems to have two different secondary qualities.

> **?** How could colours exist in the dark?

We can expand this point, recalling Russell's example of the shiny table (p. 30). All perceptual variation shows that we experience physical objects having conflicting secondary qualities. So secondary qualities only *exist* in the mind of the perceiver. Primary qualities are objective, but secondary qualities are subjective.

This argument suggests that Locke's original definition of secondary qualities as powers of objects is mistaken. Secondary qualities *come into existence* through the effect of a physical object on a perceiver. They are not qualities of the physical object itself, but exist only in the act of perception. By contrast, primary qualities are qualities a physical object has that do not depend, either by definition or for their existence, on the object being perceived.

> Explain the claim that secondary qualities 'exist in the mind'.

Direct and indirect realism on secondary qualities

The 'subjective' view of secondary qualities can be used to defend indirect realism. The world as we experience it through our senses and the world as it is 'in itself', as science describes it, are quite different. We experience all the wonderful secondary properties of the senses; the world as described by science is 'particles in motion' and empty space. It must be, then, that we don't perceive physical objects directly. While we perceive the primary properties of physical objects, the secondary qualities we perceive are properties of sense-data.

Direct realism defends Locke's original definition of secondary qualities, understanding them as relational properties. When we perceive secondary qualities, we still perceive the objects but *as they appear to us*. Just as a stick can have the property of 'looking crooked' under certain conditions, it can have the property of 'looking brown'. In fact, to *be* brown is to look brown to normal perceivers under normal conditions. To say that physical objects aren't 'really' coloured misinterprets what it means to say that something is coloured. Science explains *what it is* for physical objects to have the properties we perceive them to have; it doesn't mean that they don't have these properties. Secondary qualities are no less real, no less part of the external world, than primary qualities; it is just that they are a different *type* of property, one defined in terms of how we perceive the world.

The indirect realist can reply that what science in fact explains is what it is *for us to perceive* these properties. Colour is conveyed to our eyes by light. But what we experience directly is nothing like what light is according to physics. For instance, a blind man can understand the physics, but can't grasp what colour is. It is not until we turn to human visual experience – something mental – that we need the concept of colour, that we come across 'colour experience'. This is the *effect* of the light reflected from physical objects, not its cause.

Russell, *The Problems of Philosophy*, Ch. 3.

? Does direct realism or indirect realism have the better theory of secondary qualities?

Scepticism about the nature of the external world again

We can now return to the question of SCEPTICISM ABOUT THE NATURE OF THE EXTERNAL WORLD (p. 44). Locke has argued that the external world has the primary qualities we experience, but not the secondary qualities.

Pages 15-23 will be discussed on p. 60.

Berkeley is an idealist – he thinks that what we perceive is *entirely* mind-dependent (BERKELEY'S IDEALISM, p. 58). There are no mind-independent physical objects in the common-sense way that realism supposes there are.

BERKELEY, *THREE DIALOGUES BETWEEN HYLAS AND PHILONOUS*, FIRST DIALOGUE 1, PP. 1-15, 23-6

Berkeley argues that Locke's view is incoherent. He begins his *Three Dialogues between Hylas and Philonous* arguing, like Locke, that secondary qualities are mind-dependent. But he then uses similar arguments to show that *primary* qualities are also mind-dependent, and so indirect realism is unsatisfactory.

Berkeley on secondary qualities (pp. 1-12)

Berkeley, in the character of Philonous, begins by arguing that 'sensible things', i.e. whatever is perceived by the senses, must be whatever is perceived *immediately* by the senses. The causes of our perceptions - the reality behind appearances - if they are not

therefore

immediately perceived, we must infer. Because this is a matter of inference, we should not say that such causes are themselves perceived. Philonous then argues that (*what* we immediately perceive are the qualities of things. He then asks whether any of these qualities exist independently of being perceived.)

The character Hylas, who plays the role of the realist, starts off as a very simple direct realist. He claims that whatever we perceive exists independently of our minds, and in the form in which we perceive it. Thus heat, as we feel it, exists in the object. Philonous points out that intense heat, or indeed intense cold, light, sound, pressure, can all be experienced as pain, but pain obviously doesn't exist 'in' physical objects. If we say these secondary qualities are in the object, then we have to say that at some point, it also has the quality of pain. Hylas responds that the heat (light, etc.) isn't itself pain, but *causes* pain. Philonous objects that we feel just one unified sensation of painful heat (painful light, etc.). In fact, *all* our perceptions of secondary qualities are accompanied by some form of pleasure or pain.

Since this is an empirical argument, we can challenge it on empirical grounds. Is Berkeley right to say that we can't distinguish between the sensation of heat and that of pain? If he is right for some sensations, is he right for all sensations? Can we not, for instance, distinguish between the sensation of sweetness and the sensation of pleasure we associate with it?

Berkeley then presents THE ARGUMENT FROM PERCEPTUAL VARIATION (p. 30). He repeats Locke's example of placing a hot and a cold hand in a bowl of tepid water. The water feels hot to the cold hand and cold to the hot hand, but the water cannot *be* both hot and cold. He later develops the argument in relation to colours:

1. A cloud from a distance looks pink, but up close, it loses its colour (or appears grey).
2. A solid physical object, viewed through a microscope, appears to have different colours than those it has when viewed normally.
3. Different animals perceive the colours of objects differently.

> 'Empirical' means relating to or deriving from experience, especially sense experience, but also including experimental scientific investigation.

> Outline and explain Berkeley's argument that secondary qualities are mind-dependent because all sensations of secondary qualities are accompanied by pleasure or pain.

4. If colours really existed in physical objects, then to change the colour, it would be necessary to change the object itself. But, of course, different kinds of light - daylight, candlelight, etc. - change the colour of an object without changing the object.

5. Therefore, all colours are appearances, not properties of physical objects.

Suppose we insist that secondary qualities 'really' exist in the object as physical particles in motion (light waves, sound waves, the chemicals of smell and taste). Berkeley points out that if we say that sound *is* a vibration of the air, then we can't *hear* sound, since vibrations are something perceived by sight or touch. If we say that colour *is* tiny particles of matter in motion (photons with a particular energy, perhaps), then we can't see 'real' colour, since we cannot see these tiny particles moving. And that is very counter-intuitive.

Berkeley's attack on the primary/secondary quality distinction (pp. 13-15)

Having persuaded Hylas to agree that secondary qualities are mind-dependent, Philonous (Berkeley) argues that the argument from perceptual variation applies equally well to primary qualities.

1. What looks small to me may look huge to a small animal.

2. What looks small from a distance looks large when viewed close up.

3. What looks smooth to the naked eye appears craggy and uneven under a microscope.

4. If you look at a circle straight on, it looks circular. But if I'm looking at it from an angle, it looks elliptical. We see it differently, but it doesn't change.

5. Even motion isn't constant. We measure the speed of motion by how quickly our minds work - to a creature that thinks much faster than us, e.g. a housefly, our fastest movements appear leisurely.

> ? How would a direct realist respond to Berkeley's argument here?

> Russell also makes this argument: see The ARGUMENT FROM PERCEPTUAL VARIATION, p. 30.

Figure 2.3
A circular object, and from an obtuse angle.

6. In the case of colour, when an object appears to have many colours, depending on how it is perceived, we can't say that it has one *real* colour which is independent of how we perceive it.

7. Therefore, 1-5 show that we can't say that an object has one *real* shape or size or motion, independent of how it is perceived.

8. Therefore, the primary qualities of objects are just as mind-dependent as secondary qualities.

Problems arising from the view that mind-dependent objects represent mind-independent objects (pp. 23-6)

Locke claims that secondary qualities are very different in reality from how they appear to us, but primary qualities in the object resemble our experience of them.

Berkeley picks up this issue on p. 23. How can our sense-data, which are 'perpetually fleeting and variable', *resemble* a physical object that is 'fixed and constant'? How can circular sense-data and oval sense-data both resemble something that has just one shape? There is no more constancy in our experience of primary qualities than in that of secondary qualities. If you want to say that *one* of these appearances resembles the object, while all the others do not, then how do we distinguish *which* is the 'true copy' - the true size, shape or motion?

The argument from perceptual variation begins by supporting indirect realism, but turns into an objection to it: if neither primary nor secondary qualities, as we experience them, resemble the external world, how do we know what the world beyond our experience is really like?

Locke's theory of resemblance faces another objection. He thought that physical objects have primary qualities 'in themselves', and that these qualities resemble what we experience. So the squareness of a physical object resembles the squareness we see. But how can something we don't experience (shape that a physical object has it *in itself*) be *like* something that is experienced (shape as we experience it)? What can we mean when we say that the shape of the table 'resembles' the shape we see? How can squareness resemble

Outline and explain Berkeley's attack on the distinction between primary and secondary qualities.

See LOCKE ON RESEMBLANCE, p. 46.

Outline and explain Berkeley's objections to Locke's theory of resemblance. What implications does this claim have for indirect realism?

the idea of squareness? Our ideas of size, shape, motion and so on, derive from our perceptual experience. The *only* idea of shape we have is the one we see (or feel). We can only make sense of the table's squareness in terms of our experience of squareness. It doesn't make sense to say a pain exists unless someone feels, or that a colour exists unless someone sees it. Nor does it make sense to say a shape exists unless someone sees or feels it.

Berkeley concludes that indirect realism is left with scepticism about the nature of the external world.

Sense-data tell us of 'relations' between objects

Indirect realists have generally agreed that Locke's idea of 'resemblance' between sense-data and physical objects is problematic. But we can still argue that sense-data *represent* physical objects (just not by resembling them). As argued in THE EXISTENCE OF THE EXTERNAL WORLD IS THE BEST HYPOTHESIS (p. 40), we should believe that sense-data are caused by an external world. Now we can add that the pattern of causal relations between the external world and our sense-data is very *detailed* and *systematic*. If you turn a penny, it looks circular, then increasingly oval, then flat (from the side). *All* of these sense-data represent the penny because they are systematically related to it. We can explain how sense-data represent physical objects in terms of this complex causation.

Going further: Russell, The Problems of Philosophy, Ch. 3

Once we have accepted that there is an external world causing our sense-data, Russell argues, our experience represents that external world only if there is something physical that exists inspace. His arguments are his solution to THE ARGUMENT FROM PERCEPTUAL VARIATION (p. 30).

However, 'physical space' – the space in which physical objects exist, the space that science deals with – is not the same as space as we experience it, 'apparent space'. Shape, for instance, is a spatial property, but the shape that I perceive an object to be is different from the shape that you perceive it to be. Or again, shape is perceived by both sight and touch. But shape as we see it is not the same as shape as we touch it; we have to learn to coordinate the two experiences. So the 'real shape' of the object is not how it appears to us, either in vision or in touch, but the shape it has in physical space.

So what is the connection between physical space and our experience of spatial things? Russell makes three claims:

1. For objects in physical space to cause our sense-data, we must exist in physical space as well. In other words, we must have bodies that can be causally affected by physical objects.
2. The *relative* positions of physical objects in real space – near, far, left, right and so on – 'correspond to' the relative positions of sense-data in apparent space. Thus, it will take us longer to walk through physical space to a house that *appears* further away than to a house that appears nearer.
3. *All* we can know about physical space, and the distribution of physical objects in physical space, is what secures this correspondence. For instance, we can't know what 'space' or 'distance' are 'in themselves'.

Russell then repeats the argument with time. 'Real' time is distinct from our 'feeling of duration' – if we enjoy something, it can seem to take no time at all, if something is boring, it seems to last forever. We cannot, therefore, know the 'real time' in which physical objects exist. But we can know about 'relative' times, i.e. whether something comes before or after something else. (However, this

> The relation between visual and tactile shape is explored in a famous puzzle known as Molyneux's question.

> Explain and illustrate Russell's distinction between 'real' and 'apparent' space.

doesn't always match the order of changesin physical objects. For example, lightning and thunder are simultaneous, but we usually hear the thunder after seeing the lightning, because sound travels more slowly than light, even though they occur together.)

Russell then repeats the argument for colour, a *secondary* quality. If two objects have the same colour under the same viewing conditions, then we may infer that there is something that the two physical objects have in common. We can extend the point to *all* qualities – primary and secondary. Thus two objects making the same sound, under the same listening conditions, may be thought to have something in common; likewise for two smells, two tastes and so on. But what it is about the physical object 'in itself' that secures all these relations of similarity and difference, we can't know (at least through sense experience).

> **?** Can indirect realism avoid scepticism about the nature of the external world?

Problems arising from the view that mind-dependent objects are caused by mind-independent objects

Russell's argument requires that our minds are causally affected by physical objects. Physical objects causally affect our sense organs, which then affect our brains. But philosophers and scientists have struggled with the next step – how does what happens in our brains causally affect our conscious perception? How can something physical and mind-independent possibly cause an idea in a mind? How could nerve signals in the brain produce sensations of sound and colour? Berkeley poses this as an objection to realism, and 300 years later, the puzzle still remains unsolved.

> Berkeley, *Three Dialogues between Hylas and Philonous*, pp. 27 and 36.

Key points: Indirect realism

- Indirect realism claims that when we perceive something having some property *F*, then there is something that has this property.

If it is not the physical object, it must be something mental – sense-data – that we perceive.

- However, we can't tell the difference between illusory and veridical perception. Therefore, we are perceiving the same thing. Since we are perceiving sense-data in the case of illusion, we should infer that we always perceive sense-data.

- Sense-data are private (by definition belonging to someone's consciousness); they only exist while they are being experienced; and they are exactly as they seem. Physical objects are public, exist when not being perceived, and can be different from how they appear.

- Indirect realism faces an objection that if all we experience are sense-data, how do we know what causes them? How do we know physical objects exist at all?

- Russell argues that we cannot prove that physical objects exist, but that this claim is the best explanation for our experience.

- Locke argues that physical objects exist from the fact that we can't choose what to perceive, and from the fact that information from one sense coheres with information from another.

- We can object that indirect realism entails that our belief in physical objects remains a hypothesis, which leaves the belief open to scepticism.

- An alternative interpretation of indirect realism claims that we perceive physical objects via sense-data, and so the existence of physical objects is not a hypothesis.

- Locke distinguishes between primary and secondary qualities. Locke's primary qualities are extension (or size), shape, motion, number and solidity. Secondary qualities are colours, sounds, tastes, smells and hot/cold.

- Locke is not consistent in how he understands the distinction. He defines primary qualities as properties that objects have in themselves and are inseparable from them. He first says secondary qualities are 'nothing but' properties that objects have that produce sensations in us, i.e. they are relational properties of objects (related to how they are perceived). But later, he talks of secondary qualities as subjective and existing in the perceiving mind – a view supported by Russell and Berkeley.

- Locke argues that sense-data resemble the world in respect to primary qualities, but not secondary qualities.
- Following Locke, indirect realists can argue that the world has only primary qualities 'in itself', but we perceive it as having secondary qualities. This is another way in which what we perceive is different from how the world is 'in itself'.
- Direct realism defends Locke's first definition of secondary qualities as relational properties. To be red is to look red to normal perceivers in normal light.
- Berkeley argues that the argument from perceptual variation applies as much to primary qualities as to secondary qualities. Therefore, primary qualities are mind-dependent as well.
- He also argues that sense-data don't, and can't, resemble mind-independent physical objects.
- Russell agrees with many of Berkeley's criticisms, but argues that sense-data can still represent physical objects. The relations between physical objects in space and time and various types of similarity (e.g. colour) correspond to relations between sense-data in these same respects.
- But Russell's theory assumes that mind-independent physical objects can cause mind-dependent perceptual experiences. How this is so remains a philosophical puzzle.

C. Berkeley's idealism

The immediate objects of perception are mind-dependent objects

Esse est percipi (aut percipere) – to be is to be perceived (or to perceive).

Berkeley rejects the existence of physical objects, as they are usually thought of, namely *mind-independent*. He claims that reality is dependent on minds. The ordinary objects of perception – tables, chairs, trees and so on – must be perceived in order to exist. The only things that exist are minds (that perceive) and what minds perceive. The claim that nothing exists that is independent of mind is idealism. Does it make sense, and why does Berkeley argue for it?

We have seen that Berkeley argues that both primary and secondary qualities are mind-dependent. In *Three Dialogues between*

Hylas and Philonous (p. 3), he argues that what is perceived by the senses are qualities and nothing more.

See Scepticism about the nature of the external world again, p. 50.

1. Through vision, we perceive colours, shapes, size, etc.; through hearing, sounds; through smell, odours – and so on. Each sense perceives particular types of qualities.
2. When we perceive physical objects, we don't perceive anything *in addition* to its primary and secondary qualities.
3. Therefore, everything we perceive is either a primary or a secondary quality.
4. Both primary and secondary qualities are mind-dependent.
5. Therefore, nothing that we perceive exists independently of the mind: the objects of perception are entirely mind-dependent.

Explain and outline Berkeley's argument that everything we perceive is mind-dependent.

This doesn't show that physical objects are ideas – they could be unperceived. But Berkeley goes on to argue that the idea of a physical object as something that exists independently of our perception of it is an idea so problematic that we should reject it entirely.

Once we grant Berkeley's claim that all we perceive are primary and secondary qualities, it becomes more difficult to reject his later arguments for idealism. One way to challenge his idealism, therefore, is to argue that we can be said to perceive physical objects themselves, and not just their qualities.

Look at this table. Think of the difference between looking at it in black and white, and how it would look in colour. Now try to picture it without its solidity. Now try to picture it without its shape.

Figure 2.4 Partially completed jigsaw on table.

Figure 2.5 Table.

Figure 2.6

BERKELEY, *THREE DIALOGUES BETWEEN HYLAS AND PHILONOUS*, FIRST DIALOGUE, PP. 15-23, SECOND DIALOGUE

Four arguments against mind-independent objects

1. On p. 15, Hylas has not been persuaded that primary qualities are just as mind-dependent as secondary qualities. So Philonous tries another approach:

    a. A physical object will need to be of some size or other.
    b. What distinguishes one size from another size is something we perceive.
    c. Therefore, we can't form an idea of size as something that exists independent of our perception.
    d. We can't separate the idea of something having a size from ideas of secondary qualities. Try to picture something with a size, and you will also picture something with a shape and a colour and other qualities that we sense.
    e. Therefore, we cannot coherently form a conception of a physical object that has primary properties alone.

Berkeley's argument is unclear, but seems unpersuasive. Locke rejects (d). While we can't conceive of something as merely having size or size and shape, we can have a coherent conception of something as having only size, shape and solidity – all primary qualities. Colour is not necessary – just ask any blind person! Locke also rejects the inference from (b) to (c). The primary qualities we perceive resemble the physical object as it exists independently. Berkeley goes on to reject this. But Locke's response shows that Berkeley's argument here depends on his other arguments.

See PROBLEMS ARISING FROM THE VIEW THAT MIND-DEPENDENT OBJECTS REPRESENT MIND-INDEPENDENT OBJECTS, p. 53.

2. On p. 19, Hylas argues that we need the idea of 'a material substratum' – the stuff or substance that possesses primary and secondary qualities and holds them together to make

one thing, one physical object. This 'material substratum' can exist unperceived. Berkeley points out that it is *never* perceived, since it is distinct from its primary and secondary qualities, and we have said that all we perceive are primary and secondary qualities. So what can we say about it? Once you list all the qualities of a table, what is left of the table? For instance, size is a quality – if the matter of the table is distinct from its qualities, then in itself, it has no size! When substance exists unperceived, it exists without any qualities at all.

Locke saw the point, and accepted that the idea of substance was the idea of something unknown. A realist view of physical objects involves a mystery. Worse, Berkeley argues, is quite literally inconceivable – we can say nothing about how it exists at all. (He repeats the point on p. 36.)

> Locke, *An Essay concerning Human Understanding*, Bk 2, Ch. 23.

3. Don't we just *see* that physical objects exist? On p. 21, Berkeley argues that neither our senses nor reason supports such a claim.

    a. As argued previously, all we perceive are primary and secondary qualities, not mind-independent physical objects.
    b. Therefore, our experience cannot verify the hypothesis that there is a mind-independent physical world.
    c. Worse still, the hypothesis of 'physical substance' is not one that is even *suggested* by experience.
    d. So close attention to experience supports the claim that all there is (all we can say there is) is what we can experience.
    e. What we experience are ideas.
    f. Therefore, our experience supports idealism, not realism.

> Is the concept of 'physical substance' coherent?

> Outline and explain Berkeley's argument from experience to idealism.

4. Berkeley's next argument is captured in the last remarks of the First Dialogue: supposing that the objects of perception can and do exist independently of being perceived leads to scepticism, something discussed above in Scepticism about

THE EXISTENCE OF THE EXTERNAL WORLD (p. 40) and SCEPTICISM ABOUT THE NATURE OF THE EXTERNAL WORLD AGAIN (p. 50). How is it that we can connect up our experiences to something 'beyond' them – which, following the objection just made, we can't even describe or understand? How we can know that ideas really do represent (and represent accurately) something that exists completely independently of them?

Compare and contrast Berkeley's four arguments. Which do you think is the strongest and why?

Berkeley's 'master' argument

On p. 21, Berkeley provides another argument against the possibility of the objects of perception being mind-independent. It has come to be known as his 'master' argument, since he appears to set great weight upon it. Thus, Philonous says, 'I am willing to let our whole debate be settled as follows: If you can conceive it to be possible for any mixture or combination of qualities, or any sensible object whatever, to exist outside the mind, then I will grant it actually to be so'. Hylas responds that he is thinking of a tree existing unperceived by anyone. Philonous objects, what Hylas is thinking depends on his mind. He isn't actually thinking of a tree that exists independently of any mind; he is imagining a tree standing 'in some solitary place' where no one perceives it. But all the time, he is *thinking* of such a tree. We cannot think of a tree that is neither perceived nor conceived of. We can think of the idea of a tree, but not of a tree that exists independently of the mind.

However, Berkeley seems to have confused a *thought* with what the thought is *about*.

1. Thoughts cannot exist outside the mind – thoughts are psychological events or states.
2. Therefore, my *thinking* of a tree is not mind-independent. It is impossible (inconceivable) is that there is a thought of a tree when no one is thinking of a tree.
3. But what a thought is *about*, e.g. a tree, is not the same thing as the thought itself.

4. Therefore, just because my thinking of a tree is mind-dependent, it does not follow that *what I am thinking of* is also mind-dependent. It is not impossible (inconceivable) to think that a tree may exist when no one is thinking of it. (Or, at least, the 'master' argument doesn't show this – if mind-independent physical objects are inconceivable for some *other* reason, then this thought is impossible.)

Outline and assess Berkeley's 'master' argument.

Going further: a problem with causation

Berkeley develops yet another argument in the Second Dialogue, pp. 32ff. Hylas claims that matter is *whatever* is the cause of our perceptions. Berkeley objects:

1. Matter in the normal sense of the word, i.e. as mind-independent and possessing primary qualities, cannot exist (as argued previously).
2. Therefore, to talk any sense about matter, we must think of it in terms of our perceptions of it.
3. What we perceive – primary and secondary qualities – are ideas.
4. But *all ideas are passive*, they do not *cause* anything, they do not *do* anything – they are what are perceived.
5. It is the mind, and only the mind, that can cause, that is active – the mind that perceives, thinks, wills, and so on.
6. Therefore, whatever causes our perceptions must be a mind, not matter.

Does Berkeley show that there is no reason to think that mind-independent physical objects exist?

Berkeley's idealism

Berkeley has argued that what we perceive is not mind-independent in any way. But this does *not* lead to scepticism (pp. 29 and 40). His claim only supports scepticism if we continue

I shall not discuss the advantages Berkeley claims for idealism in relation to religious belief, but discuss only his strictly philosophical arguments.

to think that physical objects (reality) are mind-independent. But what we think of as physical objects – indeed, what we must mean by 'physical object' if the term is to be coherent – are bundles of ideas. They exist as mind-dependent things. Idealism has no need to discover how our perceptions of physical objects relate to reality. In experiencing ideas, we are experiencing the world.

But without mind-independent physical objects, what explains why we perceive what we do?

1.   As (the ideas that comprise) physical objects are mind-dependent, there are three possible causes of my perceptions: ideas, my mind, and another mind.
2.   Ideas themselves don't cause anything.
3.   If physical objects depended on *my* mind, then I would be able to control what I perceive.
4.   But I can't. Perception is quite different to imagining; we are more passive – the sensations just occur to us, and we can't control them. Imagination is voluntary, but perception is involuntary.
5.   Therefore, (the ideas that comprise) physical objects don't depend on my mind.
6.   Therefore, (the ideas that comprise) physical objects must exist in another mind, which then wills that I perceive them.
7.   Given the complexity and systematicity of our perceptions, that mind must be God.

Berkeley is aware that this view is counter-intuitive. But, he argues, it follows from his previous arguments. The rest of his defence of idealism amounts to answering possible objections and correcting misunderstandings. There is nothing impossible about his conclusion. We know from our own experience that minds can give rise to thoughts. At the end of the Third Dialogue, Berkeley points out how many metaphysical puzzles can be solved by adopting idealism: for example, we can establish the existence of God and dissolve problems about the ultimate nature of matter, how matter can cause ideas in a mind, and how matter could ever produce mind.

Discuss the difference between perception and imagination.

For a different account of the relation between perception, physical objects and God, see GOING FURTHER: DESCARTES ON THE EXISTENCE OF THE EXTERNAL WORLD, p. 111.

Outline and explain Berkeley's argument for the claim that our perceptions are caused by God.

Objections and replies

BERKELEY, *THREE DIALOGUES BETWEEN HYLAS AND PHILONOUS*, THIRD DIALOGUE

We've seen how idealism can emerge from objections to realism. But it is no improvement if it faces equally powerful objections of its own. In this section, we discuss six objections and Berkeley's responses. The six objections relate to unperceived objects, illusions, scientific investigation, objectivity, solipsism and the role of God. They appear in a different order in the text, but are organised here for ease of understanding.

Unperceived objects

On p. 45, Hylas says 'to be perceived is one thing and to exist is another'. If things cannot exist when we are not perceiving them, then when they are not being perceived, they cease to exist! This is very counter-intuitive.

The objection was famously put in the form of a limerick:

There was a young man who said, God
must find it exceedingly odd
when He finds that the tree
continues to be
when no one's about in the Quad.

Berkeley responds that when *we* are not perceiving them, physical objects still exist in the mind of God. This reply is summarised (a little inaccurately) in the second part of the limerick:

Dear Sir, your astonishment's odd.
I'm always about in the Quad,
And that's why the tree
continues to be
Since observed by, yours faithfully, God.

Outline and explain the objection to idealism from unperceived objects and Berkeley's reply.

The inaccuracy is the suggestion that God *observes* the tree. Berkeley says that the tree (which is a bundle of ideas) is *comprehended by and exists in* the mind of God. God does not observe the tree, since it is not external to God's mind.

Idealism does not give an adequate account of illusions and hallucinations

See THE ARGUMENT FROM ILLUSION, p. 33.

On p. 47, Hylas asks how idealism can explain illusions. Since we perceive ideas, there must be an idea that corresponds to the illusion. But we don't want to say that the physical object is as it looks in the illusion. If we see an oar half-submerged in water, it looks crooked, but it isn't. But the oar is just what we see; and what we see is crooked, not straight.

Berkeley's response is that we aren't misperceiving – what we perceive in the case of the half-submerged oar *is* crooked. However, this is misleading if we infer that the oar would feel crooked if we touched it or would look crooked when pulled out of the water. So illusions mislead us regarding the ideas we might *associate* with what we perceive.

This entails that the oar *is* crooked when half-submerged. Because Berkeley argues that reality is the ideas we perceive; there is no appearance-reality distinction. But to say the oar is crooked is very odd indeed – it just sounds false!

Compare and contrast the idealist and the direct realist explanations of illusions (p. 33).

In *Three Dialogues*, Berkeley doesn't consider or respond to this objection. Elsewhere in his writings, however, he replies that the problem here is with language. He agrees that we shouldn't *say* 'The oar is crooked', since what we understand that to mean is that it would look crooked under normal conditions. And this is false. So to avoid this implication, we should say 'The oar looks crooked' – and this is correct.

What about hallucinations? Berkeley discusses these, in the form of dreams, on p. 45. Hallucinations are products of imagination. Normally, imagination is voluntary and perception is not (see BERKELEY'S IDEALISM, p. 63). But hallucinations are *involuntary*, so Berkeley provides two other criteria that mark off hallucinations from perception. First, they are 'dim, irregular, and confused'. Second, even if they were as 'vivid and clear' as perceptions, they are not coherently connected with the rest of our perceptual experience.

To this, we might object that these criteria mark a difference of *degree* – perceptual experiences can be more or less clear or dim, more or less coherently connected with other experiences. But surely the difference between hallucination and perception is a difference in *kind*. In perception, you experience something that exists outside your mind, in hallucination, you don't. In response, Berkeley could agree – the ideas you perceive originate in God, but in hallucination they don't. His criteria are only supposed to indicate *how we can tell*.

Does Berkeley's idealism give an adequate account of illusions and hallucinations?

Going further: scientific investigation

On p. 50, Hylas objects that science presupposes the existence of matter. How, according to idealism, can we understand scientific investigation and explanation of the world?

Before looking at Berkeley's reply, it is worth joining this thought with another. In science, we manipulate the objects we perceive – we open up the body of an animal and see its heart or again, we put something under the microscope and see its microstructure. As we do so, we experience *new* ideas, ones not previously experienced of this physical object. What is Berkeley's explanation of what is happening?

His response is surprising. What we see through a microscope is not, strictly speaking, the same thing that we perceive with the naked eye. Each idea is something distinct. But language couldn't function this way. So we use words referring to what we perceive to pick out *bundles* of ideas that are typically connected together.

What we are investigating when we are investigating physical objects is not the 'true nature' of some unified thing, but the connections between our perceptual experiences. Scientific explanations and the 'laws of nature', then, are accounts of how our perceptions are connected to each other.

This has a further surprising result. Physical objects are just bundles of ideas. But ideas can't cause anything. So physical objects don't cause anything. So an animal's organs don't *cause* it to stay alive. Of course, we can *say* that the heart pumps blood – but this is not strictly true. Science doesn't discover causal relations between physical objects; it only discovers *regularities* in our perceptual experience. These regularities are laid down in the mind of God, from which all our perceptions originate.

Explain Berkeley's account of scientific investigation and explanation.

Idealism cannot secure objective space and time

See SENSE-DATA TELL US OF 'RELATIONS' BETWEEN OBJECTS, p. 54.

Russell argues that realism requires physical objects to exist in objective space and time. We can turn this around – for there to be objective space and time, there need to be mind-independent physical objects. But according to Berkeley, physical objects are ideas, and so there is no gap between appearance and reality. So the physical objects I experience must exist in the space and time that I experience.

On p. 53, Hylas objects that if you and I look at the same tree, the idea that exists in my mind is numerically different from the idea that exists in your mind. You see the tree that appears to you; I see the tree that appears to me. In that case, no two people ever see the same, one thing.

Berkeley's first response is that we see the same tree in the sense of 'exactly resembling'. The tree you see is qualitatively identical to the tree I see. But this reply runs counter to common sense. Surely you and I can look at *one* and the same tree.

Realism, of course, says we can; the tree is a physical object, publicly accessible, and independent of either of our minds. The tree you see is numerically identical to the tree I see.

Berkeley's second response is better. Indirect realism faces the same problem – you experience your sense-data of the tree, I experience mine. But indirect realism can respond that we both experience one and the same tree via our different sense-data. Idealism can similarly say that we both perceive a copy of the idea of the tree in *God's* mind. And this is enough to say that we perceive the same thing.

(The ideas that make up) physical objects and the relations of space and time between them exist in God's mind. Now, as Russell says, 'objective' space and time is the space and time that characterise physical objects as science describes them. So, following Berkeley's account of science, objective space and time are regularities in relations between what we experience, and these regularities are part of the mind of God. So idealism can secure objective space and time – in the mind of God.

Idealism leads to solipsism

Solipsism is the view that only oneself, one's mind, exists. There are no mind-independent physical objects and there are no other minds either. We can object that Berkeley's FOUR ARGUMENTS AGAINST MIND-INDEPENDENT OBJECTS (p. 60) – starting from the claim that everything I perceive is mind-dependent – lead to the conclusion that all that exists is *my own experience*. Or at least, experience gives me *no reason* to believe that anything apart from my experience exists (or can exist). If all I perceive are ideas, what reason do I have to think that other minds exist? For that matter, what reason do I have to think that *minds* exist? After all, I do not perceive minds.

Berkeley doesn't discuss this objection from solipsism explicitly, though Hylas expresses a version of it on p. 43, and Berkeley makes a number of remarks we can draw upon. He accepts that 'strictly speaking', I have no *idea* of a mind. But because I am a mind – a 'thinking substance' – I know I exist.

Explain the distinction between numerical and qualitative identity.

Does Berkeley successfully explain how our perceptual experience can be objective?

1. The mind is that which (actively) perceives, thinks and wills, while ideas are passive.
2. I am aware of myself as capable of this activity.
3. Therefore, I am not my ideas, but a mind.
4. Being a mind myself, I have a 'notion' of what a mind is.
5. Therefore, it is possible that other minds exist.
6. My perceptions don't originate in my mind.
7. Therefore, they are caused by some other mind.
8. The complexity, regularity, etc., of my experience indicates that this mind is God.

See BERKELEY'S IDEALISM, p. 63.

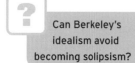

Can Berkeley's idealism avoid becoming solipsism?

As for other finite minds - other people - Berkeley doesn't spend much time on the matter, but indicates that there is evidence in my experience that they exist. Their existence, as Russell also argues (THE EXISTENCE OF THE EXTERNAL WORLD IS THE BEST HYPOTHESIS, p. 40), is a matter of inference.

Whether God can be used to play the role He does

However persuasive one finds Berkeley's arguments regarding perception, one may object to his appeal to God. It is important to note, however, that Berkeley does not *assume* that God exists, and then wheel him in to resolve philosophical difficulties in his theory. Rather, the existence of God is an inference, supported by the arguments. The cause of our perceptions is a mind, because we can only conceive of minds being active: 'I have no notion of any action other than volition, and I can't conceive of volition as being anywhere but in a spirit' (p. 48). The 'variety, order, and manner' of what I perceive shows that the mind that produces these ideas is 'wise, powerful, and good, beyond anything I can comprehend' (Second Dialogue, p. 31). I derive the idea of God from my knowledge of my own mind, 'heightening its powers and removing its imperfections' (p. 43).

But the exact relationship between ideas in the mind of God and what we perceive is puzzling (p. 58). Berkeley has said that physical objects exist in the mind of God, but

1. What I perceive is in my mind, not God's mind.
2. God can't have the sorts of perceptual experiences I have – God doesn't perceive as I do, and does not undergo sensations, such as pain (p. 49).
3. The ordinary objects of my perception change and go out of existence, but God's mind is said to be unchanging and eternal.
4. Therefore, what I perceive couldn't be part of God's mind.

Berkeley makes the following points in response:

1. What I perceive is a copy of the idea in God's mind.
2. The ideas of physical objects exist in God's mind not as perceptions, but as part of God's understanding. So while God doesn't *feel* pain, he knows what it is for us to feel pain.
3. The whole of creation exists in God's mind, eternally.
4. What I perceive, which changes, is what God *wills* me to perceive, and 'things ... may properly be said to begin their existence ... when God decreed they should become perceptible to intelligent creatures'.

Is Berkeley's idealism true?

Key points: Berkeley's idealism

- Idealism claims that all that exists are minds and ideas. What we think of as physical objects are, in fact, bundles of ideas.
- Everything we perceive is either a primary or a secondary quality. We don't perceive anything in addition to these. Since both are mind-dependent, everything we perceive is mind-dependent.
- Berkeley argues that the idea of a world with just primary qualities makes no sense, e.g. something that has size and shape must also have colour (a secondary quality). Locke argues that something that has size and shape must also have solidity, a primary quality, so a world of just primary qualities does make sense.

- The idea of mind-independent objects doesn't make sense: if we argue that we need a 'material substratum' in which qualities exist, we have no conception of this independent of its qualities.
- Idealism solves the objection to indirect realism that we cannot know how the world is. In experiencing ideas, we are experiencing the world.
- Berkeley's 'master argument' claims that we cannot conceive of anything existing independent of all minds. When we think of such a thing, our thinking of it makes it not mind-independent. We can object that Berkeley confused thought with what a thought is about.
- If physical objects are no more than their primary and secondary qualities, and these are ideas, then we cannot say that physical objects cause our perceptions, because ideas are passive. Therefore, what causes our perceptions must be a mind, not matter.
- I do not cause my perceptions. We can distinguish between what I imagine and what I perceive by the facts that the latter are not voluntary and they are part of a coherent order of nature. So what I perceive must originate in another mind. Given its complexity etc., that mind must be God.
- Berkeley deals with objects unperceived by us by saying that they exist in the mind of God.
- Illusions are misleading not because we misperceive, but because we make false inferences about what we would perceive. To mark the fact that the perception is not 'normal', we say that what we see 'looks' a certain way rather than 'is' a certain way.
- Idealism can mark off hallucinations from perception as less clear and not connected coherently with the rest of our perceptual experience.
- Berkeley explains scientific investigation as discovering not the real nature of physical objects, but connections between our ideas. It does not discover causal connections, but regularities.
- We can object that idealism entails that no two people ever perceive the same thing, since each perceives the ideas in their own mind. Berkeley responds that we perceive similar things, and these are copies of the one idea in God's mind.

- We can object that I don't know that any other minds exist. Berkeley argues that we can reason that the ideas I perceive originate in the mind of God, and that my experience contains evidence that there are also other minds like mine.
- How can what I perceive exist in God's mind? Berkeley explains that I perceive copies of ideas that exist eternally in God's understanding when God wills me to do so.

Summary: perception

In this section on perception, we have considered three theories:

1. Direct realism: we directly perceive physical objects, which exist independently of the mind.
2. Indirect realism: via sense-data, we indirectly perceive physical objects, which exist independently of the mind.
3. Idealism: we directly perceive 'physical objects', but these do not exist independently of the mind – they are collections of ideas.

In our discussion and evaluation of these theories, we have looked at the following issues:

1. How do we explain variations between what people perceive?
2. What do we perceive in an illusion or hallucination?
3. Are hallucinations the same kind of mental state as perceptions or a completely different kind which merely seems the same?
4. Can we coherently describe our perceptual experiences without presupposing the existence of physical objects?
5. What are primary and secondary qualities? Is there a valid distinction between them? Do secondary qualities exist 'in the mind' while primary qualities exist 'in the object'?
6. Do the arguments from illusion, secondary qualities, or perceptual variation support the existence of sense-data?
7. If we perceive only sense-data directly, can we know whether physical objects exist?

8. If there is an external world, can we know that sense-data accurately represent it? Can we know what physical objects are like?

9. Can we form a coherent idea of physical objects existing independently of the mind? Do we have any experience that supports this claim?

10. Do physical objects cease to exist when unperceived?

11. Can idealism satisfactorily distinguish between ideas that form 'reality' (physical objects) and subjective ideas?

12. Can idealism be explained in terms of the claim that physical objects are ideas existing in the mind of God?

II. The definition of knowledge: what is propositional knowledge?

What is knowledge? In this section, we discuss the claim, deriving from Plato's dialogue *Theaetetus*, that knowledge is a belief that is both true and justified. This claim was widely accepted until 1963, when Edmund Gettier published a very strong objection. We will look at his objection and four responses to it. Two try to defend the theory and two reject it in favour of a different account of what knowledge is. But first, we need to clarify some terminology.

A. Terminology

There are different types of knowledge. The first is 'acquaintance knowledge'. This is knowledge *of* someone or some place. For example, I know Oxford well. The second is 'ability knowledge', knowing *how* to do something. For example, I know how to ride a bike. These first two types of knowledge are very interesting, and raise some important philosophical puzzles, but we will be concerned only with a third type of knowledge, 'propositional knowledge'. Propositional knowledge is knowledge *that* some claim – a proposition – is true or false. A proposition is a declarative statement, or more accurately, what is expressed by a declarative statement, e.g. 'eagles are birds'. Propositions can go after the phrases 'I believe that …' and 'I know that …'. So I know that eagles are birds. From now on, our question is, what is it to know that a proposition is true or false?

Explain and illustrate the three types of knowledge.

Key points: terminology

- There are different types of knowledge: acquaintance, ability, and propositional knowledge. Theories of knowledge discussed here are about propositional knowledge.

B. The tripartite view

The tripartite definition of knowledge

The tripartite definition of knowledge claims that knowledge is justified, true belief. It claims that if you know some proposition, *p*, then

1. the proposition *p* is true;
2. you believe that *p*;
3. your belief that *p* is justified.

And if you have a justified true belief that *p*, then you know that *p*.

NECESSARY AND SUFFICIENT CONDITIONS

The tripartite definition aims to provide a complete analysis of the concept of propositional knowledge. Its three conditions, taken together, are intended to be 'equivalent' to knowledge. So if someone knows some proposition, they should fulfil exactly those three conditions. And if they fulfil those conditions, then they know the proposition. The conditions are 'necessary and sufficient conditions' for their knowledge that *p*.

Necessary and sufficient conditions are related to conditional statements, which take the form 'if *x*, then *y*'. Such statements relate the truth of two propositions, e.g. 'it is raining' and 'I am getting wet', e.g. 'If it is raining, then I am getting wet'. The conditional asserts that if the first statement (known as the antecedent) is true, then the second statement (the consequent) is also true. Suppose the conditional is true: *if* it is raining, then I am getting wet. It follows that if the antecedent is true (it is raining), then the consequent is true (I'm getting wet). It also follows that if the consequent is false (I am not getting wet), then the antecedent is false (it is not raining).

The tripartite definition of knowledge claims that *if* all the three conditions it lists are satisfied – if you have a justified true belief that *p* – then you know that *p*. You don't need anything else for knowledge; the three conditions, together, are *sufficient*. It also says that *if* you know that *p*, then you have a justified true belief that *p*. There is no other way to know that *p*, no other analysis of knowledge. So, it claims, each of the three conditions is *necessary*. If *p* is false, or you don't believe that *p*, or your belief that *p* is not justified, then you don't know that *p*.

So the definition puts forward *two* conditionals: if all three conditions are satisfied, then you know that *p*; and if you know that *p*, then all three conditions are satisfied. This means whenever you have one, you have the other. Knowledge and justified true belief *are the same thing*. Justified true belief is necessary for knowledge (you can't have knowledge without it), but it is also sufficient for knowledge (you don't need anything else).

> Explain the tripartite definition of knowledge.

Are the conditions individually necessary?

> The method of finding counterexamples is important in philosophy. If a theory makes a general claim, we only need to find a single instance in which this is false to show that something is wrong with the theory.

We can raise two kinds of objection to the tripartite definition of knowledge by searching for counterexamples. First, it may be that one of the conditions is not necessary for knowledge – can we have knowledge without justified true belief? Second, it may be that all of the conditions together are still not sufficient for knowledge – can we have justified true belief without knowledge? We will discuss the first question in this section, and the second question in the next section.

JUSTIFICATION IS NOT A NECESSARY CONDITION OF KNOWLEDGE

Why think that justification is necessary for knowledge? Could knowledge be just true belief? The difficulty with this suggestion is that people can have true beliefs without having any *evidence* or *justification* for their beliefs. True beliefs can be formed or held on irrational grounds. For example, someone on a jury might think that the person on trial is guilty just from the way they dress. Their belief, that the person is guilty, might be true; but how someone dresses isn't evidence for whether they are a criminal! Or again true beliefs can just be *lucky*. For example, there is a lot of evidence that astrology does not make accurate predictions, and my horoscope has often been wrong. Suppose on one occasion, I read my horoscope and believe a prediction, although I know there is evidence against thinking it is right. And then this prediction turns out true! Did I *know* it was right?

In both examples, it is counter-intuitive to say that the belief counts as knowledge, because the person has no reason, no evidence, no justification, for their belief. Knowledge, then, needs some kind of support, some reason for thinking that the proposition believed is true. This is what is meant by saying that knowledge needs to be *justified*.

We can object that sometimes we use the word 'know' just to mean 'believe truly', without worrying about justification. If I ask, 'Do you know who wrote the *Meditations*?', I'm only interested in whether you have the true belief that it was Descartes. But we could reply that this is just a loose use of the word 'know'; strictly speaking, unless your belief is justified, it isn't really knowledge. Alternatively, we could say that true belief can count as knowledge (at least sometimes) in this sense; but there is another, stronger sense of 'knowledge', which is what we are interested in here.

TRUTH IS NOT A NECESSARY CONDITION OF KNOWLEDGE

Could knowledge be simply justified belief? There are two very different possibilities here. First, perhaps we can know what is false. Second, perhaps we shouldn't talk about truth or falsehood at all.

People can believe propositions that aren't true. For example, someone may claim that flamingos are grey, and *think* that they

We'll return to this debate in RELIABILISM, p. 89.

Some philosophers have thought that another difference between knowledge and belief is *certainty*. Knowledge must be certain; beliefs don't have to be. If a belief is certain, then it can't count as knowledge. Whether this is right will be discussed in INFALLIBILISM, p. 86.

Does true belief on its own ever amount to knowledge?

know this. But they are mistaken: flamingos are not grey, but pink. Of course, they *believe* that flamingos are grey, they may even be *certain* that flamingos are grey. But beliefs can be false, and if they are, then they are not knowledge. You can't know something false.

What if many people, perhaps a whole society, share a particular belief and have good reasons for doing so? For instance, almost everybody used to believe that the Earth is flat. It does, after all, look that way. Should we say that people used to know that the Earth is flat? Or should we say that they didn't know it, they only believed it?

Another puzzle arises with how specific we make the claim. One of the most important revolutions in scientific thinking was the shift from Newtonian physics to Einstein's theory of relativity. Now, our everyday experience is very accurately described by Newtonian physics (because we are not moving at speeds close to the speed of light). However, strictly speaking, Newtonian physics is false. So do we know the claims of Newtonian physics, which after all, we rely on and use all the time, very successfully?

One response is to note that the claims of Newtonian physics are *roughly* true, or 'true enough' in the context of everyday life. So rather than saying we don't know them, because strictly speaking they are false, we can say that we do know them, roughly speaking. This response rules out the opposite claim regarding the flat Earth – it is not even roughly true that the Earth is flat, so people only believed, but didn't know, that it was flat.

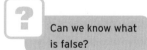
Can we know what
is false?

Kuhn, *The Structure of
Scientific Revolutions*

Going further: doing away with truth?

Thomas Kuhn argues that science repeatedly involves large shifts in thought, such as the shift from Newtonian to Einsteinian physics. One way of thinking, which Kuhn calls a 'paradigm', is replaced by another. When this happens, Kuhn claims, we can't compare the two paradigms in such a way as to say that one is true and the other is false, because 'paradigm shifts' involve changes in the concepts that we use to understand and explain reality. And there is not just one *right* set of concepts that matches reality.

It is natural to think that a scientific theory (paradigm) can be evaluated as true or false, or at least better (more true) or worse (more false), by comparing its claims with evidence derived from observation. But, argues Kuhn, there is no 'theory-neutral' way of describing the world which we can use to compare and judge between two paradigms.

1. How scientists describe what they observe depends on the concepts they use.
2. The main concepts of a paradigm acquire their meaning in relation to the paradigm as a whole.
3. Therefore, a different paradigm, even if it uses the same term, interprets the concept differently, because it plays a new and different role.
4. Therefore, different paradigms are talking about different things.
5. There is no neutral way of describing the world.
6. Therefore, we cannot compare different paradigms' claims to say that one is more 'correct' or 'true' than another, as they could both be correct *in their own terms*.

If we insist that knowledge involves truth, then it will be difficult to talk of scientific knowledge. So we should say that knowledge is justified belief.

We can object that if we do not assume that scientific theories are getting closer to the (objective) truth, we cannot explain the success of science. Technology has advanced considerably – the best explanation for this is that the scientific theories which underpin technology are more accurate than before. Kuhn responds that there is progress, including the solving of problems, but he argues that the idea that we are getting 'closer to the truth' makes no sense. Science responds to the challenges it faces at any particular time; this does not mean that there is an 'ultimate goal' – truth – towards which it is moving.

A different objection is to argue that there have been no revolutions as Kuhn describes them. Changes in scientific theory

> Outline and explain how Kuhn's theory of science can be used to argue that knowledge doesn't involve truth.

involve considerable continuity and overlap, e.g. in beliefs about methodology and evidence. If there have been no Kuhnian revolutions, then scientific theories exhibit enough similarity for us to compare them and judge which is better.

A third objection accepts that we can't talk about Truth (with a capital 'T'), how the world 'really' is independent of our concepts or experience or way of thinking about it. But we can still argue that within each way of thinking, there are true (small 't') and false beliefs. And only those beliefs that are true, using the concepts available within that paradigm, can count as knowledge. Knowledge is not justified True belief, it is justified true belief.

> **?** What is the relationship between truth and knowledge?

BELIEF IS NOT A NECESSARY CONDITION OF KNOWLEDGE

There are two strengths of the objection that belief is not necessary for knowledge. The weak objection is that sometimes it is possible to know something without believing it. The strong objection is that knowledge is never a form of belief.

The weak objection: suppose John is sitting an exam, but he's very nervous and has no confidence in his answers. Suppose when answering 'Which philosopher wrote the *Meditations*?', he writes 'Descartes'. He's right, and the answer isn't a lucky guess – he has remembered what he learned. So it is plausible to say that John knows the answer, he knows more than he thinks – he's just unconfident. But because he's unconfident, we should say that John doesn't *believe* that the answer is Descartes. So he knows the answer without believing it.

We can defend the tripartite definition by replying in one of two ways. We can say that John doesn't know the answer, e.g. because he can't produce a justification for giving that answer. Or we can say that John does believe that the answer is 'Descartes', although this belief is *unconscious* or 'tacit'. This unconscious belief amounts to knowledge.

Going further: knowledge is not a form of belief

Timothy Williamson argues that knowledge is not a form of belief, but an entirely different mental state. Either you believe something or you know it; but you don't know something by believing it.

Williamson, *Knowledge and Its Limits*

We can understand this by comparing it to THE DISJUNCTIVE THEORY OF PERCEPTION (p. 48). According to that theory, we only *see* that the tea is on the table if the tea is on the table. If we hallucinate this, that is an entirely different kind of mental state. Perception is not hallucination + added conditions (e.g. that what appears to you is how things are). Perception is a 'factive' mental state – you can only be in a perceptual state, such as seeing something, if the world is the way you perceive it to be.

Knowledge is the same. You can only know that *p* if *p* is true. Belief, by contrast, is a mental state that can be true or false – you can have a belief that *p* whatever the world is like. Knowledge is factive, belief is not.

The tripartite definition explains this difference by saying that knowledge is belief with additional conditions (truth, justification). But we will see (RESPONSES, p. 85) that every attempt to spell out the conditions meets objections. This is a reason to think that knowledge is not a kind of belief at all. Knowledge is *unanalysable* – there are no necessary and sufficient conditions that accurately describe what knowledge is. (If some analysis of knowledge is convincing, this theory loses much of its motivation.)

Williamson argues that knowledge is the most general factive mental state. What this means is that any factive mental state is a way of knowing. So seeing is factive – a way of knowing something is to see that it is the case. Another example is remembering. You don't remember something if what you think you remember is not actually true. So remembering is a way of knowing (about the past). And so on with other factive states.

What is a factive mental state?

Williamson argues that we should understand belief in terms of knowledge. To believe that *p* is to take *p* to be true. You can't believe that elephants are grey while also believing that your belief that elephants are grey is false! Put another way: to believe that *p* is to treat *p as if* you know that *p*. Again, we can draw a parallel with disjunctivism, which understands hallucination as a mental state in which it appears to you *as if* something is *F*. To understand what hallucination is, you have to first understand what it is to perceive that something is *F*. Likewise, we can only understand what beliefs are if we first understand what knowledge is.

One objection to Williamson's theory points to those occasions on which we make mistakes. Suppose I thought I knew something, but it turns out I didn't. We would usually say that I had, nevertheless, *believed* it. I believed it, but I thought I knew it; this shows that we can mistake belief for knowledge. If knowledge isn't a kind of belief, this would be puzzling. But Williamson can reply, as the disjunctivist does in the case of hallucination, that just because belief and knowledge can be subjectively indistinguishable does not tell us anything significant about what knowledge is.

> Outline and explain two ways in which knowledge and belief may be related.

Are the conditions jointly sufficient?

Edmund Gettier famously presented cases in which we want to say that someone has justified, true belief but *not* knowledge. They show that the three conditions of the tripartite definition are not sufficient for knowledge.

GETTIER, 'IS JUSTIFIED TRUE BELIEF KNOWLEDGE?'

Gettier starts by claiming, uncontroversially, that DEDUCTIVE ARGUMENT (p. 8) preserves justification. Suppose you are justified in believing that *p* (say, that Socrates is a man and that all men are mortal), and *p* entails another proposition, *q* (that Socrates is mortal). If you deduce *q* from *p*, you are also justified in believing that *q*.

He then gives two counterexamples to the tripartite definition. We'll just look at the first one. Smith and Jones are applying for the same job. Smith has excellent reason to believe that Jones will get the job, e.g. Smith has been told this by the employer. Smith also has excellent reason to believe that Jones has ten coins in his pocket, e.g. Smith has just counted them. Therefore, both of these beliefs are justified. Smith then puts the two beliefs together and deduces that the man who will get the job has ten coins in his pocket. This belief is *justified*, because it is inferred deductively from justified beliefs. It turns out that Jones doesn't get the job, Smith does. It also so happens that, unknown to him, Smith also has ten coins in his pocket. So Smith's belief that the man who will get the job has ten coins in his pocket is *true*.

Smith's belief is both true and justified, but we shouldn't say that Smith *knows* that the man who will get the job has ten coins in his pocket. Smith inferred his belief from a *false* belief, namely that Jones would get the job. So the *reason* Smith has for his belief is false. What makes his belief true (Smith, who has ten coins in his pocket, gets the job) has come apart from what justifies his belief (that Jones, who has ten coins in his pocket, will get the job). There is no connection between what justifies his belief and his belief's being true.

Other examples of justified true belief without knowledge became known as 'Gettier cases'. They all describe situations in which we have justified true belief, but not knowledge, by demonstrating how the belief is only *accidentally* true, given the evidence that justifies it. So justified true belief is not *sufficient* for knowledge. That means it is not the *same* as knowledge. If knowledge isn't justified true belief in these cases, then knowledge is *never* justified true belief.

> Outline and explain Gettier's objection to the tripartite theory of knowledge.

Key points: the tripartite view

- The tripartite definition of knowledge claims to give necessary and sufficient conditions for knowledge. If you have a justified true belief that *p*, you know that *p*; the conditions are sufficient for knowledge. And if you know that *p*, you have a justified, true belief that *p*; the conditions are necessary for knowledge.
- If justified true belief is both necessary and sufficient for knowledge, it is the same thing as knowledge.
- Although we sometimes use the word 'know' to mean 'believe truly', knowledge is not true belief. True beliefs may or may not be justified. To be knowledge, a true belief must be justified.
- Beliefs can be mistaken, but strictly speaking, no one can know what is, strictly speaking, false. However, if a belief is widespread and roughly accurate, we can say that it is knowledge.
- Kuhn argues that we cannot say that science gets closer to the truth. Because there is scientific knowledge, we can infer that knowledge must be justified belief.
- We can object either that Kuhn does not establish his claim or that truth should not be understood in terms of how the world is, independent of our way of thinking about it.
- Someone may know something without consciously believing it, e.g. if they are unconfident. But we can respond that their knowledge is an unconscious justified true belief.
- Williamson argues that knowledge is not the same mental state as belief because knowledge is factive and belief is not. An important argument for his view is that it is not possible to analyse knowledge in terms of belief.
- Gettier argues that it is possible to have justified true belief with knowledge. And so justified true belief is not knowledge. A Gettier case is one in which what makes a person's belief true is not related to what justifies it.

C. Responses

Gettier's argument poses a serious challenge to the tripartite definition. In the resulting debate over what knowledge is, most attention has focused on the claim about justification. One thought is that we need to *strengthen* what we mean by justification in the case of knowledge. Another is that we need to *replace* the justification condition with something else. But we start with a simpler idea.

Add a 'no false lemmas' condition (J+T+B+N)

Smith doesn't know that the man who will get the job has ten coins in his pocket, we said, because he inferred this belief from a false belief, namely that Jones will get the job. So all we need to do is rule this out in the definition of knowledge by adding an extra condition. You know that *p* if

1. *p* is true
2. you believe that *p*
3. your belief that *p* is justified
4. you did not infer that *p* from anything false.

Condition (4) is called the 'no false lemmas' condition. A lemma is a claim part way through an argument. Smith concluded that Jones will get the job from being told by the employer; and he then used that information to conclude that the man with ten coins in his pocket will get the job. So 'Jones will get the job' is a lemma.

This addition certainly deals with Gettier's examples. But it doesn't deal with the underlying worry about truth and justification 'coming apart'. There are Gettier cases in which you don't make an inference, so condition (4) is satisfied, but you still don't have knowledge. Here's a famous example that we will return to later. Henry is driving through the countryside. He doesn't know it, but in this part of the country – call it 'Barn County' – there are lots of fake barns, just barn facades. But they have been built so that they look just like real barns when seen from the road. As he drives along,

Alvin Goldman, 'Discrimination and Perceptual Knowledge'

Henry often thinks 'There's a barn', or 'Hey, there's another barn'. These beliefs don't count as knowledge because they are false. But just once, Henry thinks 'There's a barn' when he is looking at the one and only real barn in the area. This belief is true. And it is justified – it is formed from normal perception and Henry, of course, has no reason to suspect that he is the victim of an elaborate hoax. If our normal perceptual beliefs are justified, then so is Henry's belief. But it is not knowledge, because – as in Gettier cases – it is only a matter of *luck* that Henry's belief is true in this one instance.

Henry hasn't inferred that there's a barn from something false. First, forming beliefs from perception isn't a matter of inference – we simply believe what we see. Second, suppose it were a matter of inference. Suppose Henry thinks 'It appears to me as though there is a barn. Appearance is a good guide to reality. Therefore, there is a barn'. None of these claims is false, so he has not inferred 'There is a barn' from any false lemmas. (If Henry relies on the belief 'Appearance is a good guide to reality *around here*', then this would be a false lemma. But who thinks like this?!)

> **?**
> Does the 'no false lemmas' response to Gettier succeed? If so, how? If not, why not?

Infallibilism

The tripartite definition of knowledge does not tell us what it is for a belief to be justified. Gettier has assumed that Smith's beliefs – that Jones will get the job and that he has ten coins in his pocket – are justified. Because they are justified, his deduction that the man who will get the job has ten coins in his pocket is justified. But we can challenge Gettier's assumption. Perhaps Smith's initial beliefs are *not* justified or, better, not justified *enough* to count as knowledge. If so, then his deduction will not be justified enough either.

Smith has excellent reasons for both his beliefs about Jones getting the job and having ten coins in his pocket. But infallibilism argues that knowledge is *certain*. Only certainty can provide the degree of justification needed to turn true belief into knowledge. We can either say that a belief is not justified if it is not certain or that it is not sufficiently justified to count as knowledge if it is not certain. The implication that we should draw from Gettier cases is that our beliefs are rarely sufficiently justified to count as knowledge.

DESCARTES, *MEDITATION* I

Descartes begins *Meditation* I by declaring that he has known for a long time that in order to establish anything 'in the sciences that was stable and likely to last' (p. 1), he would have to start from the foundations. He does not need to reject as *false* everything he thinks he knows, but he needs to avoid believing things 'that are not completely certain and indubitable'. To establish this certainty, he seeks to test his beliefs by doubting them. As he tries to call his beliefs into question, he repeatedly asks how he can *know* they are true. So he understands knowledge in terms of what is 'completely certain and indubitable'. If we can doubt a belief, then it is not certain, and so it is not knowledge.

So what can we doubt? Descartes doubts the beliefs formed on the basis of what he perceives and even whether he knows if he is awake or not. He then wonders if he can know what exists at all. Of course, his 'habitual opinions' are *highly probable*, but they are not certain. To remind himself of this, he supposes that he is the victim of a massive deception by an evil demon, telepathically controlling his experiences and thoughts.

> Locke adopts a similar standard when he says that we only have knowledge of how the physical world is *at the time we experience it*. Anything else is merely belief with a high degree of probability (*An Essay concerning Human Understanding*, Bk 4, Ch. 9, §9).

> For a discussion of the arguments, see ARGUMENTS AGAINST KNOWLEDGE EMPIRICISM: THE LIMITS OF EMPIRICAL KNOWLEDGE, p. 101.

DISCUSSION

By 'indubitable', Descartes doesn't mean that he has a *feeling* of certainty. That could vary from one person to another, e.g. you might *feel certain* that God exists or that your friends will never betray you. We can all make mistakes, and be certain of something when it is not certain. For Descartes, for a belief to be indubitable, it must be *infallible* in some way. This is where Descartes' method of doubt comes in. Using his best, most careful judgement, what he judges must be true – it is impossible that he could be making a mistake.

> For more on this idea, see CLEAR AND DISTINCT IDEAS, p. 107.

1. No one can know what is false.
2. Therefore, if I know that *p*, then I can't be mistaken about *p*.
3. Therefore, for justification to secure knowledge, justification must guarantee truth.

4. Therefore, if I am justified in believing that *p*, I *can't possibly* be mistaken.
5. Therefore, if it is possible that I am mistaken, then I can't be justified in believing that *p*.
6. Therefore, infallibilism is true.

How does infallibilism respond to Gettier? Is the response persuasive?

Infallibilism defends the tripartite definition of knowledge and rules out Gettier cases, because in these cases I do not have *justified* true belief.

However, it is rare that our evidence rules out the *possibility* of error. Infallibilism entails that we have very little knowledge (even if we still have many beliefs that are very probably true). Descartes brings *everything* into question. Unless he can build his way back out using only infallible beliefs, then infallibilism leads to scepticism, rather than secure knowledge. It would be better to find a definition of knowledge that allowed us more of it.

For objections, see GOING FURTHER: DO 'I' EXIST? (p. 107) and KNOWLEDGE EMPIRICIST ARGUMENTS AGAINST INTUITION AND DEDUCTION (p. 114).

Going further: rejecting the argument for infallibilism

The argument for infallibilism rests on a logical error. Premise (2), 'if I know that *p*, then I can't be mistaken about *p*', has more than one meaning, depending on how one understands 'can't':

> 2'. It can't be the case that if I know that *p*, I *am* mistaken that *p*.

We should agree with this, because of (1) 'No one can know what is false'.

> 2''. If I know that *p*, (I am in a position that) I *can't possibly* be mistaken that *p*.

This is what infallibilism assumes in moving from (2) through (3) to (4). It is a much stronger claim than (2'), because it says that not only am I *not* mistaken, but I *can't possibly be* mistaken that *p*. Obviously, there are many cases of perception or memory in which I *could* be mistaken that *p*, but in fact I am not, and my true belief rests on evidence, so there are good reasons why I am not mistaken.

The argument for infallibilism slips from (2') (inferred from (1)) to (2'') (to support (4)). But this is a mistake, confusing one claim for another. The two claims are distinct, since one is a claim about whether I *am* mistaken, and the other is a claim about whether I *could be* mistaken. So the argument fails. To accept infallibilism, we need some other, independent reason to believe (2'').

This is called the fallacy of equivocation.

[?] Does infallibilism rest on a mistake?

Reliabilism (R+T+B)

If we allow justification to amount to less than certainty, then Gettier shows that justified true belief is not knowledge. But if we strengthen justification so that it is certainty, as infallibilism argues, then it looks like we end up with scepticism, or at least, much less knowledge than we normally take ourselves to have. So perhaps the solution is to reject the idea that knowledge requires justification.

Reliabilism claims that you know that *p* if

1. *p* is true;
2. you believe that *p*;
3. your belief is caused by a reliable cognitive process.

A reliable cognitive process is just one that produces a high percentage of true beliefs. Examples include perception, memory and testimony. True beliefs caused by such processes count as knowledge. (Of course, if these processes cause a false belief – if you misperceive or misremember or someone lies to you – then your belief isn't knowledge, but that's because it is *false*.)

One advantage of reliabilism is that it allows young children and animals to have knowledge. It is odd to say, of many animals, that they have reasons or evidence for their beliefs – they don't have that kind of sophisticated psychology. But they get around the world very well indeed, so it is also odd to deny that they have knowledge. Reliabilism explains both points. Justification is irrelevant to knowledge, which children and animals have because their true beliefs are caused by reliable processes.

However, simple reliabilism doesn't solve Gettier's challenge. Let's return to Henry, driving through Barn County. We said Henry doesn't know that he is looking at the one and only real barn when he thinks 'There's a barn'. But reliabilism has to say he *does* know. His belief is caused by a very reliable process, namely vision, and it is caused by precisely *what makes it true*. The problem is that in Barn County, this reliable process has produced a true belief in circumstances in which the belief still seems only accidentally true.

One solution is to make reliabilism more complex. In normal situations, Henry can discriminate between barns and things that aren't barns just fine, so he knows a barn when he sees one. But in Barn County, he can't reliably discriminate between real barns and facades. That's why he doesn't know that what he sees is a barn when it is. This more sophisticated reliabilism says that you know that *p* if

1. *p* is true;
2. you believe that *p*;
3. your belief that *p* is caused by a reliable cognitive process;
4. you are able to discriminate between 'relevant possibilities' in the actual situation.

RELIABILITY AS TRACKING THE TRUTH

We defined a reliable process as one that produces a high percentage of true beliefs. Robert Nozick provides a different definition in terms of 'tracking the truth'. You know that *p* if

1. *p* is true;
2. you believe that *p*;
3. in the situation you are in, or a similar situation, if *p* were not true, then you would not believe that *p*;
4. in the situation you are in, or a similar situation, if *p* were true, then you would believe that *p*.

What is reliabilism?

See ADD A 'NO FALSE LEMMAS' CONDITION (J+T+B+N), p. 85.

Outline and explain the argument for adding a fourth condition to simple reliabilism.

Robert Nozick, *Philosophical Explanations*, pp. 172ff.

(3) tends to be more important for solving the counterexamples we've been looking at. In normal cases, Henry knows that he is looking at a barn, because if it wasn't a barn he was looking at it, he wouldn't believe that it was. But in Barn County, Henry does not know he is looking at a barn, because he would believe it was a barn even if it were a facade. So in normal cases, Henry knows that there is a barn by sight; but in Barn County, he doesn't.

(3) does not imply that you *could not* be mistaken, no matter what. As stated, it means that in the situation you are in and others that are likely to come up, you are able to tell whether or not *p* is true.

> Explain the claim that knowledge 'tracks the truth'. Does it solve Gettier cases?

Going further: denying the principle of closure

According to reliabilism, I know I have two hands. It's true, and I can see and feel them. But now consider a rather extreme thought experiment. Descartes envisages the possibility that he is being telepathically deceived by an evil demon, so that although it seems to him that there is a world of physical objects, including his own body, when in fact there is no such world. The modern variant of this is to imagine oneself as a brain in a vat, being fed perceptual experiences by a supercomputer. According to reliabilism, do I know that this isn't true, that I'm not a brain in a vat? I believe that I am not, but can I tell reliably? The answer must be 'no', because if I *were* a brain in a vat, I would continue to believe that I am not. My experiences, after all, would be exactly as they are now, in the real world. So I don't know that I am not a brain in a vat.

These two results – that I know I have two hands, but I don't know that I am not a brain in a vat – produce a paradoxical conclusion. Deduction is a reliable cognitive process. If you start with true beliefs (the premises), and validly deduce another belief (the conclusion), then that belief *must* be true. 'The principle of closure' says that if I know the premises, and I validly

See INFALLIBILISM, p. 86.

See DEDUCTIVE ARGUMENT, p. 8.

deduce the conclusion from the premises, then I know the conclusion. So here is a valid deduction:

Premise 1: I have two hands.
Premise 2: If I have two hands, then I am not a brain in a vat.
Conclusion: Therefore, I am not a brain in a vat.

Reliabilism claims that I know premise (1), and of course, I know premise (2), because it is true by definition. But although I know both premises, and the premises entail the conclusion, reliabilism says that I do *not* know the conclusion. But that must mean that deduction does not always preserve knowledge! Many philosophers have found this an absurd conclusion that shows that reliabilism cannot be a correct analysis of what knowledge is.

It is tempting to think that if I do not know that I am not a brain in a vat, then I do not know that I have two hands. Because it is possible that I am mistaken about not being a brain in a vat, then it is possible that I am mistaken about having two hands. But this line of thought returns us to INFALLIBILISM (p. 86) and with it, scepticism. That is why reliabilists want to say that if I am not a brain in a vat, then the process that causes my belief that I have two hands is reliable. So I can know I have two hands without knowing whether I am a brain in a vat.

> **?** Is it coherent to deny the principle of closure?

> **?** Is knowledge true belief produced by a reliable cognitive process?

Virtue epistemology (V+T+B)

Virtue epistemology is a recent development out of reliabilism. The idea of a 'virtue' in this context relates to intellectual virtue. An intellectual virtue can be understood as a particular intellectual skill or ability or trait that contributes to getting to the truth. There are two types of virtue epistemology, each of which emphasises the importance of different kinds of intellectual virtue.

'Reliabilist' versions of virtue epistemology developed directly out of reliabilism. They focus on the virtues of cognitive *faculties*, such as acuity of perceptual organs, reliability of memory, and rationality of thought processes. 'Responsibilist' versions of virtue epistemology focus on the virtues of intellectual *traits*, such as caring for the truth, open-mindedness and intellectual courage. Responsibilist virtue epistemologists focus more on the conditions of a virtuous knower than on definitions of knowledge. So we will discuss only reliabilist virtue epistemology.

Reliabilist virtue epistemology claims that you know that *p* if

1. *p* is true;
2. you believe that *p*;
3. your true belief is a result of you exercising your intellectual virtues.

The fact that you have true belief represents a 'cognitive achievement' of yours for which you deserve 'credit'. You have the true belief 'owing to [your] own abilities, efforts, and actions, rather than owing to dumb luck, or blind chance, or something else'. We can draw an analogy with skill at sports. Suppose an archer shoots an arrow at a target. We can assess the shot in three ways:

> John Greco,
> 'Knowledge as Credit
> for True Belief'

> Ernest Sosa, *Apt Belief
> and Reflective
> Knowledge*

1. Accuracy: did the arrow hit the target?
2. Adroitness: was the arrow shot well? Was the shot competent?
3. Aptness: did the arrow hit the target *because* it was shot well?

It is possible for a shot to be accurate without being adroit – it can be lucky. It is possible for a shot to be adroit without being accurate – even an expert can miss sometimes or be unlucky. And it is possible for a shot to be accurate and adroit without being apt. Suppose it was shot well, but then a gust of wind blows the arrow all over the place before finally, by chance, it hits the target. That's quite different from when the arrow hits the target because of the skill of the archer.

We can now apply this to belief:

1. Accuracy: is the belief true?
2. Adroitness: is the way that the person formed the belief an exercise of their intellectual virtues?

3. Aptness: is the belief true *because* the person used their intellectual virtues in forming it?

Explain the claim that knowledge is apt belief.

See GOING FURTHER: DENYING THE PRINCIPLE OF CLOSURE (p. 91) for another objection to reliabilist virtue epistemology.

I) Is knowledge true belief that results from exercising one's intellectual virtues? 2) Is there a satisfactory solution to Gettier problems?

According to Sosa, knowledge is apt belief – belief that is true because it is formed by an exercise of intellectual virtue. This is more than being both true *and* the result of virtuous intellectual activity. The virtuous intellectual activity explains *why* the person holds a true belief.

Does this solve our puzzle cases? Consider Henry again. Normally, of course, when Henry sees and recognises a barn, he believes it is a barn because he sees and recognises it, so his belief is apt. In Barn County, he uses these *same* abilities to acquire the true belief 'there's a barn'. That means that his belief is still apt. But, we said, that belief doesn't count as knowledge.

The reliabilist virtue epistemologist can reply in two ways. Either Henry *doesn't* have the ability to recognise barns in Barn County, because of all the fake barns, as demonstrated by all his false beliefs about the other barn facades. His true belief can't be the result of an ability he doesn't have – so it isn't apt. Or we can say that because of all the fake barns around, the fact that his belief is true in this one case is the result of *luck*. Again, Henry's belief is not the result of his abilities.

Key points: responses

- The 'no false lemmas' amendment to the tripartite definition of knowledge adds the fourth condition that you don't infer your belief from anything false. While this deals with Gettier's own examples, there are other counterexamples, such as Barn County, in which someone arrives at a justified true belief without relying on a false inference, but the resulting belief still isn't knowledge.
- Infallibilism strengthens the justification condition, claiming that to be knowledge, a belief must be certain. Descartes adopts this standard in order to doubt all his beliefs to find out, in the end, what we can know to be true.

- He doubts his perceptions and whether he is awake. He questions what he can know even if an evil demon is controlling his experiences and thoughts.
- Infallibilism argues that if I cannot know what is false, then when I know that *p*, I *can't be* mistaken. Justification therefore requires certainty. But this argument is wrong. If I know that *p*, it can't be that I *am* mistaken. But it can happen that I am not mistaken even though I *could* be.
- Infallibilism leads to scepticism, because most beliefs are not certain.
- Reliabilism claims that knowledge is true belief caused by a reliable process, when the subject can use the process to discriminate between relevant possibilities. Nozick argues that knowledge 'tracks the truth', in particular, if *p* were not true, you would not believe that *p*.
- Both versions of reliabilism, and reliabilist virtue epistemology, deny the principle of closure, the claim that I know whatever I deduce from what I know. While this is counter-intuitive, denying the principle of closure can be used to reject scepticism.
- Reliabilist virtue epistemology analyses knowledge as true belief that is acquired as a result of a person exercising their intellectual virtues. Sosa describes this as 'apt' belief.
- We can object that this doesn't solve Gettier cases, but reliabilist virtue epistemologists try to amend their theory to succeed.

Summary: the definition of knowledge

In this section on knowledge, we have considered the claim that knowledge is justified true belief, Gettier's objections, and four responses to Gettier. In our discussion and evaluation of these theories, we have looked at the following issues:

1. There are different types of knowledge. Our concern is only with propositional knowledge.
2. Could there be knowledge that is not justified?
3. Could there be knowledge without truth?
4. Could knowledge be a different mental state from belief?

5. Is justified true belief sufficient for knowledge in all cases?
6. Is justified true belief that hasn't been inferred from anything false sufficient for knowledge?
7. Does knowledge require certainty? Can I know that *p* if it is possible that I am wrong about *p*?
8. Is knowledge true belief that is caused by a reliable cognitive process?
9. Is the principle of closure – the claim that if I know the premises of a deductive argument and validly infer the conclusion, then I know the conclusion – true?
10. Is knowledge 'apt' belief, true belief that results from my exercising my intellectual virtues?

III. The origin of concepts and the nature of knowledge: where do ideas/concepts and knowledge come from?

In this section, we turn to the question of what we know and how we know it. Central to the debate is whether we gain all our knowledge from experience, or whether there are other ways of gaining knowledge. This is the debate between empiricism, which argues that our knowledge is all derived from experience, and rationalism, which argues that it is not. (The two terms are defined below.) After looking at knowledge, we discuss something that knowledge presupposes, namely concepts. Do these also all derive from experience, or are some concepts built into the structure of the mind?

A. Knowledge empiricism

Knowledge empiricism

The syllabus defines knowledge empiricism as the claim that all synthetic knowledge is a posteriori, while all a priori knowledge is (merely) analytic. This definition involves two technical distinctions that we need to understand.

TWO IMPORTANT DISTINCTIONS

Analytic/synthetic

The contrast between analytic and synthetic propositions is a contrast between *types of proposition*. A proposition is *analytic* if it is true or false just in virtue of the meanings of the words. Many analytic truths, such as 'squares have four sides', are obvious, but some are not, e.g. 'In five days' time, it will have been a week since the day which was tomorrow three days ago' (think about it!). A proposition is *synthetic* if it is not analytic, i.e. it is true or false not just in virtue of the meanings of the words, but in virtue of the way the world is, e.g. 'ripe tomatoes are red'.

A priori/a posteriori

This contrast is, in the first instance, between *types of knowledge*. It concerns how we know whether a proposition is true. You have *a priori* knowledge of a proposition if you do not require (sense) experience to know it to be true. An example is 'Bachelors are unmarried'. If you understand what the proposition means, then you can see straightaway that it must be true. You don't need to find bachelors and ask them if they are married or not. Propositions that can only be established through experience are *a posteriori*. An example is 'There are more than 6 billion people on the Earth'.

When applied to propositions, the a priori/a posteriori distinction is about how to check or establish knowledge. It is not a claim about how we come to *understand* the proposition. To learn what a proposition means, to acquire the concepts or words involved, we may well need sense experience. But that is a different issue from how, once we understand it, we check if it is true.

We can also apply the a priori/a posteriori distinction to concepts. An a posteriori concept is one that is derived from experience. An a priori concept is one that cannot be derived from experience. We will discuss some examples in CONCEPT INNATISM (p. 137).

EMPIRICISM V. RATIONALISM

On first reflection, it might seem that the two distinctions line up neatly: only analytic propositions are known a priori; and all synthetic

On propositions, see TERMINOLOGY, p. 74.

1) Explain the analytic/synthetic distinction. 2) Come up with three different examples of analytic propositions and three of synthetic propositions.

Explain and illustrate the distinction between a priori and a posteriori knowledge.

propositions are known a posteriori. 'Bachelors are unmarried' is not only known a priori, but is also analytic. 'You are reading this book' is synthetic and can only be known through sense experience. But is this alignment correct?

All analytic propositions are known a priori. Because they are true (or false) just in virtue of the meanings of the words, we don't need to check them against sense experience to know whether or not they are true. But are all propositions that are known a priori analytic? Could there be a priori knowledge of *some* synthetic propositions? The debate over whether there is a priori knowledge of any synthetic propositions is a debate between empiricism about knowledge and rationalism.

Empiricism claims that all knowledge of synthetic propositions is a posteriori, while all a priori knowledge is of analytic propositions. Anything we know that is not true by definition or logic alone, we must learn and test through our senses.

Rationalists deny this, claiming that there is some a priori knowledge of synthetic propositions, either because this knowledge is innate (see KNOWLEDGE INNATISM, p. 118) or because we can gain such knowledge using reason rather than sense experience (see INTUITION AND DEDUCTION THESIS, p. 104). Many rationalists add that the synthetic a priori knowledge we gain through reason or innately cannot be arrived at in any other way. They may also argue that it is superior, for example by being more certain, to the knowledge or beliefs we gain through the senses.

We should refine this a little: empiricists deny, and rationalists assert, that we can gain a priori knowledge of synthetic propositions that are about things *other than one's own mind*. Many propositions about my mental states are synthetic, e.g. 'I feel sad' or 'I am thinking about unicorns'. But they don't require *sense* experience to be known; in fact, does knowing my own thoughts involve *experiencing* them at all? We don't need to worry about this. Rationalists and empiricists alike accept that we *just do* know that we have certain thoughts and feelings. The argument is about knowledge of things other than our own minds.

? Can you suggest any examples of synthetic a priori knowledge?

The terms 'rationalism' and 'empiricism' have been used in different ways at different times, and sometimes quite misleadingly. However, the common definition is the one given in the syllabus.

As we will see, rationalists have historically connected these two defences of a priori knowledge of synthetic propositions.

Outline and explain the difference between rationalism and empiricism about knowledge.

HUME, *AN ENQUIRY CONCERNING HUMAN UNDERSTANDING*, §4, PT 1

Although the syllabus refers to §4, only Pt 1 is relevant.

Hume's 'fork'

Hume defends knowledge empiricism, arguing that we can have knowledge of just two sorts of claim: the relations between ideas and matters of fact. He uses two related criteria to make the distinction, though it is easier to grasp what he means by taking them in a different order:

1. Relations of ideas 'can be discovered purely by thinking, with no need to attend to anything that actually exists anywhere in the universe' (p. 11). Matters of fact, by contrast, are 'propositions about what exists and what is the case' (p. 12).
2. Relations of ideas are statements that are 'either intuitively or demonstratively certain' (p. 11). Hume gives the example of $3 \times 5 = 30/2$ – a statement about the relations of numbers. Relations of ideas that are demonstratively certain are known by deduction. Matters of fact, by contrast, are not known by deduction, because they are statements that can be *denied without contradiction*. But any claim that can be shown to be false by deduction implies a contradiction.

See DEDUCTIVE ARGUMENT, p. 8.

The second point needs explanation. A contradiction both asserts and denies something. A true analytic proposition cannot be denied without contradiction. To say that vixens are not foxes is a contradiction in terms; it is to say that female foxes are not foxes. In a deductive argument, if you assert the premises, but deny the conclusion, then again, you contradict yourself, e.g. '$3 \times 5 = 15$ and $30/2 = 15$, but $3 \times 5 \neq 30/2$'. Hume is claiming that we gain knowledge of relations of ideas through merely understanding concepts and through deductive inference from such understanding. To deny any claims we know this way would involve a contradiction.

(We can also use deduction to infer matters of fact from other matters of fact, e.g. Socrates is a man and all men are mortal, so Socrates is mortal. But 'Socrates is mortal' isn't known by deduction in Hume's sense, since the premises rely on sense experience.)

We can now connect the two criteria. What we know that is intuitively or demonstratively certain is also what can be discovered purely by thinking – relations of ideas. On the other hand, propositions about what exists we can know only from experience – matters of fact.

On Hume's description of relations of ideas, the history of philosophy is full of debate about what qualifies. Rationalists, such as Plato and Descartes, argue that a great deal can be known through (rational) intuition and demonstration, including the existence of God. We need to interpret Hume as saying that a priori knowledge (relations of ideas) is analytic (and what can be deduced from analytic truths), while all knowledge of synthetic propositions (matters of fact) is a posteriori.

Matters of fact

The foundation of knowledge of matters of fact, Hume argues, is what we *experience* here and now, or can remember (p. 12). We gain it by using observation and employing induction and reasoning about probability. All knowledge that goes beyond what is present to our senses or memory rests on *causal inference*. We take our experience to be an effect of whatever fact we infer. If I receive a letter from a friend with a French postmark on it, I'll believe that my friend is in France – because I *infer* from the postmark to a place. I do this because I think that where something is posted causes it to have the postmark of that place; and if the letter was posted by my friend, then I believe that he is in France.

And how do I know all this? How do I know what causes what? Not by a priori reasoning or deduction. If you encounter some object that you've never experienced before, you cannot work out what effects it will have just by examining it. Just by examining a magnet – having never experienced one before –

See Intuition and deduction thesis (p. 104).

Outline and explain the key differences between relations of ideas and matters of fact.

See Inductive argument, p. 8.

could you deduce what effect it will have on metal? Just by examining bread, could you work out that it doesn't nourish tigers (p. 13)? Just by seeing a billiard ball roll towards another billiard ball, could you conclude that the second one will move away? Even if you imagine that this is what will happen, that's arbitrary, groundless.

It is only our *experience* of what causes what that enables us to make causal inferences in particular cases. It is only our experience that enables us to infer from the existence of some cause to its effect, or from some effect to its cause. I have experienced letters being posted, I have seen different postmarks, I have found that postmarks relate to where you post something, and so on. Reason can impose some order on the particular causal relations we discover through experience, but that's all (p. 14). Reason can simplify our causal principles, e.g. by identifying different instances (the movements of billiard balls and the vibrations of molecules, say) as examples of the same kind of thing (kinetic energy). But we can't, for example, discover 'ultimate' causes – the causes of why causes have the effects they do – through reasoning.

> Outline and explain Hume's theory of our knowledge of matters of fact.

Arguments against knowledge empiricism: the limits of empirical knowledge

Empiricists deny that there is any a priori knowledge of synthetic propositions. The only knowledge we have is either

1. a priori knowledge of analytic propositions and what can be deduced from them; or
2. a posteriori knowledge of synthetic propositions.

Any claim that is neither analytic nor known a posteriori, we do not know. We may object that this rules out many claims that we think we know. For instance,

1. (According to empiricism) All knowledge of synthetic propositions is a posteriori.
2. 'Physical objects exist' is a synthetic proposition.
3. But we cannot know, through sense experience, that physical objects exist.
4. Therefore, (according to empiricism) we cannot know that physical objects exist.
5. Therefore, either we cannot know that physical objects exist or empiricism is false.
6. But we can know that physical objects exist.
7. Therefore, empiricism is false.

> If this argument is right, then empiricists face SCEPTICISM ABOUT THE EXISTENCE OF THE EXTERNAL WORLD (p. 40). The key premise here is (3). Why believe this?

DESCARTES, *MEDITATION* I

Descartes provides us with an argument for (3). He begins by using THE ARGUMENT FROM ILLUSION (p. 33). He notes that he has, in the past, been deceived by his senses - things have looked a way that they are not (p. 1). Things in the distance look small, for instance. Or picking up our previous example, a stick half-submerged in water looks crooked. But, Descartes remarks, such examples from unusual perceptual conditions give us no reason to doubt all perceptions, such as that I am looking at a piece of paper with writing on it. More generally, we might say that perceptual illusions are *special cases* (and ones we can frequently explain). Otherwise we wouldn't be able to talk about them as illusions. So they don't undermine perception generally.

Descartes then doubts whether he knows he is awake (p. 1). I could be dreaming that I'm looking at a piece of paper. I could even have the thought, while I'm dreaming, that I'm not dreaming! There is no reliable way to tell whether I'm awake or asleep. This argument attacks all sense perception, even the most mundane and most certain. I cannot know that I see a piece of paper because I cannot know that I am not dreaming of seeing a piece of paper.

We can object that there *are* reliable ways of distinguishing waking perception from dreaming, such as the far greater coherence of perception. But what Descartes means is that I cannot know, of my perception now, whether I am awake or asleep. The objection assumes that I can rely on my memory of what I have experienced to compare it with my dream. But what if I'm dreaming that I remember this?

Descartes then claims that even if he were dreaming, and may be imagining particular physical objects, dreams are constructed out of *basic ideas* and these must correspond to something real – ideas of body, extension, shape, quantity, size, motion and time.

He also reaffirms the truths of mathematics.

But he then casts doubt on even these claims by questioning whether God may have deceived him (p. 2). Is it possible that he could go wrong in adding two and three? To the objection that God is good and wouldn't deceive Descartes like this (a point Descartes returns to later in the *Meditations*), Descartes introduces a further doubt. Suppose that God does not exist. Suppose, worse, that all my experiences are produced in me by an evil demon who wants to deceive me (p. 3). If this were true, I wouldn't know. So I cannot know that this is not true. Descartes uses the evil demon supposition to make sure that he doesn't believe anything he can't know. And it throws into doubt all beliefs about the external world, as they are based on his experience, which he is supposing the evil demon controls. So, (3) above: we cannot know, through sense experience, that physical objects exist. (Descartes doesn't here repeat that his beliefs about mathematics are also thrown into doubt. When he comes to consider them again, he defends them.)

How Descartes manages to respond to this supposed situation is discussed in Descartes, *Meditations* II, III, V, VI (p. 106).

For Descartes' solution, see Descartes on the existence (and nature) of God, p. 109.

Descartes' list here is a list of primary qualities, and matches Locke's, with the addition of time. See Locke, An essay concerning human understanding, Bk 2, Ch. 8, p. 44.

See Descartes on the existence (and nature) of God, p. 109.

On Descartes on knowledge, see Infallibilism, p. 86.

Outline and explain Descartes' argument that we cannot know, through sense experience, that physical objects exist.

The argument (1–7) that opens this section can be adapted to generate objections to empiricism in other areas of knowledge. For example, can we know that God exists? If 'God exists' is a synthetic claim, according to empiricism, we could only know that God exists from sense experience. But can we? Hume argued that we can't – the reasoning involves claims that sense experience cannot establish. So we can't know whether God exists. Another example is morality.

See Ontological arguments (p. 181), The argument from design (p. 200) and The cosmological argument (p. 220).

Moral claims, such as 'Murder is wrong', don't *appear* to be analytic. But could we know them through *sense* experience? Which of our senses pick up on 'wrongness', and how? If empiricists can't show that moral claims are either analytic or a posteriori, then they will be forced to conclude that there is no moral knowledge either.

This issue is picked up at A2, in WHAT IS THE STATUS OF ETHICAL LANGUAGE?

Intuition and deduction thesis (rationalism)

We noted earlier that rationalists claim that we have knowledge of synthetic propositions that does not depend upon sense experience. They argue that there are two key ways in which we gain such knowledge:

See EMPIRICISM V. RATIONALISM, p. 97.

a. we have a form of rational 'intuition' or 'insight' and the power of deduction which together enable us to grasp certain truths intellectually;
    and/or
b. we know certain truths 'innately'.

Historically, rationalists have connected these two non-empirical forms of knowledge, and a complete account of how we gain such a priori knowledge involves both. But we will look at (a) in this section, bearing in mind that, in many cases, the account will need to be completed by the discussion of (b) in KNOWLEDGE INNATISM (p. 118) and PROPOSED EXAMPLES OF INNATE CONCEPTS (p. 140).

First, the terms: you can check that you understand what deduction is by reading (or rereading) DEDUCTIVE ARGUMENT, p. 8. What about 'intuition'? This *doesn't* mean a 'gut feeling' or 'instinct'. It refers to *rational* intuition. For example, when you consider a deductive argument, do you understand why, if the premises are true, then the conclusion must be true? How is it that you can 'see' the conclusion follows – that it *must* be true if the premises are? This grasping of rational truths takes us towards the idea of 'rational intuition', though it covers much more than deductive reasoning. At the heart of rational intuition is discovering the truth of a claim just by thinking about it.

Explain the concepts of rational intuition and deduction.

NECESSARY AND CONTINGENT TRUTH

See HUME'S 'FORK', p. 99.

To understand this better, we need another distinction. Hume says that matters of fact can be denied without contradiction. In other words, statements of matters of fact *could* be either true or false. A proposition that *could* be true or false is contingent. Of course, it will *be* either true or false, but the world could have been different. It is true that you are reading this book; but you could have been doing something else – it could have been false. So it is contingently true. It is contingently true that there are more types of insect than there are of any other animal. This wasn't always true, and one day it might be false again.

A proposition is necessary if it *must* be true (if it is true), or *must* be false (if it is false). Mathematical propositions are necessary: 2 + 2 must equal 4; it is not possible (logically or perhaps mathematically possible) for 2 + 2 to equal any other number. Likewise, analytic truths are necessary: if a proposition is true by definition, then it *must* be true.

Historically, philosophers agreed that a priori knowledge is necessary and a posteriori knowledge is contingent. Why? A posteriori knowledge is knowledge of how the world is, and surely the world could always have been a different way – so all propositions about the world *could* have been true or false. Could necessary truths be established a posteriori? (Recall again that, for a priori knowledge, sense experience may be *necessary*, e.g. to enable us to understand the claim. But it is not *sufficient* – sense experience is not how we establish or justify the claim.) Leibniz points out that our sense experience only provides us with information about particular instances – that *these* two apples and these two apples make four apples; that *this* triangle has internal angles that add up to 180 degrees; and so on. But 'however many instances confirm a general truth, they aren't enough to establish its universal necessity' – because how things are doesn't tell us how things must be. If we reject this, and argue that '2 + 2 = 4' is just a generalisation of our experience so far, then we are saying that it is possible, one day, that 2 + 2 will equal some other number. But this is inconceivable. So, we should say that mathematical knowledge is a priori, established through reasoning alone.

Of course, it is possible that the figure '2' could have been *used to mean* the number 3. But then '2 + 2' wouldn't mean 2 + 2; it would mean 3 + 3. To test whether a proposition is true or false, in all cases, you have to *keep the meanings of the words the same*. If '2' means 2, and '4' means 4, then 2 + 2 must equal 4.

Leibniz, *New Essays on Human Understanding*, p. 2

Explain and illustrate the distinction between necessary and contingent truth.

So, whatever turns out to be a necessary truth must be known through a priori reasoning. If any necessary truths are not analytic, then we have some synthetic a priori knowledge.

Empiricists will object that these claims are analytic or we don't know them. See KNOWLEDGE EMPIRICIST ARGUMENTS AGAINST INTUITION AND DEDUCTION, p. 114.

DESCARTES, *MEDITATIONS* II, III, V, VI

Descartes' *Meditations* provide an extended study in establishing knowledge through rational intuition and deduction. We focus on three central claims: his arguments for the existence of the self, of God, and of physical objects. We will also consider his elaboration on the idea of rational intuition through his concept of 'clear and distinct' ideas.

Descartes on the existence (and nature) of the self (*Meditation* II, pp. 3–6)

At the end of DESCARTES, MEDITATION I (p. 102), we left Descartes supposing that he was being deceived by an evil demon. At the start of *Meditation* II, he argues that, even if the evil demon is deceiving him, 'he will never bring it about that I am nothing while I think I am something' (p. 4). Why not? Descartes cannot doubt that he exists: if he were to doubt that he exists, that would prove he does exist – as something that thinks. So he knows that he exists. He can't know that he exists *as a body* – his sense perception of his body, and of bodies in general, could be no more than a dream. But he cannot doubt that he thinks. The *cogito*, 'I think', is Descartes' first stepping stone to knowledge.

Could he nevertheless *be* a body, without knowing it? Descartes can't say, but at least his *knowledge* of what he is can't *depend* on his being a body, since he knows he exists but not whether he has a body. What he is is a thinking thing, 'a thing that doubts, understands, affirms, denies, wants, refuses, and also imagines and senses' (p. 5). This provides further knowledge of the self. I know which type of thought I am engaging in: I can't mistakenly think that I'm imagining when I'm conceiving, can't think I'm doubting when I'm willing and so on.

Outline and explain Descartes' argument for the *cogito*.

Descartes discusses this further in *Meditation* VI. It is studied in A2 Philosophy of Mind, SUBSTANCE DUALISM.

The last activity Descartes lists is 'senses'. But doesn't sense perception involve having a body? So doesn't the fact that I sense establish the existence of physical objects? No, because, Descartes notes, I have sensory experiences in my dreams as well, when I am not seeing or hearing at all. 'Sensing' is just having sensory experiences. Understood like this, independent of their cause, these experiences are nothing more than a form of thinking, and so don't depend on having a body.

> So Descartes adopts a type of sense-data theory. At this point, Descartes is an idealist (see THE IMMEDIATE OBJECTS OF PERCEPTION ARE MIND-DEPENDENT OBJECTS, p. 58), but once he proves the existence of physical objects, he becomes an indirect realist (see INDIRECT REALISM, p. 38).

Going further: do 'I' exist?

What does it mean to say 'I exist' or 'I think'? Descartes claims that 'I' am a thinking *thing*. I am the *same* thing from one thought to another. But can Descartes know this? The evil demon may deceive him: perhaps there is only *a succession of thoughts*, nothing that persists between thoughts which is a *single* thing.

Descartes' response, in an appendix to the *Meditations* called 'Objections and Replies', is to say that thoughts logically require a thinker. Perhaps it is true that there can't be a thought unless something thinks it. But that doesn't entail that the 'thinker' is a subject that persists from one thought to another. As soon as Descartes says that to be a thinker is to doubt, will, imagine, and so on, he assumes we can say these activities belong to the *same* subject, that he (the same thinker) does all this. But perhaps the evil demon is simply creating a series of false thoughts, among which is the thought that a thinker, a substance, an 'I', exists. Descartes' claims about *what* he is could be false.

> This objection is further developed in GOING FURTHER: HUME ON SUBSTANCE AND SELF, p. 150.

> See IDEALISM LEADS TO SOLIPSISM (p. 69) for a similar defence by Berkeley.

> Does Descartes establish the existence of a self?

Clear and distinct ideas (*Meditation* III, pp. 9–10)

At the start of *Meditation* III, Descartes reflects on the *cogito*. He finds that his certainty in it rests on how the idea presents itself to his mind. So he argues (p. 9),

A note on terminology: this phrase, 'clear and distinct', is the usual translation of Descartes' Latin phrase *clarus et distinctam*. However, the text on the anthology uses 'vivid and clear'. Because 'clear and distinct' is much more common, I shall stick with it.

1. 'In this first item of knowledge there is simply a clear and distinct perception of what I am asserting.'
2. If clarity and distinctness do not guarantee truth, then I cannot know that I exist.
3. I do know that I exist.
4. Therefore, 'as a general rule ... whatever I perceive very clearly and distinctly is true'.

This argument lays the foundations for Descartes' theory of *rational intuition*. Descartes has defended the *cogito* as a claim that he knows to be true just by thinking about it. What enables him to know it is that it is an idea that is 'clear and distinct'.

What does this mean? Descartes doesn't say in the *Meditations*, but gives this definition in his *Principles of Philosophy* (Pt 1, §45): an idea is clear 'when it is present and accessible to the attentive mind - just as we say that we see something clearly when it is present to the eye's gaze and stimulates it with a sufficient degree of strength and accessibility'. An idea is distinct if it is clear and 'it is so sharply separated from all other ideas that every part of it is clear'. In the *Meditations*, again drawing on an analogy with vision, Descartes connects clear and distinct ideas to what he calls 'the natural light': 'Things that are revealed by the natural light - for example, that *if I am doubting then I exist* - are not open to any doubt, because no other faculty that might show them to be false could be as trustworthy as the natural light' (p. 11). So, for Descartes, rational intuition is the 'natural light', our ability to know that clear and distinct ideas are true.

Our perception of physical objects isn't, in fact, clear and distinct, though they can *seem* so (p. 10). On reflection, Descartes sees that what was clear was 'merely the ideas', i.e. the sensory experiences, but not what causes them. Mathematical claims, such as '2 + 3 = 5', remain clear and distinct, and Descartes cannot doubt them. Or rather, he can only doubt such a claim when he thinks not about the claim, but about the power of God (or an evil demon) to deceive him. So, *at the time we consider*

?

What, according to Descartes, is a 'clear and distinct' idea?

it, a thought which is clear and distinct we must believe to be true. But in order to be sure, when we are not focusing on it, that the clear and distinct thought really is true, we need to know that we are not being deceived by God (or an evil demon). Descartes' next task, therefore, is to show that we can know this.

Descartes on the existence (and nature) of God (*Meditations* III, V)

Descartes provides two a priori arguments for the existence of God, his TRADEMARK ARGUMENT (p. 144) and his ontological argument (p. 185). As both of these arguments are discussed elsewhere, we won't repeat them here. But it is worth turning to read at least the explanation of Descartes' arguments now.

Both arguments try to prove the existence of God from just the idea of God. Descartes begins by providing an analysis of his idea of God, claiming that it is an idea of a being that is, among other things, supremely powerful and supremely perfect. These claims are intended to be analytic, true in virtue of the concept of God.

Descartes needs to show not only that God exists, but also that God wouldn't deceive us (nor allow an evil demon to deceive us).

1. God exists.
2. By definition, God is supremely perfect.
3. 'The natural light makes it clear that all fraud and deception depend on some defect' (p. 17).
4. (By definition, something that is supremely perfect can have no defects.)
5. Therefore, it is not possible for God to deceive us.

By this, Descartes does not mean that we cannot make mistakes! He means that God 'has given me the ability to correct any falsity there may be in my opinions' (p. 30). We are assured that once we have done all we can to avoid error, and form beliefs on the basis of clear and distinct ideas, then we will not go wrong. But we are not assured of anything more than this.

Descartes doesn't spell it out, but God's existence is enough to rule out deception by an evil demon as well.

1. God is supremely powerful.
2. If God is supremely powerful, then an evil demon could only deceive us if God allowed it.
3. If an evil demon is deceiving me, then I have no way of correcting my false opinions.
4. If I have no way of correcting my false opinions, then God is a deceiver.
5. Therefore, if God permits an evil demon to deceive me, then God is a deceiver.
6. God is not a deceiver.
7. Therefore, God will not permit an evil demon to deceive me.

But can we know what God will or won't do or allow? Descartes allows that we cannot know God's purposes (p. 19), but we don't need to. If we have no way of correcting our false beliefs, this would frustrate what we are, namely rational minds seeking the truth using clear and distinct ideas. We don't need to know what God's purposes are in order to know that this would amount to God being a deceiver, which is contradictory to being supremely perfect.

At the very end of the *Meditations*, Descartes also uses God's not being a deceiver to solve the objection that he may be dreaming. He accepts that we can tell the difference between dreaming and being awake, because memory connects up perceptions coherently, but not dreams, and because we can confirm our perceptions using different senses (p. 34). This response is only available *now* (and not in *Meditation* I) because God is not a deceiver. Without that, we couldn't rely on memory in this way.

See DESCARTES, MEDITATION I, p. 102.

Outline and explain Descartes' argument for the claim that we are not deceived by God.

Going further: Descartes on the existence of the external world (Meditation VI)

If perception doesn't show that physical objects exist, e.g. if we don't perceive physical objects immediately, then in order to prove they exist, we need to undertake a number of preliminary steps.

1. We need to understand our *concept* of a physical object – what is it that we think exists?
2. We need to show that this is a *coherent* concept, not something self-contradictory (like the concept of a round square).
3. We need to show that it is *possible* that physical objects exist.

With all that in place, we can then argue that

4. Physical objects do, in fact, exist, and we can know this.

We discuss Descartes' arguments for (1) and (2) in DESCARTES ON THE CONCEPT OF A PHYSICAL OBJECT (p. 142). He argues for (3) and (4) in *Meditation* VI. (3) is straightforward.

1. I have a clear and distinct idea of what a physical object is.
2. (God exists and is supremely powerful.)
3. The only reason for thinking that God cannot make something is that the concept of it is contradictory.
4. Therefore, God can make physical objects.
5. Therefore, it is possible that physical objects exist.

See ARGUMENTS AGAINST KNOWLEDGE EMPIRICISM: THE LIMITS OF EMPIRICAL KNOWLEDGE, p. 101.

Critically compare Descartes' arguments with Russell's argument.

To prove (4), Descartes first considers two arguments that aim to show that THE EXISTENCE OF THE EXTERNAL WORLD IS THE BEST HYPOTHESIS (p. 40). But he is dissatisfied because neither of them gives us certainty, which he thinks is necessary for knowledge (see INFALLIBILISM, p. 86).

The first argument is from imagination (p. 27). He begins by showing that the faculty of imagination is different from the faculty of understanding.

1.   The imagination uses images, e.g. imagining a triangle. But the understanding does not. When working mathematically with a chiliagon – a two-dimensional figure with 1,000 sides – we cannot imagine the figure.
2.   Imagining takes more effort than understanding.
3.   Therefore, imagination and understanding are different.
4.   Imagination is not essential to me, while understanding is. I cannot be me (a thinking thing) without understanding, but I can be me without imagination.
5.   The best explanation for all these differences is that imagination depends upon having a body. Imagination draws its ideas from the body, which makes its ideas sensory images and difficult to work with, and makes imagination not essential to a thinking thing. Being purely mental, understanding draws its ideas from itself, making them non-imagistic and easy to work with, and understanding is essential to a thinking thing.
6.   Therefore, it is probable that the body exists.

It is, however, only *probable*, so the argument doesn't give us knowledge of the existence of physical objects.

The second argument is from perception (p. 28). It is natural to think that we know that physical objects exist because we perceive them. Our perceptions are both

Outline and explain Descartes' argument from imagination for the existence of physical objects.

involuntary and 'much more lively and vivid' than imagination or memory. One explanation is that they are caused by physical objects that exist independent of our minds. But Descartes reminds us of his ARGUMENTS AGAINST KNOWLEDGE EMPIRICISM: THE LIMITS OF EMPIRICAL KNOWLEDGE (p. 101) from perceptual illusion and dreaming (p. 29). The *mere fact* that perceptual experiences are vivid and involuntary isn't enough to show that they are caused by mind-independent physical objects.

It does, however, provide the starting point for his next argument (p. 30). I have added in missing premises in brackets, some of which Descartes assumes because he has argued for them previously.

1. I have involuntary perceptual experiences of physical objects.
2. (These experiences are caused by some substance.)
3. If the cause of my perceptual experiences is my own mind, my perceptual experiences are voluntary.
4. Because I know my mind, I would know if my perceptual experiences are voluntary.
5. Therefore, because I know that my perceptual experiences are involuntary, I know that the cause of my perceptual experiences is not my own mind.
6. Therefore, the cause must be some substance outside me – either God or physical objects.
7. If the cause is God, then God has created me with a very strong tendency to have a false belief (that physical objects exist) that I cannot correct.
8. If God has created me with such a tendency, then God is a deceiver.
9. (God is perfect by definition.)
10. (Therefore,) God is not a deceiver.

Berkeley identifies exactly these features to distinguish perception from imagination, but he is an idealist. See IDEALISM DOES NOT GIVE AN ADEQUATE ACCOUNT OF ILLUSIONS AND HALLUCINATIONS, p. 66.

Descartes' argument for this claim is given in his TRADEMARK ARGUMENT, p. 144.

See DESCARTES ON THE EXISTENCE (AND NATURE) OF THE SELF, p. 106.

On 7-12, see DESCARTES ON THE EXISTENCE (AND NATURE) OF GOD, p. 109.

See DESCARTES'
TRADEMARK ARGUMENT
(p. 144) and DESCARTES'
MEDITATION V (p. 185).

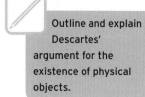

**Outline and explain
Descartes'
argument for the
existence of physical
objects.**

11. (Therefore, God did not create me with a tendency to have false beliefs that I cannot correct.)
12. (Therefore, if God exists, I do not have such a tendency.)
13. Therefore, if God exists, the cause of my perceptual experiences of physical objects is the existence of physical objects.
14. (God exists.)
15. Therefore, there is an external world of physical objects that causes our perceptual experiences.

This argument is one of the best examples of the use of rational intuition and deduction. It is surprising to think that we cannot know from sense experience that physical objects exist. It is even more surprising to be told that we can nevertheless know that physical objects exist using a priori reasoning.

KNOWLEDGE EMPIRICIST ARGUMENTS AGAINST INTUITION AND DEDUCTION

Rationalists claim that we have a priori knowledge of some synthetic propositions. Empiricists can respond by arguing

1. that the propositions aren't synthetic, but analytic; or
2. that we don't know them a priori; or
3. that we don't know them at all.

Is mathematics analytic?

In NECESSARY AND CONTINGENT TRUTH (p. 105), we argued that mathematical truths are necessary and therefore known a priori. Empiricists can accept that mathematical knowledge is a priori, if they also argue that it is analytic. In other words, mathematical knowledge is reached by analysing the concepts involved. But if this is true, how are mathematical 'discoveries' possible? How can we 'discover' something that is true in virtue of the meaning of the concepts?

Empiricists reply that analytic knowledge doesn't need to be obvious; mathematical truths are very complex, so it takes work to establish that they are true.

In the twentieth century, empiricists such as Bertrand Russell argued that although mathematical truths were not analytic, they were nevertheless 'logical' truths. His argument depended on technical developments in logic and in mathematics. Philosophers still disagree about the success of Russell's attempt – and attempts by other philosophers since – to reduce mathematics to logical truths. While some attempts are promising, no reduction has been completed.

> If you are mathematically minded, research Fermat's last theorem on the internet.

Going further: geometry

The truths of geometry don't seem to be analytically true. The fact that it takes at least three straight lines to enclose a space in two dimensions seems to be a truth about *space*, rather than the *concept* of space. Yet it has mathematical certainty, and can be proved by mathematical geometry. How could such certainty come from sensory experience alone?

In fact, there is more than one geometry of space. It is in classical, or Euclidean, geometry that it takes three straight lines to enclose a two-dimensional space. But mathematicians have worked out perfectly good, consistent *non-Euclidean* geometries in which this and other 'truths' are not true (if you curve the two-dimensional plane, e.g. the surface of the Earth, you can enclose a space with two straight lines – longitude). So, empiricists argue, geometry applied to the real world has two elements: conceptual definitions, which are analytic truths; and then an a posteriori claim about which type of geometry applies to space. So there are geometrical truths about the nature of space, but they are not necessary – space could have been otherwise, e.g. non-Euclidean. In fact, in some cases in advanced physics, Euclidean geometry does not describe space accurately.

> Are mathematical propositions synthetic and known a priori?

Does Descartes know what he claims to know?

If Descartes' deductions of the existence of himself, God and physical objects fail, then he hasn't shown that we have knowledge through a priori reasoning.

We saw one objection to his claim that he exists in GOING FURTHER: DO 'I' EXIST? (p. 107). This challenged Descartes' claim that he *knows* that he is a thinking thing. A second objection is that he can know this, but it does not count as synthetic a priori knowledge. The reason is because it derives from our *experience* of ourselves. We noted in EMPIRICISM V. RATIONALISM (p. 97) that the debate between them is about knowledge of synthetic propositions about the world *outside one's mind*. One reason for this is because it is unclear to say that knowledge of one's own mind is either a priori or a posteriori. Thus I know I exist because I experience myself, not because of anything about 'clear and distinct' ideas being certainly true.

Objections to Descartes' arguments for the existence of God are discussed together with those arguments in DESCARTES' TRADEMARK ARGUMENT (p. 144) and DESCARTES, *MEDITATION* V (p. 185).

Descartes' argument for the existence of physical objects depends on his arguments for the existence of God. If these fail, then he hasn't shown that physical objects exist.

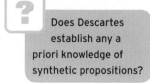

Locke calls this 'reflection'. See THE *TABULA RASA*, p. 132.

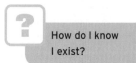

How do I know I exist?

Does Descartes establish any a priori knowledge of synthetic propositions?

Going further: the Cartesian circle

It is worth evaluating Descartes' use of CLEAR AND DISTINCT IDEAS (p. 107), as this is his account of rational intuition itself. An objection called 'the Cartesian circle' argues Descartes cannot establish that clear and distinct ideas guarantee truth.

In *Meditation* III (p. 10), Descartes says that he is certain of his clear and distinct ideas when he considers them. But when he turns away from the idea itself to consider the power of God to deceive him, he can doubt that it (or any clear and distinct idea) is certain. Now, when trying to prove the existence of God, Descartes relies on what he can clearly and distinctly perceive, because this is the only way he can know anything. But given his own admission, it seems that Descartes needs to prove that God exists before he can claim to know what he clearly and distinctly perceives. It seems that he says

- I am certain that God exists only because *I am certain of whatever I clearly and distinctly perceive*; and yet
- *I am certain of whatever I clearly and distinctly perceive* only because I am certain that God exists.

But this is circular. Descartes cannot rely on clear and distinct ideas before proving God exists, but he cannot prove that God exists without relying on clear and distinct ideas. So he is stuck – he cannot take clear and distinct ideas to guarantee truth.

> Explain the Cartesian circle.

But perhaps the objection misinterprets Descartes. I *can* be certain of what I clearly and distinctly perceive without knowing that God exists, but *only at the time* that I focus on that specific thought. In other words, while I am clearly and distinctly perceiving some *particular proposition*, then I can be certain of that proposition. But when I turn my attention away from it, I no longer perceive it clearly and distinctly, I only *remember* that I did so. And this is no guarantee of truth. However, once he has shown that God exists, Descartes claims, he can know the *general principle* that whatever is clear and distinct is true. He doesn't need to focus on a particular clear and distinct idea to know it is true; he can know it is true by knowing that it is clear and distinct.

But is Descartes entitled to claim that he can be certain of what he clearly and distinctly perceives, even at the time he perceives it, while it is still possible that he is being deceived by God (or an evil demon)? He can respond that God (or the demon) cannot bring about anything 'in which I see a plain contradiction' (p. 10), and to deny a clear and distinct idea (e.g. to say that 2 + 3 does not equal 5) is a contradiction.

The best interpretation of this is that clear and distinct ideas are *necessarily* true, at least at the time when one thinks them. Empiricists can then argue that they are necessarily true either

Can we know that whatever can be clearly and distinctly perceived is true?

because they are analytically true or because thinking them, e.g. 'I think', is what makes them true. There is still no rational intuition of synthetic a priori claims.

Innatism about knowledge and concepts has historically been associated with rationalism. However, I will restrict the term 'rationalism' to the INTUITION AND DEDUCTION THESIS (p. 104), because many empiricists have recently adopted a form of innatism. See GOING FURTHER: EXPERIENCE TRIGGERS INNATE KNOWLEDGE, p. 125.

Knowledge innatism

Knowledge innatism argues that there is at least some innate knowledge. Exactly what 'innate' means in this context is disputed. But the claim is that some knowledge is part of the mind, already 'in' the mind from birth, rather than gained from experience. If there is any innate knowledge, it cannot be a posteriori, but must be a priori.

What is innate knowledge?

PLATO, *MENO* (81E FF.)

Plato's dialogue *Meno* is mostly about virtue. But it includes an extended example and discussion of innate knowledge. The anthology source doesn't have section or page numbers, but our interest begins with Socrates saying 'You argue that man cannot enquire either about that which he knows, or about that which he does not know; for if he knows, he has no need to enquire; and if not, he cannot; for he does not know the very subject about which he is to enquire'. Plato's solution to this puzzle is to say that learning is a form of *remembering*. He demonstrates this by asking Meno's slave boy a series of questions about a theorem in geometry.

Socrates draws a square in the ground that is 2 feet × 2 feet. Its total area is therefore 4 square feet. How long are the sides of a square with a total area of 8 square feet? The slave boy has not been taught geometry, and yet is able to work out the right answer in response to Socrates *only asking questions*. The boy first guesses that the sides will each be 4 feet long, but when asked what 4 feet × 4 feet is, he realises that the area of this square is 16 square feet, not 8 square feet. The answer must be between 2 feet and 4 feet – he guesses 3 feet. But again, when asked what 3 feet × 3 feet is, he realises this square would be 9 square feet, not 8 square feet.

Socrates then draws three more squares of 2 feet × 2 feet, arranging them with touching sides to make one big square of 4 feet × 4 feet. He then draws a diagonal line across each small square, dividing them into triangles. The four diagonals are arranged to form a (square) diamond in the middle of the big square. Through questioning, he gets the slave boy to agree that each triangle is half of 4 square feet, i.e. 2 square feet. There are four such triangles making up the diamond, which is therefore 8 square feet. The sides of the diamond are the diagonals of the original 2 foot × 2 foot squares. So a square with an area of 8 square feet has sides the length of the diagonal of a square that is 4 square feet.

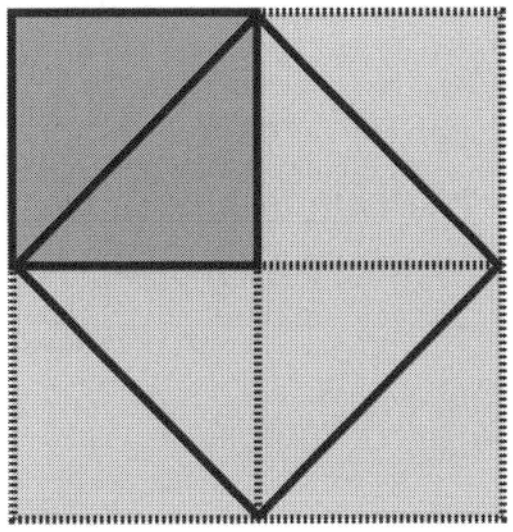

The boy wasn't taught any geometry, yet he correctly answers each stage of the proof (or realises his mistake). How? He didn't gain the knowledge from experience, so he must have recovered the answers from within his mind. The argument for innate knowledge is that we have knowledge that we can't have gained from experience.

(Socrates goes on to argue that the mind must exist from before birth, to have gained this knowledge in a previous form of existence. Socrates' questions triggered the knowledge he had from before birth, but had forgotten – just as memories can be triggered by some event or question. However, we don't have to draw *this* conclusion about the pre-existence of the mind. Other explanations of innate knowledge are possible.)

Figure 2.7
Meno square.

Explain and outline Plato's argument for innate knowledge.

See GOING FURTHER: INNATE KNOWLEDGE AND THE 'NON-NATURAL', p. 128.

LOCKE, *AN ESSAY CONCERNING HUMAN UNDERSTANDING*, BK 1, CHS 1-3

Locke's arguments against innate knowledge

Locke argues that we have no innate knowledge. He begins by asking how we acquire our ideas. By 'idea', he means 'whatever

See also IMPRESSIONS AND IDEAS, p. 133.

What, according to Locke, is an idea?

Empiricists can accept that these claims are a priori if they are analytic – which arguably, they are. However, Locke's target here is the claim that they are innate.

By 'idiots', Locke means people with severe learning disabilities.

it is that the mind can be employed about in thinking' (Bk 1, Ch. 1, §8). Or again, an 'idea' is any 'immediate object of perception, thought, or understanding' (Bk 2, Ch. 8, §8). So he uses the word to cover a very wide range of mental phenomena. An idea can be

1. a complete thought, taking the form of a proposition, e.g. 'bananas are yellow';
2. a sensation or sensory experience, e.g. a visual sensation of yellow; or
3. a concept, e.g. 'yellow'.

Our focus here is on propositions, as these are what we can know or not know.

Locke understands innate ideas as 'thoughts printed on to the soul at the point of existence, which it brings into the world with it' (Bk 1, Ch. 2, §1). As examples of potential innate knowledge, taken from the debate at the time, he offers 'Whatever is, is' and 'It is impossible for the same thing to be and not to be'. He assumes that innate knowledge must be universal – every human being has it (§3). However, he immediately objects that just because some claim is universally accepted, that doesn't mean it is innate – it may be that we could explain in some other way why everyone agrees. His argument against innate knowledge is this:

1. If there is innate knowledge, it is universal (§3).
2. For an idea to be part of the mind, the mind (the person) must know or be conscious of it: 'it seems to me nearly a contradiction to say that there are truths imprinted on the soul that it doesn't perceive or understand. No proposition can be said to be in the mind which it has never known or been conscious of' (§5).
3. Therefore, innate knowledge is knowledge that every human being is or has been conscious of.
4. Children and 'idiots' do not know theorems in geometry or 'It is impossible for the same thing to be and not to be'. (They do not know these claims, because they do not understand them) (§4).

5. Therefore, these claims are not innate.
6. There are *no* claims that are universally accepted, including by children and 'idiots'.
7. Therefore, there is no innate knowledge.

What if we redefine as 'innate' any knowledge that we can gain? Locke objects that this is a misuse of the term (§5) – everything we come to know, including through sense experience, will be innate! What we should say is that the *capacity* for knowledge is innate. This is true – we are born with the ability to know things – but it doesn't mean that there is innate *knowledge*. Compare: the capacity to see (vision) is innate, but that doesn't mean that *what* we see is innate as well!

A third definition: innate knowledge is what everyone knows and agrees to when they gain the use of reason (§6). But why think that what we can discover by reasoning is *innate*? If the knowledge is innate, and so we already have it, why do we need to 'discover' it (§§8–10)? But even if we grant the definition, there is still no innate knowledge, because children can reason *before* they understand mathematical and logical truths.

A fourth definition: innate knowledge is gained at some point after the use of reason (§13). This is hopeless – it doesn't mark off innate knowledge from all kinds of other knowledge, including what we learn from sense experience.

A fifth definition: innate knowledge is assented to promptly as soon as it is understood (§§17–18). It is 'self-evident'. But there are many such claims that rely on sense experience, e.g. 'white is not black'. So they can't be innate. We can explain the rapid agreement in other terms, namely that the proposition is analytic (and obvious).

In Ch. 3, Locke makes similar arguments regarding the possibility of innate moral knowledge. In particular, he argues that there are no moral principles that everyone agrees to (§2), and that if moral principles were innate, they would be self-evident, so that asking for reasons would be 'absurd', but as it is, we can always legitimately ask for reasons supporting a moral rule (§4).

> Explain the difference between the ability to know and knowledge.

Outline and explain Locke's reasons for rejecting innate knowledge.

In Ch. 4, Locke provides a further argument against innate knowledge. To have innate knowledge requires that one has the concepts involved in the proposition one knows (§1). If we first had to acquire the concepts, then the knowledge can't be innate. But there are no innate concepts. We will look at these arguments in LOCKE'S ARGUMENTS AGAINST INNATE CONCEPTS (p. 138).

A number of points Leibniz makes concern innate concepts, rather than innate knowledge. We discuss these in LEIBNIZ, NEW ESSAYS ON HUMAN UNDERSTANDING, PREFACE AND BK 1, p. 140.

LEIBNIZ, *NEW ESSAYS ON HUMAN UNDERSTANDING*, BK 1, CHS 1-2

Leibniz wrote his *New Essays* as a commentary on and response to Locke. I shall comment on the argument by theme, rather than in the order in which Leibniz introduces his ideas. The argument starts on p. 16. Leibniz accepts, for now, the distinction between 'mental content' (knowledge, beliefs, experiences, etc.) that comes from the senses and mental content that doesn't. His defence of innate knowledge rests on three central claims:

1. We can know things without being conscious of them. Locke is wrong to claim that an idea can only be in the mind if we are conscious of it (p. 18).
2. There is an important distinction between NECESSARY AND CONTINGENT TRUTH (p. 105). Necessary truths are a priori, while 'truths of fact' are a posteriori (p. 17).
3. Innate knowledge exists as 'a disposition, an aptitude, a preformation' in the mind towards developing, understanding and knowing certain thoughts (p. 21).

Unconscious knowledge

On p. 18, Leibniz picks up Locke's example of 'It is impossible for the same thing to be and not to be', and rejects Locke's claim that this is not universally accepted. Everyone uses this knowledge all the time, but 'without explicitly attending to it'. Indeed, we can't really think without it, since it is needed to distinguish the concept of one thing from the concept of something different. 'General principles [such as the example given] enter into our thoughts, serving as their inner core and as their mortar. Even if we give no thought to them, they are necessary for thought. The mind relies on these principles constantly' (p. 23).

This claim entails that knowledge can be unconscious. But this shouldn't be controversial. Memory 'stores' ideas and usually, but not always, retrieves them when we need them. This shows two things: we can know things without being conscious of them; and retrieving this knowledge can need assistance. So even Locke, who says that an idea can only be part of the mind if it is something the person can be conscious of, must accept that there is nothing impossible about unconscious knowledge.

Locke can reply that this is true, but irrelevant to the question of innate knowledge, because in memory, we are recalling what has been conscious. But, says Leibniz, why accept that what is unconscious must always have once been conscious or gained from experience (p. 20)? Why think that we can know everything about our minds straightaway? (Leibniz rejects Plato's argument that innate knowledge is remembered from a previous existence. The proposal won't work, because it won't account for our knowledge of necessary truths (see below), which we cannot gain from experience, even experience before birth.)

With this argument, Leibniz has responded to Locke's objection that no knowledge is universal. But as Locke also commented, that is not yet enough to show that universal knowledge is innate. Leibniz's second argument provides a reason to think that it is.

> This point forms the third of LOCKE'S ARGUMENTS AGAINST INNATE CONCEPTS, **p. 138.**

Necessary truth

On p. 19, Leibniz tackles Locke's objections to his third definition of 'innate knowledge'. He distinguishes between necessary and contingent truths and then argues that all necessary truths are innate. He argues, as explained on p. 105, that experience cannot

Here, then, is the link between a priori knowledge that is innate and a priori knowledge that is gained by rational intuition and deductive reasoning.

See NECESSARY AND SUFFICIENT CONDITIONS, p. 75.

give us knowledge of necessary truths (p. 21). Now, because these truths are not conscious, we need to discover them. We do so by attending to 'what is already in our minds', and Leibniz approvingly cites Plato's example in *Meno*. In fact, in a broad sense of 'innate', all the knowledge we gain by a priori reasoning from 'basic' innate knowledge can also be called innate.

This doesn't mean, however, that we can discover our innate knowledge without any sense experience. We need sense experience in order to form abstract thoughts; we rely on words, letters, sounds, which we learn from experience. That makes sense experience *necessary* but not *sufficient*.

Leibniz makes a similar point about sense experience when talking about God (p. 18). He accepts that many aspects of the knowledge of God could be gained from teaching. But our experience of the universe doesn't bring us 'the whole way to the idea of God that we have and require'. If nothing else, we have a prior *inclination*, a *receptivity*, to the idea of God. (This will lead to Leibniz's third main claim.)

Leibniz's response to Locke's fifth definition of innate knowledge also draws on the distinction between necessary and contingent truth (p. 22). Claims like 'white is not black' aren't innate, it is true. But they are applications of a necessary truth that *is* innate, namely 'It is impossible for the same thing to be and not be at the same time', to particular cases and concepts acquired from sense experience.

Locke might object that the particular cases, such as 'white is not black' are known *before* the abstract principle. Leibniz responds that in the particular cases, we *unconsciously deploy* our knowledge of the abstract principle that something can't both be and not be at the same time.

Innate knowledge as a disposition

On p. 20, Leibniz tackles Locke's second definition of 'innate knowledge', that it is merely a capacity for knowledge. While innate knowledge does not exist 'fully formed' or explicitly in our minds, it is more than mere capacity. In gaining knowledge of necessary truths, the mind needs to actively engage with itself, albeit at the prompting of sense experience. Thus, he says on p. 24, 'The actual knowledge of [necessary truths] isn't innate. What is innate is what might be called the potential knowledge of them, as the veins of the marble outline a shape that is in the marble before they are uncovered by the sculptor'. Because it takes work to uncover what is within us, we should say that innate knowledge is learned. But the point is that we don't learn it from sense experience.

What, according to Leibniz, is innate knowledge?

Morality

In Ch. 2, Leibniz applies these ideas to moral knowledge. Innate moral principles are ones that we know through reasoning. However, in addition, we have an unclear sense of them through 'instinct', such as the instinct to 'pursue joy and flee sorrow'. Moral knowledge is especially difficult to come to know, because it can conflict with our desires, which leads us to conceal what we know from ourselves. Hence the fact that people behave badly is no proof against universal, innate moral knowledge. Geometry would be disputed and violated as much if it conflicted with what we wanted as well!

Outline and explain Leibniz's defence of innate knowledge.

Going further: experience triggers innate knowledge

No major philosopher has ever defended innate knowledge using one of Locke's definitions. Instead, they all reject Locke's claim that it is impossible for knowledge to exist 'in the mind' unless we are or have been conscious of it. Innate knowledge is knowledge *which cannot be gained from experience*, e.g. geometry (Plato) and other necessary truths (Leibniz). Since we are not consciously aware of this knowledge from birth, there is some point at which we first come to be aware of it. And so innatists argue that experience *triggers our awareness* of the knowledge, or some relevant concept that it depends upon.

How is experience 'triggering' knowledge different from simple *learning* from experience? The idea of triggering is often used in the study of animal behaviour. For example, in some species of bird, a baby bird need only hear *a little bit* of the bird song of its species before being able to sing the *whole* song itself. There has been far too little experience of hearing the song sung by other birds for the baby bird to learn from experience; rather the experience has triggered its innately given song.

Peter Carruthers notes that there are many developments in our cognitive *capacities* that are genetically determined. For example, infants cannot see further than approximately 12 inches when first born. Within 8 weeks, they can see much further. This development of the eye is genetically encoded. The same could be true for certain types of *knowledge*. At a certain genetically determined point in development, children begin to think in a particular way for the first time, but that way of thinking has not been derived from experience. For example, around 3-4 months, babies *quickly* shift from thinking of objects as only existing while they experience them to thinking of objects as something that can exist outside their experience. So, for example, they begin looking for things they have dropped. Or again, babies *very quickly* relate to other people as having minds – beliefs, desires, intentions. In both cases, they couldn't have learned this from experience. So the knowledge is innate.

This is not to say that experience has no role. A child must be exposed to the relevant stimuli – interactions with objects and people – for the knowledge to emerge. What shows that the knowledge is innate is that it cannot be derived from experience.

The argument is not that we have the *capacity* to gain this knowledge. Locke allowed that general capacities for knowledge are innate. Rather, the claim is that our capacities aren't 'general' – they are 'preshaped' towards thinking about the world in some

Carruthers, *Human Knowledge and Human Nature*, p. 51

Genes always cause their effects through interaction with the environment. For example, there are genes for height, but height also depends on someone's diet.

ways rather than others. So experience merely triggers our acquiring this knowledge, rather than being the source of the knowledge.

Outline and explain the role of 'triggering' in the theory of innate knowledge.

ARGUMENTS AGAINST KNOWLEDGE INNATISM

Alternative explanations

If we are to deny that there is any innate knowledge, then for any proposed claim, we need to argue either that we do not have the knowledge claimed or that we obtain it some other way. But we do know the necessary truths of logic and mathematics, and the argument that we cannot establish them on the basis of experience is convincing. So how do we know things like '2 + 2 = 4' and 'It is impossible for the same thing to be and not to be' if we do not know them innately?

See KNOWLEDGE EMPIRICIST ARGUMENTS AGAINST INTUITION AND DEDUCTION, p. 114.

The answer, says the empiricist, is the same as before: necessary truths are a priori but *analytic*. We acquire the concepts involved from experience, and then in understanding the concept, we come to know the necessary truths. So we don't need to say that the mind is structured with a predisposition to form these concepts and know these truths.

Outline the argument that because necessary truths are analytic, knowledge of necessary truths is not innate.

This empiricist explanation will only be successful on two conditions. First, we have to show that necessary truths are, in fact, analytic. We discussed this question in KNOWLEDGE EMPIRICIST ARGUMENTS AGAINST INTUITION AND DEDUCTION (p. 114). Second, we have to show that we do, in fact, acquire the relevant concepts from experience. We will discuss this in CONCEPT INNATISM (p. 138).

What is the best explanation for our knowledge of necessary truths?

The truths of logic and mathematics may be analytic. But this is less easy to believe about moral truths. Locke, however, argues that they are, or at least can be deduced from, analytic truths, and so moral truths can be shown to be as 'incontestable' as mathematical truths. Hume, by contrast, argues that there is no moral knowledge because there is no moral truth. Instead, moral claims are expressions of our feelings, rather than propositions that can be true or false.

Locke, *An Essay concerning Human Understanding*, Bk 4, Ch. 3

Hume's theory is discussed at A2 in WHAT IS THE STATUS OF ETHICAL LANGUAGE?

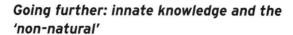

Going further: innate knowledge and the 'non-natural'

A second objection we can raise to innate knowledge is this: if it does not derive from experience, then where does it come from? How is it that it is already part of the mind?

Historically, defenders of innate knowledge appealed to explanations that require us to accept something beyond the 'natural' world, the world that science discovers and describes. Plato appeals to the existence of the mind before birth. Leibniz develops a complex metaphysical theory that includes the existence of God and makes the mind independent of the body – indeed, he rejects our common-sense understanding of physical objects entirely. Descartes argues that innate knowledge derives from concepts implanted in our minds by God. And so on.

It is important to note that Plato, Leibniz and Descartes are not *assuming* their theories of the mind and the existence of God. They supply *arguments* for thinking that there is innate knowledge, and then *argue* that the best explanation for innate knowledge requires their theories of the mind or God. In other words, their commitment to 'non-natural' things is an *implication* of their arguments, not an assumption. (The syllabus is therefore misleading in talking of the 'reliance' of knowledge innatism on the non-natural.)

The objection, then, is that innate knowledge requires a more complicated and less plausible account of what exists. Therefore, if we can explain our knowledge without appealing to innate knowledge, we should reject the hypothesis of innate knowledge.

However, recent philosophers, such as Carruthers, have argued that innate knowledge does not require these non-natural explanations. We can provide an *empirical* explanation in terms of evolution. Knowledge is innate in the sense of it being encoded genetically that we will develop the relevant concepts and use the knowledge at a certain point in cognitive development under certain conditions. Evolution has prepared our minds to form an understanding of the world in terms of mind-independent

See DESCARTES ON THE CONCEPT OF A PHYSICAL OBJECT, p. 142, and DESCARTES' TRADEMARK ARGUMENT, p. 144.

See HYPOTHETICAL REASONING, p. 9.

physical objects and the existence of other minds with beliefs and desires, and we can argue that these beliefs constitute knowledge because they are reliable.

This reply, however, is much more plausible for claims about physical objects and other minds than it is for the kinds of necessary truths Leibniz and Locke discuss. How could evolution give us knowledge of necessary truths if necessary truths cannot be established through experience? So if necessary truths are known innately, perhaps some non-natural explanation will be needed.

See Reliabilism, p. 89.

Is there any innate knowledge?

Key points: knowledge empiricism

- Analytic propositions are true or false just in virtue of the meanings of the words. Synthetic propositions are not analytic and are made true or false by how the world is.
- A priori knowledge is knowledge of propositions that is not established on the basis of (sense) experience. A posteriori knowledge is gained and justified through sense experience.
- Empiricism about knowledge claims that all a priori knowledge is of analytic propositions and all synthetic propositions are known a posteriori.
- Rationalism about knowledge claims that we have a priori knowledge of some synthetic propositions. We have this knowledge either innately or through rational intuition and deduction.
- Hume claims that we know only 'relations of ideas' and 'matters of fact'. Relations of ideas are established by pure thought and are 'intuitively and demonstratively certain'. The negation of a relation of ideas is a contradiction. Matters of fact are about the world and are known through experience and induction, especially causal inference.
- Rationalism objects that empiricism leads to scepticism, as sense experience cannot justify many of our beliefs about the world, God or morality.

- Descartes' argument from illusion throws doubt on always believing what our senses tell us. His argument from dreaming throws doubt on all sense perception, and therefore, on whether physical objects exist. His argument from the evil demon makes these doubts more vivid.
- Rational intuition involves discovering the truth of a claim just by thinking about it.
- A proposition that *could* be true or false is contingent. A proposition is necessary if it *must* be true (if it is true) or *must* be false (if it is false). Necessary truths are known a priori.
- Descartes uses rational intuition and deduction to argue for the existence of himself, God and physical objects.
- He argues that he cannot doubt his own existence, and that he is a thinking thing. 'I think', the *cogito*, is Descartes' first item of knowledge. His nature is thinking, i.e. doubting, understanding, affirming, denying, wanting, refusing, imagining and sensing.
- We can object that Descartes cannot know that thoughts require a thinker as something that persists between thoughts.
- Descartes' theory of 'clear and distinct' ideas is an account of rational intuition. A clear idea is 'present and accessible to the attentive mind'; a distinct idea is clear and also sharply separated from other ideas so that every part of it is clear.
- We can know that an idea that is clear and distinct is true while we consider it. We can only know that all ideas that are clear and distinct are true once God's existence is proven.
- Descartes argues that we know that God is not a deceiver, because we know that God is perfect. This does not mean that God guarantees every belief we have. It means that we have the means to correct any mistakes we make. If we believe only what we can clearly and distinctly perceive to be true, we will not go wrong.
- Because God is not a deceiver, and God is omnipotent, God would not let an evil demon deceive us. We can now also tell dreaming from being awake by the way our memory connects up our waking experiences.
- Imagination uses images deriving from the senses and requires effort. These are reasons to think bodies exist, but not a proof.

- We have involuntary sensory experiences of bodies. But this is also not enough to show that bodies exist.

- However, because sensory experiences are involuntary, we can know that they are not caused by our own minds. Because God is not a deceiver, we also know that they are not caused by God, but by physical objects themselves. Therefore, we know that physical objects exist.

- To reject claims of synthetic a priori knowledge, empiricists must argue that the claims are either analytic or a posteriori or not knowledge.

- Empiricists argue that mathematics is analytic, or in the case of geometry, a combination of analytic claims and a posteriori synthetic claims (about space).

- Empiricists can argue that Descartes knows he exists, but this is not an a priori claim. They also present various objections to his arguments for the existence of God.

- The Cartesian circle claims that Descartes relies on knowing clear and distinct ideas in order to prove that God exists, but relies on God in order to know clear and distinct ideas are true. Descartes can reject the second claim and argue that he knows clear and distinct ideas because they are necessarily true.

- Knowledge innatism claims that we have some knowledge, not derived from experience, as part of our minds.

- Plato argues that learning is a form of remembering, and provides an example of a boy discovering a geometrical truth just by being asked questions. As he is not taught anything, the questions must have triggered knowledge he already had.

- Locke argues that there is no innate knowledge. He provides five definitions of innate knowledge, and rejects them all. In particular, there is no knowledge that everyone has, whether from birth or when gaining the use of reason.

- Leibniz argues against Locke's view that we can only have ideas of which we are conscious. Memory shows otherwise, and there is no reason to think that all our unconscious knowledge is acquired from experience.

- Leibniz argues that experience cannot give us knowledge of necessary truths, and so this knowledge is innate. However, experience is needed to trigger innate knowledge, which exists as a disposition towards developing and using knowledge of necessary truths.

- Innatists generally understand innate knowledge as knowledge which can't be gained from experience, but which is triggered by experience.
- Empiricists argue that all purported examples of innate knowledge can be explained either as knowledge of an analytic proposition (e.g. necessary truths) or not knowledge at all (e.g. moral knowledge).
- Empiricists also object that innate knowledge requires the existence of 'non-natural' things. But more recent defenders of innate knowledge offer an explanation in terms of evolution.

B. Concept empiricism

The syllabus defines concept empiricism as the claim that all concepts are derived from experience. Opposing this is concept innatism, which claims that some of our concepts are innate. We will discuss the positive case for concept empiricism first, before continuing the debate over innatism that we began by looking at KNOWLEDGE INNATISM (p. 118).

All concepts are derived from experience

'*Tabula rasa*' is Latin for 'blank slate'. The phrase recalls the time when children would have slates (or tablets (*tabula*)), like small blackboards, to write on. Until the teacher told them to write something, the slates would be blank.

LOCKE, *AN ESSAY CONCERNING HUMAN UNDERSTANDING*, BK 2, CH. 1

The *tabula rasa*

Locke argues that at birth – or more accurately, since there can be consciousness and thought before birth, prior to any experience – the mind is a '*tabula rasa*' (or as the anthology translation puts it 'white paper') (§2).

It contains no ideas – no thoughts or concepts. If you observe newborn babies, says Locke, you'll find no reason to disagree (§6). All our ideas, then, derive from one of two sources:

1. Sensation (§3): our experience of objects outside the mind, perceived through the senses. This gives us ideas of 'sensible qualities'.
2. Reflection (§4): our experience of 'the internal operations of our minds', gained through introspection or an awareness of what the mind is doing. This provides the ideas of perception, thinking, willing, and so on. These ideas may well arrive later in childhood (§8).

See THE DISTINCTION BETWEEN PRIMARY AND SECONDARY QUALITIES, p. 44.

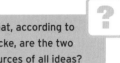

What, according to Locke, are the two sources of all ideas?

IMPRESSIONS AND IDEAS

HUME, *AN ENQUIRY CONCERNING HUMAN UNDERSTANDING*, §2

Locke's use of the term 'idea' to cover sensations and concepts (and propositional thoughts!) is very confusing (see LOCKE'S ARGUMENTS AGAINST INNATE KNOWLEDGE, p. 119). The *sensation* of yellow isn't the same thing as the *concept* YELLOW. When we see something yellow, this perceptual experience is quite different from the role YELLOW plays in the thought 'If it is yellow, it is coloured'.

When I am referring to a concept, I will put the word in capitals.

Hume's terminology is a little clearer. What we are immediately and directly aware of are 'perceptions'. 'Perceptions' are divided into 'impressions' and 'ideas', the difference between the two being by marked by a difference of 'forcefulness' and 'vivacity' (p. 7), so that impressions relate roughly to 'feeling' (or 'sensing') and ideas to 'thinking'. Although he doesn't say so explicitly here, Hume, following Locke, divides impressions into those of 'sensation' and those of 'reflection'. Impressions of sensation derive from our senses, impressions of reflection derive from our experience of our mind, including emotions.

Hume argues that ideas are 'faint copies' of impressions. Think what it is like to see a scene or hear a tune; now, what it is like to imagine or remember that scene or tune. The latter is weaker, fainter. (Thinking, for Hume, works with ideas as images

? What, according to Hume, is the difference between impressions and ideas?

Show Hume's theory in a diagram or table, giving examples.

in the same way as imagination and memory.) However, Hume immediately qualifies his claim about liveliness – disease or madness can make ideas as lively as impressions. So Hume's claim that ideas are also *copies* of impressions is important. (On p. 9, Hume provides a third distinction between ideas and impressions: we are liable to confuse and make mistakes about ideas, but this is more difficult with impressions.)

So just as there are impressions of sensation and reflection, so there are ideas of sensation (e.g. RED) and ideas of reflection (e.g. THINKING). What Hume means by 'idea' here, we can refer to as *concepts*. So his theory of how we acquire ideas, namely by copying them from impressions, is a theory of how we acquire concepts.

So Locke and Hume have slightly different versions of how we first acquire ideas with which we can think. We start with sense experiences of the physical world and experiences of our own minds; for Locke, this gives us ideas; but this makes it sound as if the experiences themselves are the ideas with which we think. Hume corrects this: it is copies of sensory impressions that we use in thinking.

Why think that all ideas derive from impressions? Hume gives two arguments (p. 8). The first relates to 'simple' and 'complex' ideas – we'll return to this in SIMPLE AND COMPLEX CONCEPTS (p. 136). The second is that without having a particular type of experience, a person lacks the ability to form an idea of that experience. Thus, a blind man does not know what colour is and a mild man cannot comprehend the motive of revenge.

The missing shade of blue

However, Hume notes that there is an exception to his principle that all simple ideas are copies of impressions. If you present someone with a spectrum of shades of blue with one shade missing, then using their imagination, they will be able to form an idea of that shade. This idea has not been copied from an impression. Hume dismisses the example as unimportant, but it is not. If it is possible that we can form an idea of a shade of blue without deriving it from an impression, is it possible that we could form other ideas without preceding impressions?

The question is important because Hume uses his 'copy principle' repeatedly in his philosophy. He closes §2 (p. 10) by saying that in metaphysics, we become confused because the ideas we work with, e.g. SUBSTANCE, are 'faint and obscure', so we don't understand them well. But if ideas derive from impressions, we can solve metaphysical debates by asking, of the words used, 'From what impression is that supposed idea derived?' If we can't find the associated impression, we can conclude that the word is used without a proper meaning, and reject the debate.

See GOING FURTHER: HUME ON SUBSTANCE AND SELF, p. 150.

However, if we *can* form ideas without copying them from impressions, then we can't use Hume's copy principle to cut through metaphysical debates as he suggests. So can the copy principle be defended against the counterexample of the missing shade of blue?

Outline and explain the importance of 'the missing shade of blue'.

Going further: amending the copy principle

There are two possible solutions that allow the case of the shade of blue, while maintaining a strong link between ideas and impressions. The first solution weakens the copy principle: any ideas that are not copied from impressions are only *meaningful* if they *could* be copied from impressions. In other words, what the idea is an idea of is something we can encounter in experience. The missing shade of blue clearly meets this condition, but perhaps many metaphysical ideas will not.

The second solution keeps the copy principle as it is – ideas are copied from impressions – but explains how and why the missing shade of blue is an 'exception'. The simple impressions of different shades of blue are related to each other, as they can be arranged according to how they resemble each other. From the arrangement, we can form the idea of the missing shade *drawing on other similar impressions we already have*. This only works when impressions are structured by resemblance like this. If we have no relevantly similar impressions which strongly resemble the missing impression, we cannot form the missing idea. This is the same reason that a blind man cannot form an idea of colour, and so it fits well with Hume's theory.

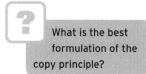

What is the best formulation of the copy principle?

SIMPLE AND COMPLEX CONCEPTS

LOCKE, *AN ESSAY CONCERNING HUMAN UNDERSTANDING*, BK 2, CH. 2

Locke argues that the basic building blocks of all thought are simple ideas, or more precisely, in Hume's terminology, simple impressions – single colours, single shapes, single smells and so on. For each, there is a corresponding simple idea (for clarity, I shall talk, from now on, about concepts). A simple impression or simple concept 'contains nothing but one uniform appearance or conception in the mind, and is not distinguishable into different ideas' (§1). Of course, we experience many such simple impressions at once, e.g. we feel wax that is at once both warm and soft. But there is no confusing the sensation of warmth with the sensation of softness – they are quite distinct.

As the building blocks of thought, these simple concepts can be used to construct complex concepts (§2).

1. We can *unite* or *combine* the impressions of the qualities we perceive into the concept of a single object – we identify one and the same thing, a dog, say, as having a particular colour, shape, smell. So we can think of 'that thing', where the concept of 'that thing' is made up of many concepts of colour, shape, smell. This is a complex concept.
2. We can also form complex concepts by *abstraction*, e.g. the concept DOG doesn't correspond to any one particular dog.

When we abstract, we ignore certain specific features and concentrate on others; so to develop the concept DOG, we ignore the different colours and sizes of dogs and pick out features they have in common, like four legs, tail, bark, hairy.

3. We can put together simple concepts in an original way. While many of us have seen a picture of a unicorn, *someone* had to invent the concept without seeing a picture. They did it by putting together concepts of HORSE and HORN and WHITENESS.

> Outline Locke's theory of the origin of concepts.

HUME, *AN ENQUIRY CONCERNING HUMAN UNDERSTANDING*, P. 8

Hume agrees with Locke's claim that all concepts are either simple concepts or complex concepts that have been built out of simple concepts. He claims, like Locke, that all concepts can be analysed into simple concepts which each correspond to an impression. Therefore, all concepts ultimately derive from experience. For example, in direct opposition to Descartes, Hume claims that the concept GOD, based on concepts of PERFECTION and INFINITY, is extrapolated from concepts of IMPERFECTION and FINITUDE: 'The idea of God – meaning an infinitely intelligent, wise, and good Being – comes from extending beyond all limits the qualities of goodness and wisdom that we find in our own minds'.

    If you disagree with his theory, it should be easy to find a counterexample, a complex concept that cannot be analysed into simple concepts.

> On Descartes' view, and his response to Hume's claim, see DESCARTES' TRADEMARK ARGUMENT, p. 144.

Objections

Hume and Locke argue that *no* concept, no matter how abstract or complex, is more than a putting together, altering, or abstracting from simple concepts. Hume challenges us to find a counterexample. Very well. If he cannot give us a satisfactory analysis of how we derive whatever concept we choose as a counterexample from experience, that is a reason to think that the concept does not originate from experience. Now, attempts to analyse philosophical

> On the concept of knowledge, see THE TRIPARTITE DEFINITION OF KNOWLEDGE, p. 75, and RESPONSES, p. 85.

concepts like KNOWLEDGE, TRUTH and BEAUTY into their simple constituents have all failed to produce agreement. A good explanation for this is that they don't have this structure, and Locke and Hume's theory of the origin of concepts is wrong.

Concept innatism

Concept innatism argues that some of our concepts are innate. This means that not all concepts are derived from experience; some are somehow part of the structure of the mind. Before looking at positive arguments for concept innatism, let us complete the arguments supporting concept empiricism by looking at objections to the claim that there are innate concepts.

LOCKE'S ARGUMENTS AGAINST INNATE CONCEPTS

LOCKE, *AN ESSAY CONCERNING HUMAN UNDERSTANDING*, BK 1, CH. 4

When Locke begins his attack on innate concepts, he has already discussed and rejected innate knowledge. It is an important part of his argument that whatever concepts we have, we are conscious of. Furthermore, he assumes (and everyone in the debate agrees) that innate concepts must be universal – every human being has them. If we put these two thoughts together, an innate concept must be one that every human being is or has been conscious of.

Locke gives three main reasons for rejecting the existence of innate concepts, given his definition of what they are:

1. If we observe newborn babies, we have no reason at all to think that they have any concepts beyond, perhaps, ones deriving from their experience in the womb, such as WARMTH and PAIN (§2). Certainly, we can't think that such advanced concepts as IDENTITY or IMPOSSIBILITY are concepts babies are familiar with and conscious of.

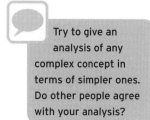

Try to give an analysis of any complex concept in terms of simpler ones. Do other people agree with your analysis?

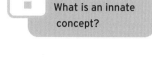

What is an innate concept?

See LOCKE'S ARGUMENTS AGAINST INNATE KNOWLEDGE, p. 119.

Locke chooses these examples because innatists argue that 'It is impossible for the same thing to be, and not to be' is innate knowledge. On this and GOD, see LEIBNIZ, *NEW ESSAYS ON HUMAN UNDERSTANDING*, BK 1, CHS 1-2, p. 122.

2. Another favourite of innatism is the concept of GOD. But not only is this not a concept that babies have, it is not a concept that all human beings have – whole societies, historically, have been atheist (§8). The concept of GOD is not innate, but learned by children from their teachers (§13).

3. The only way a concept can be part of the mind without the mind being conscious of it is if it is lodged in memory (§20). To remember something is to have been conscious of it in the past. If you aren't remembering a concept, then it is new to your mind – arising from some impression of sensation or reflection. Innate ideas would have to be neither remembered nor new. How could there be such a thing?

> Outline and explain Locke's argument against innate concepts.

Rejecting Locke's definition

We noted in GOING FURTHER: EXPERIENCE TRIGGERS INNATE KNOWLEDGE (p. 125), defenders of innate knowledge disagree with Locke's definitions of innate knowledge. The same applies to innate concepts. They reject his claim that it is impossible for concepts to exist 'in the mind' unless we are or have been conscious of them. Innate concepts are concepts which cannot be gained from experience, and arguments defending innatism try to show that experience cannot explain how we have or use the concept. Experience is necessary to trigger our development of the concept, but it is not sufficient to explain our having the concept.

The idea of experience 'triggering' the concept needs to be understood carefully. The claim is not that we simply have the *capacity* to form the concept. Rather, we are predisposed to form *just this concept*, which we cannot form on the basis of experience alone.

On this understanding of innate concepts, it is no objection that babies don't have the relevant concept of GOD or IDENTITY – it needs to be triggered by experience before it develops.

> What is it for experience to trigger an innate concept?

LEIBNIZ, *NEW ESSAYS ON HUMAN UNDERSTANDING*, BK 1, CH. 3

Leibniz's defence of innate concepts follows his defence of innate knowledge. He begins with the argument made above. He accepts Locke's claim that innate knowledge requires innate concepts. Therefore, if we want to say that 'It is impossible for the same thing to be and not be' is innate knowledge, we will have to say that concepts such as IDENTITY and IMPOSSIBILITY are innate (p. 32). But, to answer Locke's first objection, this means that we have, from birth, the disposition to form these concepts. Indeed, they are essential to all thought, even though it takes time for us to make them *explicit* in our thinking.

In answer to Locke's second objection, Leibniz points out that to lack the *word* for God is not to lack the concept of GOD (p. 33). Some societies have no word for 'being', but that doesn't mean they don't have thoughts that use the concept. Again, it may take considerable work of reflection to develop the concept of GOD and know that God exists (Ch. 1, p. 18). We are disposed, from our experience of nature, to develop the idea of a higher power. But this isn't yet the full concept of GOD as we have it. Our experience triggers a concept that goes beyond it; our minds are 'receptive' to the idea of God.

In answer to Locke's third objection, Leibniz repeats his theory that innate knowledge and concepts exist as dispositions in the mind (p. 33) – so neither new, in the sense of originating outside the mind, nor remembered.

See LEIBNIZ, *NEW ESSAYS ON HUMAN UNDERSTANDING*, BK 1, CHS 1-2, p. 122.

? Are Locke's objections to innate concepts convincing?

The list in the syllabus is only intended to identify possible examples, rather than being required. I discuss others here, drawing on authors in the anthology.

PROPOSED EXAMPLES OF INNATE CONCEPTS

In this section, we'll look at examples of innate concepts from Leibniz, Plato and Descartes. We will cover just their arguments defending these examples, and look at objections to their arguments in CONCEPT EMPIRICIST ARGUMENTS AGAINST CONCEPT INNATISM (p. 148).

LEIBNIZ, *NEW ESSAYS ON HUMAN UNDERSTANDING*, PREFACE AND BK 1

Leibniz gives a number of examples of concepts that he claims are innate. His longest list is in the Preface. On p. 4, he comments on Locke's division of concepts into those that originate in sensation and those that originate in reflection, which Leibniz calls 'intellectual ideas'. He comments, 'to reflect is simply to attend to what is within us, and something that we carry with us already is not something that came from the senses! So it can't be denied that there is a great deal that is innate in our minds'. Thus, he says the concepts of BEING, UNITY, SUBSTANCE, DURATION, CHANGE, ACTION, PERCEPTION and PLEASURE are all innate, because we are ourselves beings, unities, substances, that endure through time, that change, act, perceive and experience pleasure. In fact, all the concepts we acquire through reflection can be called 'innate'. (He reaffirms the claim for BEING on p. 24 and for SUBSTANCE on p. 33.)

However, reflecting on our own nature cannot be a general explanation for all innate concepts, e.g. some concepts involved in necessary truths, such as IMPOSSIBILITY, and concepts from geometry, such as SQUARE (p. 23). If these are innate, it is not because I am impossible or a square! It must be something to do with their role in innate knowledge.

See THE *TABULA RASA*, p. 132.

Explain Leibniz's claim that reflection provides us with innate concepts.

Plato on universals

Plato provides an argument for the claim that *very many* concepts are innate. Whatever we experience through sense experience is a *particular* thing. We see this red bus, that green apple and so on. We never experience 'redness' per se, but only ever this or that example of redness. Or, changing the example to something more complex, when we experience something beautiful, we experience this or that instance of beauty. Red and beauty are properties of things, properties that more than one thing can have. Some philosophers think of properties as 'universals' – something that different particular things can have in common (red bus, red pillar box, beautiful melody, beautiful painting).

Plato, *The Republic*, Bk 5 (476f.)

How do we acquire concepts of universals? If we only ever experience this particular beautiful thing or that particular beautiful thing, we never experience *beauty itself*.

Furthermore, our concept of BEAUTY is a concept of a kind of perfection. But everything that we experience through our senses is imperfect. Nothing is perfectly beautiful – it is always not beautiful in some way or at some time. So how could we have derived the concept of BEAUTY from experience?

Plato provides another example in the *Phaedo*. In judging that two sticks are of equal length, we use an idea of EQUAL that we cannot have gained from experience. Nothing is *exactly* equal in experience, but only 'almost equal'. But the concept ALMOST EQUAL contains the concept EQUAL. So where does EQUAL come from? (We can give the same argument for Leibniz's examples of SQUARE and CIRCLE. We never experience a *perfect* square or circle.) Plato argues that if we do not learn our concepts of universals from experience, we must already have them – they are innate. We are able to classify our experiences, e.g. that two sticks are equal, by comparing them with our innate concept of EQUAL. And the same is true for judging that things manifest BEAUTY or not.

Outline and explain
Plato's argument
in favour of innate
concepts.

Descartes on the concept of a physical object

How do we come to have the concept of SUBSTANCE, of something that continues to exist as one and the same thing through time, that possesses properties but is not reducible to properties, because while its properties change, it remains the same thing? We have two particular concepts of substance, namely PHYSICAL SUBSTANCE (physical objects) and MENTAL SUBSTANCE (minds or selves). Do these concepts come from sense experience or are they innate?

See also GOING FURTHER: EXPERIENCE TRIGGERS INNATE KNOWLEDGE, p. 125.

See DESCARTES ON THE EXISTENCE (AND NATURE) OF THE SELF, p. 106.

We saw above that Leibniz thinks that I derive the concept (MENTAL) SUBSTANCE simply from my being a substance. Descartes also argues that I know I am a substance by reflection on myself.

What about PHYSICAL SUBSTANCE – the idea of a physical object?

DESCARTES, *MEDITATION* II, PP. 6-8

Descartes discusses the concept of a physical object when discussing the nature of his mind. He has argued that 'sensing' is just having sensory experiences - whether physical objects are the cause of these experiences is not clear and distinct. This is puzzling, so he considers perceptual experiences further, focusing on the example of perceiving a piece of wax (p. 6). His question is, 'exactly what is it that I think a piece of wax, as a physical object, is?' (In the argument that follows, 'imagination' is the faculty that deals with images, including those derived from sense experiences.)

1. When I melt a piece of wax, it loses all of its original sensory qualities (the particular taste, smell, feel and shape it has).
2. Yet I believe it is the same wax.
3. Therefore, what I think of as the wax is not its sensory qualities.
4. What I think is the wax is what remains through the changes of its sensory qualities.
5. This is a body, something that is extended - i.e. has size and shape and takes up space - and changeable, i.e. its sensory and spatial properties can change (p. 7).
6. I know that the wax can undergo far more possible changes, including changes in its extension, than I can imagine.
7. Therefore, my concept of the wax as extended and changeable does not derive from my imagination (and therefore it does not derive from perceptual experiences).
8. Therefore, I 'perceive' (comprehend) the wax as what it is (as opposed to its sensory qualities) by my mind alone.
9. Only this thought of the wax, and not the perceptual experience of it, is clear and distinct.

Descartes finishes by commenting that the wax he comprehends by his understanding is the same wax that is presented by images from the senses. Although we say we 'see' the wax (through vision), in fact we judge (through understanding) that it is present from what we see.

Outline and explain Descartes' argument for the claim that the concept of PHYSICAL OBJECT is not derived from sense experience.

Descartes' question is not about the wax itself, but about his experience, knowledge and concept of it. This is shown by his comment, on p. 8, that '[w]hat I see might not really be the wax; perhaps I don't even have eyes with which to see anything'. He doesn't, in *Meditation* II, know that there are physical objects. But he knows he has experiences of them. And it is this – his concept of what he experiences – that he is exploring. The argument is intended to show that the concept of a physical object does not derive from sense experience, but is part of the understanding. We can now add that this means that it is innate.

For his proof that they exist, see GOING FURTHER: DESCARTES ON THE EXISTENCE OF THE EXTERNAL WORLD, p. 111.

Descartes only turns to the question of whether anything corresponds to our concept of PHYSICAL OBJECT in *Meditation* V. He argued, in *Meditation* III, that whatever is clearly and distinctly perceived is true. His concept of PHYSICAL OBJECT, refined by the wax argument to mean a body that is extended and changeable, is clear and distinct. Therefore, it is a coherent concept and if physical objects exist, then they are indeed extended and changeable.

Descartes' trademark argument

DESCARTES, *MEDITATION* III, PP. 10-17

In the 'trademark argument', Descartes tries to prove that God exists just from the fact that we have a concept of GOD. This concept, which he argues is innate, is like a 'trademark' that our creator has stamped on our minds (p. 17).

Descartes identifies three possible sources of any idea (p. 10):

1. it derives from something outside my mind, such as I experience in sense perception;
2. I have invented it;
3. it is innate. (Descartes explains this as 'it derives from my own nature', but he also uses the usual rationalist argument that it can't be explained by our experience (or invention).)

Explain Descartes' three sources of ideas.

We cannot in general be certain which of the three types of cause an idea has (p. 11). Which is the source of the concept GOD?

Before answering that question, Descartes embarks on a long defence of the claim that a cause must have at least as much 'reality' as its effect, and that the cause of an idea must have as much reality as what the idea is an idea *of*. Both the claim and the argument are very puzzling, so we set them aside to explore below. For now, here is a common-sense example: if we discover a picture of a sophisticated machine, even though it's just a *picture*, we think it must be the product of an advanced society or a highly fertile imagination. It is what it is a picture *of* that makes us think the cause is sophisticated. Where could the 'sophistication' of the machine in the picture come from except a mind that is itself just as sophisticated? The cause must have as much 'reality' as the machine in the picture.

With this in place, Descartes argues:

1. I have the concept GOD.
2. The concept GOD is a concept of something infinite and perfect (pp. 11-12).
3. As a mind, a thinking substance, I can think up (create) many ideas, including ideas of people and physical objects (pp. 13-14).
4. But I am finite, while the concept GOD is of something infinite (p. 14).
5. Therefore, it is a concept of something with more reality than my own mind.
6. The cause of the concept GOD must have as much reality as what the concept is of.
7. Therefore, my mind could not have created it.
8. The only possible cause is God.
9. Therefore, God exists.

Descartes considers and rejects an objection to (4), namely that I have all the perfections I attribute to God, and so could invent the concept (p. 15). But given that I am in doubt, I clearly do not have infinite knowledge - I am not infinite, but finite.

See GOING FURTHER: DEGREES OF REALITY, p. 146.

Bernard Williams, *Descartes*, pp. 138-9

Outline and explain Descartes' trademark argument.

Another objection and reply, concerning infinity, is discussed in GOING FURTHER: DESCARTES ON GOD AND INFINITY, p. 151.

This argument is discussed in DESCARTES, MEDITATION III, pp. 15–16, 223.

After a long argument regarding the cause of his own existence, Descartes returns to the question of the source of his concept GOD (p. 16). He has argued that he cannot have invented it, and he adds now that it doesn't come from the senses. So it must be innate.

Going further: degrees of reality

Descartes' argument rests on premises (5)–(7), but these are difficult and highly controversial. The idea of 'degrees of reality' is strange to us, but was a standard part of medieval metaphysics.

1. A 'substance' is defined as something that can exist independently, such as the mind, God and physical objects.
2. An 'attribute' is a property of a substance – the attribute of mind is thought, while extension is an attribute of physical objects.
3. A 'mode' is a particular determination of a property. So ideas are modes of the mind – specific ways of thinking.

A substance has more reality than an attribute, because a property cannot exist without a substance, and so is dependent on it. There can be no thoughts without a thinker. Modes, therefore, also have less reality than substances. Ideas are modes of the attribute 'thought', which is possessed by thinking substances.

Descartes applies these thoughts to cause and effect. He simply takes it to be a clear and distinct idea that the cause of something must contain at least as much reality as its effect (p. 12). From this, he derives the claim that something can't come from nothing (p. 13). But in fact, it is easier to work the other way around – something can't come from nothing, and so whatever is part of the effect must have originated in the cause. For instance, a stone can only be created by something that contains the qualities of the stone (what is needed to make a stone). Or again, something hot can't derive its heat from something cold.

Ideas are more complicated. As modes of thought, the 'intrinsic reality' of all ideas is the same, and less than the reality of my mind, which is a substance. But ideas also represent something, e.g. an object, a size, a tune, a mind, God. Some of these things – object, mind, God – are substances; others – a size, a tune – are modes. The degree of reality of the thing that the thought is about determines the idea's 'representative reality' (p. 11). Just as we need to able to explain where the heat in something hot comes from, so we need to be able to explain the representative reality of an idea. Just as heat comes from something hot, so an idea with a certain representative reality must come from something with at least as much intrinsic reality (p. 12). So ideas of substance can only be caused by substances; ideas of modes can be caused by either modes or substances.

We can now apply this to the concept GOD. As a concept, it is a mode, and so it seems my mind – a substance – could cause it, just as my mind causes many other ideas. But the special features of what GOD is a concept *of*, namely something infinite and perfect, mean that it has a representative reality *greater* than the intrinsic reality of my mind. If I invented the concept, GOD would contain things – infinity and perfection – that are not in its cause, because I am imperfect and finite. But this is impossible – there must be as much reality in the cause as in the effect. So only God, being perfect and infinite, could create a concept of something perfect and infinite.

> **?**
> What does Descartes mean by 'representative reality'?

CONCEPT EMPIRICIST ARGUMENTS AGAINST CONCEPT INNATISM
Alternative explanations

Because empiricists reject innate concepts, they must argue that the examples of concepts given above are not, in fact, innate. The syllabus indicates two ways of doing this. First, they can argue that the concept is, in fact, derived from experience. Second, they can argue that there is 'no such concept'. In fact, this second objection cannot work – clearly the concept *exists*. But empiricists can try to show that the concept is *incoherent*, the result of some kind of mental error. This would explain its origin as neither derived from experience nor innate. We shall take the examples in turn.

1. Leibniz

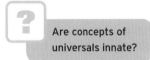

Do concepts I gain from reflecting on my own nature count as innate?

Locke can rightly object that reflection upon what I am does not establish innate concepts. My *existence* and my *ability* to perceive are innate, but that doesn't mean that the *concepts* of SUBSTANCE and PERCEPTION are innate. Locke argues that we must first *experience* our own mind and its activities (in reflection) to develop the concepts – hence they are not innate. It is a confusion to argue that because we derive the concepts from our mental activities that we do not therefore derive them from experience.

2. Plato

Are concepts of universals innate?

For Plato's universals, Locke and Hume can reply that they are derived *by abstraction* from experience. They can argue, for example, that the concept ALMOST EQUAL does not contain the concept EQUAL. Instead, ALMOST-EQUAL is a simple concept derived from sense experience of comparing objects. For instance, we have experiences of two sticks not being the same length. We form the concept EQUAL (as in equal length) by abstracting from the experience of differing lengths – two sticks are equal when they differ by no length. The concept BEAUTY is likewise an abstraction from what beautiful things have in common.

3. Substance: mind

It may be that I *am* a substance. But this doesn't entail that I can derive the concept of SUBSTANCE from myself by reflection. I need to experience myself in reflection *as a substance*. Berkeley argues that we do, that we can have a 'notion', and so a concept of MENTAL SUBSTANCE or MIND. I am not only aware of my mental activities, but aware of my mind as that which is active in thinking, perceiving and willing. So I am aware that my mind is not reducible to the activities themselves. So, Berkeley argues, we can derive the concept of SUBSTANCE from our own minds, but the concept is not innate, as it is derived from our experience of ourselves.

See IDEALISM LEADS TO SOLIPSISM, **p. 69**.

We discuss a different objection in GOING FURTHER: HUME ON SUBSTANCE AND SELF (p. 150).

4. Substance: physical objects

Empiricists can make a number of objections to Descartes' argument regarding the concept of PHYSICAL OBJECT.

a. They can argue that the concept of extension, as a primary quality, must derive from our sense experience, both vision and touch. We can form it *by abstraction* from our many changeable experiences. Such abstraction may require the operation of the understanding, but that is allowed on an empiricist account of the origin of concepts. Descartes' inference from (6) to (7) (p. 143) needs further support.

b. Berkeley would reject Descartes' premise (5), arguing that we can make no sense of physical objects having primary qualities without also having secondary qualities. However, it is not clear that Berkeley is right about this.

See THE IMMEDIATE OBJECTS OF PERCEPTION ARE MIND-DEPENDENT OBJECTS, **p. 58, and** FOUR ARGUMENTS AGAINST MIND-INDEPENDENT OBJECTS, **p. 60**.

c. Berkeley also argues that the concept PHYSICAL OBJECT cannot be a concept of mind-independent SUBSTANCE, some *thing* that persists through changes, as Descartes claims in premise (4). We do not experience physical substances, only their primary and secondary properties, and both are mind-dependent. That anything exists beyond these changeable properties is not an idea that sense experience supports. But rather than conclude that the concept is innate, we should conclude that it is *confused*.

Is the concept of PHYSICAL OBJECT innate?

Going further: Hume on substance and self

Hume, *A Treatise of Human Nature*, Bk 1, Pt 4, §2

Hume develops this last objection further. The concept of a PHYSICAL OBJECT is the concept of something independent of experience existing in three-dimensional space. But how can experience show us that something exists independently of experience? I see my desk; a few moments later, I see it again. If my two experiences are of one and the same desk, then the desk existed when I wasn't looking at it. But I don't experience the desk existing when I'm not looking at it. So how do I arrive at the idea that it is *one and the same* desk, which has persisted through time even when I wasn't experiencing it? My experience only provides the information that my two experiences of the desk are *very similar*. The desk as I first experience it is very similar, perhaps exactly similar, to the desk as I experience it the second time. But similarity, even exact similarity, is not quantitative identity. Being *qualitatively* identical is not the same as being *numerically* identical. (For example, two people can sit comfortably on identical chairs, but they can't sit comfortably on *one and the same* chair.) My sense experience can only provide the concept of a physical object that is numerically identical (with itself) *while I am experiencing it*.

See IDEALISM CANNOT SECURE OBJECTIVE SPACE AND TIME, p. 68.

Hume applies the same argument to the concept of the SELF or MENTAL SUBSTANCE. He disagrees with Descartes, Leibniz and Berkeley: we *don't* experience a continuing substance over time, we *only* experience a continually changing array of thoughts and feelings. Even if we experienced thought as active, as Berkeley maintains, how does experience enable us to move to the claim that I am one and the same active substance, persisting through time and different thoughts?

Treatise of Human Nature, Bk 1, Pt 4, §5

This objection is also discussed in GOING FURTHER: DO 'I' EXIST?, p. 107.

So far, Hume has argued that we cannot derive the concepts of MENTAL or PHYSICAL SUBSTANCE from our experience. If he is right, then we could argue that both concepts must be innate. After all, we *do* have the concept of SUBSTANCE as something that persists through change, and we have the concepts of

PHYSICAL SUBSTANCE and MENTAL SUBSTANCE. If we don't get them from experience, they must be innate.

But Hume takes his argument to show that both concepts of SUBSTANCE are *confused*, rather than innate. In coming up with the concept of a PHYSICAL SUBSTANCE that exists independently of my experiences, I have confused similarity with identity. How does this happen? Our perceptions of physical objects exhibit constancy: if I look at my desk and then shut my eyes and open them again, the desk looks exactly as it did before. On the basis of this similarity, the mind simply has a tendency to *imagine* that what I see after I opened my eyes is not just similar but identical to what I saw before I closed my eyes. The origin of the idea that the two experiences are of something identical – something that exists between and independent of perceptions – is the imagination. The imagination creates the idea of identity from similarity and unity (the idea of an individual thing, being 'one'), both of which we can derive from experience. But there is nothing in experience that matches this concept.

A similar story applies in the case of MENTAL SUBSTANCE or SELF. We've confused the similarity of our thoughts and feelings from one moment to the next with the identity of a 'thing' to which such mental states belong. The concept is not innate, it is confused.

We can object that Hume's theory makes our common-sense idea of the world wrong. If we are to avoid scepticism, we must either find a way to derive these concepts from experience or accept that they are innate.

> Outline and explain Hume's arguments that we cannot derive a concept of SUBSTANCE from experience.

> Outline and explain Hume's objection to either the concept PHYSICAL OBJECT or the concept SELF.

See Arguments against knowledge empiricism: the limits of empirical knowledge, p. 101.

Going further: Descartes on God and infinity

Empiricists can argue that we can form the idea of GOD from experience by abstraction and negation. We are familiar with things – such as ourselves – being finite and imperfect, so we can form the concepts of NOT-FINITE (INFINITE) and NOT-IMPERFECT (PERFECT).

Descartes rejects this proposal (p. 14). The idea of imperfection or lack depends upon an idea of perfection; we can't recognise that we are imperfect *unless* we have an idea of perfection with which to compare ourselves.

See PLATO ON UNIVERSALS, p. 141, for a similar argument.

This argument seems to work in other cases, e.g. REAL and REALITY. It is intuitively plausible that our concept REAL is not an abstraction from NOT-UNREAL – how could we first have experiences of what is unreal on which UNREAL is based? Our experiences are fundamentally of what is real, so REAL is the primary concept.

But does it work for PERFECTION and INFINITY? It is much harder to argue that it does. PERFECTION and INFINITY are arguably challenging and unclear concepts. What is it, exactly, to think not merely of the *absence of limits*, but of something for which there could be no limits? Yet Descartes claims that we have a very powerful – clear and distinct – positive idea of God as perfect and infinite, and not some hazy notion of something indefinitely great. Yet he also accepts that, as a finite mind, he cannot 'grasp' this thought, but he merely 'understands' it (p. 14). With this admission, his claim that the concept of GOD is clear and distinct and involves a positive conception of God's infinity and perfection is unpersuasive.

Is the idea of God innate?

(There are two other claims in Descartes' trademark argument that empiricists may object to: the assumption that all ideas have a cause; and the claim that a cause must have at least as much reality as its effect. Neither of these claims is an analytic truth, but neither is obviously justified by experience. So, on an empiricist theory of knowledge, we cannot know either claim.)

Innate concepts and the non-natural

See GOING FURTHER: INNATE KNOWLEDGE AND THE 'NON-NATURAL', p. 128.

We earlier considered the objection to innate knowledge that it requires the existence of 'non-natural' things. The same objection (and replies) applies to innate concepts – if we don't acquire them from experience, then how are they already part of the mind? Plato, Descartes and Leibniz argue that our thought and experience cannot be explained without innate concepts, and argue from there to their theories about the mind or the existence of God. But there may also be at least some innate concepts, such as PHYSICAL OBJECT, that we can explain empirically in terms of evolution.

Are there any innate concepts? ?

Key points: concept empiricism

- Concept empiricism is the view that all concepts derive from experience. In Locke's terms, all concepts derive from either sensation (sense experience) or reflection (experience of our minds). Prior to experience, the mind is a *tabula rasa*.
- Hume claims that simple concepts are (fainter) copies of impressions. However, he allows that some simple ideas, e.g. a particular shade of blue, don't have to be derived from sense impressions. We can make Hume consistent by saying that an idea does not need to be copied from an impression, but it is only meaningful if there is a possible impression it could be copied from. Alternatively, we can explain why the shade of blue is a very specific exception that cannot be generalised.
- Locke and Hume argue that complex concepts are created out of simple concepts by combining and abstracting from them.
- We can object that there are some complex concepts, e.g. KNOWLEDGE or BEAUTY, that cannot be analysed in terms of simpler concepts.
- Concept innatism claims that some concepts are innate, i.e. part of the structure of the mind and not derived from experience.
- Locke rejects innate concepts for three reasons: babies have almost no concepts, and those they have are derived from experience; no concept, even GOD, is possessed by all human beings; any idea must be either new to the mind or remembered.
- Defenders of concept innatism reject Locke's understanding of innate concepts, arguing instead that they are concepts that cannot be learned from experience, though experience may be necessary to trigger them.
- Leibniz argues that this understanding of innate concepts defeats Locke's first objection. He also argues that human beings are universally disposed to form the concept of GOD,

and that understanding innate concepts as dispositions to think in particular ways explains how an idea can be neither new nor remembered.

- Leibniz takes all concepts that are derived from reflection to be innate.
- Universals are properties that many particular objects can have as the same property, e.g. beauty. Plato argues that because we only experience particular things, we cannot derive concepts of universals from sense experience.
- Furthermore, nothing that we experience perfectly exemplifies these concepts. For example, we only ever experience things that are almost equal, never equal. So we cannot derive the concept EQUAL from experience. So it must be innate.
- Descartes argues that our concept of a physical object, e.g. a piece of wax, cannot be derived from its sensory properties, because these can change, while we think the object is the same object. Furthermore, we understand that the object can go through more changes than we can imagine.
- Our concept of a physical object is of something extended and changeable. This concept is part of the understanding.
- Descartes identifies three sources of ideas: outside my mind, invented, and innate.
- He claims that all causes must have at least as much reality as their effects. The cause of an idea must have as much reality as what the idea represents.
- He argues that only God has as much reality as what the concept GOD represents, namely something infinite and perfect. The concept can't be invented by me and doesn't derive from experience. Therefore, it is innate.
- Empiricists can object to Leibniz that concepts that are derived from reflection are not innate, but derived from the experience of our own minds. Berkeley argues that I gain the concept of MENTAL SUBSTANCE this way.
- They can object to Plato that we can form concepts of universals by abstraction.
- They can object to Descartes that the concept of extension, being a primary quality, must be formed, by abstraction, from sense experience.

- Berkeley and Hume argue that PHYSICAL SUBSTANCE is not a concept that can be derived from experience.
- Hume argues that both PHYSICAL SUBSTANCE and MENTAL SUBSTANCE derive from a confusion between similarity and identity; we experience similarity, but we imagine identity. Both are therefore not innate, but confused.
- We can object that Hume's analysis leads to scepticism. This is a good reason to think that the concepts are innate.
- Empiricists can object to Descartes that we invented the idea of God by negating ideas of imperfection and finitude. Descartes replies that our idea of God is of something that is positively, not negatively, infinite and perfect.
- We can object that this isn't persuasive. We can also object to his claim that the cause of an idea must have 'as much reality' as its object, and his assumption that all ideas have a cause.
- Concept empiricists can object that innate concepts require the existence of 'non-natural' things. But more recent defenders of innate concepts offer an explanation in terms of evolution.

Summary: the origin of concepts and the nature of knowledge

In this section on the origin of concepts and the nature of knowledge, we have looked at the debates about how we acquire concepts and knowledge. The debate over knowledge is between

1. Empiricism: our knowledge is limited to what can be derived from sense experience and analytic truths; and
2. Rationalism: there is, in addition, synthetic a priori knowledge that we have innately or acquire by the use of a priori reasoning.

The debate over concepts is between

1. Concept empiricism: all our concepts derive from experience through either sensation or reflection; and
2. Innatism: there are some concepts that we cannot derive from experience, and that are therefore innate.

In our discussion and evaluation of these theories, we have looked at the following issues:

1. What is the distinction between analytic and synthetic propositions? What is the distinction between a priori and a posteriori knowledge? And how are the distinctions linked to each other?
2. Can knowledge empiricism avoid becoming scepticism?
3. What is the distinction between necessary and contingent truths? How do we know necessary truths?
4. Can we use rational intuition and deduction to gain a priori knowledge of synthetic truths?
5. How does Descartes argue for the existence of his mind, God and physical objects? Do his arguments succeed?
6. Why and how do Plato and Leibniz argue for innate knowledge and concepts, and why and how does Locke reject them?
7. What is it to say that experience 'triggers' innate knowledge or concepts?
8. Can empiricists provide alternative explanations for all potential examples of innate knowledge?
9. How, according to empiricists, are all concepts derived from experience? Do any concepts, such as concepts of universals, substance, physical objects, God and infinity, present counterexamples?
10. If some concepts cannot be derived from experience, are such concepts innate or incoherent?

PHILOSOPHY OF RELIGION

3

In this chapter, we look at four issues. First, what is God, according to a traditional monotheistic concept of God deriving from Judaism, Christianity and Islam? Does the concept make sense? Second, we will discuss three arguments for the existence of God. The ontological argument claims to prove that God exists just by unpacking our understanding of the concept of God. The argument from design uses the apparent order and purpose of nature to infer the existence of God. And the cosmological argument claims that God is the origin of the universe. The third issue is the problem of evil, an argument that uses the existence of evil to infer that God, at least as traditionally conceived, does not exist. Finally, we look at the nature of religious language. Does religious language state facts, can it be true or false, and is it even meaningful?

By the end of the chapter, you should be able to analyse, explain, and evaluate a number of arguments for and against the coherence of the concept of God, the existence of God, and theories of religious language.

A note on referring to God: I have adopted the traditional personal pronoun 'he' in referring to God. English unfortunately has only two personal pronouns, 'he' and 'she', both gendered. If God exists, I don't believe that God is gendered in either way. My use of 'he' is purely to avoid the awkwardness of alternating 'he' and 'she' and of using 's/he'.

SYLLABUS CHECKLIST

The AQA AS syllabus for this chapter is:

I. The concept of God

✔ God as omniscient, omnipotent, supremely good, and either timeless (eternal) or within time (everlasting) and the meaning(s) of these divine attributes.

Issues, including:

✔ issues with claiming that God has these attributes, either singly or in combination, including:
   ● the paradox of the stone
   ● the *Euthyphro* dilemma
✔ the compatibility, or otherwise, of the existence of an omniscient God and free human beings.

II. Arguments relating to the existence of God

A. Ontological arguments, including those formulated by:
✔ Anselm
✔ Descartes
✔ Leibniz
✔ Malcolm
✔ Plantinga.

Issues, including those raised by:
✔ Gaunilo
✔ Hume
✔ Kant.

B. The argument from design:
✔ arguments from purpose and regularity, including those formulated by:

- Paley
- Swinburne.

Issues, including those raised by:
- ✔ Paley (himself)
- ✔ Hume
- ✔ Kant.

C. The cosmological argument:
- ✔ causal and contingency arguments, including those formu-lated by:
  - Aquinas' Five Ways (first three)
  - Descartes
  - the Kalam argument.

Issues, including those raised by:
- ✔ Hume
- ✔ Russell.

D. The problem of evil:
- ✔ how to reconcile God's omnipotence, omniscience and supreme goodness with the existence of physical/moral evil.

Responses and issues arising from those responses, including:
- ✔ the free will defence (Plantinga)
- ✔ soul-making (Hick).

III. Religious language

- ✔ logical positivism: verification principle and verification/falsification (Ayer)
  - religious statements as verifiable eschatologically (Hick)
- ✔ cognitivist and non-cognitivist accounts of religious language and issues arising from them
  - the *University* debate: Flew (on Wisdom's 'Gods'), Hare ('bliks') and Mitchell (the 'partisan')

I. The concept of God

At the heart of philosophy of religion is the concept of God. There are many concepts of God around the world, and different religions have different views on the nature of God. However, almost all agree that God is 'maximally great' – that nothing could be greater than God. This is the conception of God we will start with. But we develop it more narrowly, and the properties of God we will discuss are those which Judaism, Christianity and Islam – the three great monotheistic traditions – have thought central. Even more narrowly, we will only look at how the debate over God's attributes has been understood and developed in the Western Christian tradition. In this section, we will ask how the concept of God has been understood, whether it is coherent, and whether it is consistent with certain views of morality and human freedom.

The divine attributes

We start with the thought that nothing could be greater than God. Another way this thought has been expressed is that God is perfect. Augustine says that to think of God is to 'attempt to conceive something than which nothing more excellent or sublime exists'. Some philosophers claim that God is the most perfect being that *could* (not just does) exist.

On Christian Doctrine, Bk 1, Ch. 7

The idea of perfection has often been linked to the idea of reality. The view is that what is perfect is more real than what is not. Perfection has also been thought to involve complete self-sufficiency – i.e. not to be dependent on anything, and not to lack anything. Again, this connects with being the ultimate reality: that which is not the ultimate reality will depend on that which is, and so not be perfect. So God is traditionally thought of as the ultimate reality – the ground or basis for everything that exists.

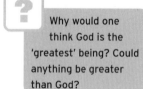

Why would one think God is the 'greatest' being? Could anything be greater than God?

God as personal

Before turning to the attributes of God listed in the syllabus, we may ask why these properties have been thought to belong to God. Part of the answer is that many religions have thought that God is 'personal'. Properties that essentially characterise a person include intellect and will. The intellect is characterised by rationality and knowledge, the will by morality, freedom and the ability to act (power). (Some philosophers argue that to lack either intellect or will is to lack perfections – things without either intellect or will are not as great as things with intellect and will. Certainly we prize these abilities very highly. So to be perfect, God must have both intellect and will, i.e. be personal.)

Intellect and will are properties of mind. If God is a person, he is so in virtue of being a mind. Being perfect, if God is a mind, then he is a perfect mind. He will have perfect intellect and perfect will. Perfect intellect involves perfect wisdom, perfect rationality and perfect knowledge (omniscience). Perfect will involves perfect goodness and perfect power (omnipotence).

However, if God were a person, he would be very unusual. As the most perfect possible being, God cannot become more perfect; nor can God become less perfect, as then he would not be the most perfect being possible, and so not God. So unlike other persons, it seems that God cannot change. Persons also have bodies. But the most perfect being can't have a body, at least literally.

> **Outline and explain one reason for thinking that God cannot change.**

1. Anything made of matter changes over time.
2. Anything made of matter has parts.
3. Whatever has parts depends on them for its existence.
4. If God were made of matter, God would change and depend on his parts.
5. Being perfect, God can't change and God doesn't depend on anything for his existence.
6. Therefore, God can't be made of matter.

For these reasons, philosophers have said God is *personal* rather than a *person*, that is, God has attributes essentially associated with

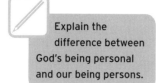

Explain the difference between God's being personal and our being persons.

being a person, but God is not a person, because he does not change and does not have a body.

Omniscience

Perfect knowledge is usually taken to mean 'omniscience'. The most obvious definition of omniscience is 'knowing everything' (Latin *omni-*, 'all'; *scient*, 'knowing'). But we need to remember that God is the most perfect *possible* being, and perhaps it is *impossible* to know everything. For example, if human beings have free will, then perhaps it is not possible to know what they will do in the future. So let us say for now that omniscience means 'knowing all the truths that it is possible to know'.

We return to this issue in KRETZMANN, 'OMNISCIENCE AND IMMUTABILITY', p. 172, and OMNISCIENCE AND HUMAN FREEDOM, p. 175.

Omniscience is not just a matter of *what* God knows, but also of *how* God knows. Aquinas argues that God knows everything that he knows 'directly', rather than through inference or through understanding a system of representation (such as language or thinking in terms of propositions). Other philosophers disagree, and argue that if God doesn't know all true propositions, then there is something that God doesn't know; so God has propositional knowledge as well as direct knowledge.

Aquinas, *Summa Theologica*, Pt 1, Q. 14, Arts 5, 6

What is 'omniscience'?

Omnipotence

Power is the ability to do things. As perfect, God will have perfect power, or the most power possible. The most obvious definition of omnipotence is 'the power to do anything' (Latin *omni-*, 'all'; *potent*, 'powerful'). But does 'anything' include, for instance, the logically impossible? Could God make $2 + 2 = 5$? Could God create a married bachelor? Some pious philosophers have wanted to say yes – logic is no limit on God's power. However, there is simply no way we can meaningfully say this.

AQUINAS, *SUMMA THEOLOGICA*, PT 1, Q. 25, ART. 3

Aquinas argues that the correct understanding of God's omnipotence is that God can do anything possible. What is impossible is a contradiction in terms – the words that you use to describe the impossible literally contradict each other. So any description of a logically impossible state of affairs or power is not a meaningful description, because it contains a contradiction. What is logically impossible is not anything at all.

Thus, the *limits* of the logically possible are not *limitations* on God's power. Even if God can't do the logically impossible, there is still nothing that God can't do.

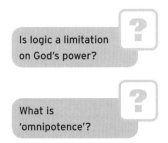

Is logic a limitation on God's power?

What is 'omnipotence'?

Supreme goodness

There are two ways of understanding perfect, or supreme, goodness. If goodness just is perfection, then saying God is perfectly good is just to say that God is perfectly perfect – or the most perfect possible being. There is more than one way to be perfect (including, as we've seen, perfect power and perfect knowledge), and God is perfect in all ways. This is a metaphysical sense of 'goodness'.

The other sense of 'goodness', which is the sense in which I will understand it in our discussion, is the moral sense. In this sense, 'God is perfectly good' means that God's will is always in accordance with moral values.

Plato and Augustine connect the two understandings of perfect goodness. What is perfect includes what is morally good; evil is a type of 'lack', a 'falling short' of goodness. If evil is a 'lack' or 'failure', what is morally good is more (metaphysically) perfect than what is not.

Explain the difference between 'metaphysical' and 'moral' perfection.

See OMNIPOTENCE AND SUPREME GOODNESS, p. 167.

Eternal and everlasting

Being perfect, God is self-sufficient, dependent on nothing else for existence. If something brought God into existence, God would be dependent on that thing to exist. If there were something that could end God's existence, then God is equally dependent on that thing (not exercising its power) to continue to exist. If God depends on nothing else, then nothing can bring God into existence or end God's existence. And so (if God exists) God's existence has no beginning or end.

There are two ways in which this can be expressed. If God exists in time, then God's existence is *everlasting* – God exists throughout all time. If God exists outside time, then God's existence is *eternal* – God is timeless. In this case, God has no beginning or end because the ideas of beginning and end only make sense in time – something can only start or stop existing in time. God is not in time, so God cannot start or stop existing.

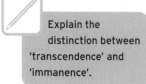

Explain the difference between the terms 'everlasting' and 'eternal'.

Going further: transcendence and immanence

These two interpretations of the relationship of God to time can be understood in a broader context of the relation of God to creation. The idea of *transcendence* marks the way God is very different from creation. First, God is 'outside' or 'goes beyond' the universe. Since God is self-sufficient and also traditionally said to be the creator of the universe, clearly God is not reducible to the universe. Second, God is not spatial or physical as the universe is, and many philosophers argue that God is eternal, transcending time. Third, while God is personal, he has intellect and will in quite a different way from persons.

However, emphasising God's transcendence can make it seem that God is very remote from us. The claim that God is *immanent* marks the close connection between God's existence and the existence of everything else. For example, it is said that God is *omnipresent*, i.e. that he exists everywhere - in everything that exists, God is 'there'. In being everywhere, God knows everything from the 'inside'. Some thinkers also argue that God is everlasting, immanent in time and so in human history, giving a sense that we work alongside God in producing what is morally good.

Explain the distinction between 'transcendence' and 'immanence'.

Immanence without transcendence - God as wholly immanent - would lead to 'pantheism', the view that God and the universe are the same thing. It would also lead to a denial of God being personal - since the universe isn't. So transcendence is necessary for the traditional conception of God; immanence is necessary to prevent that God being impossibly remote from us.

> Explain the relationship between transcendence and one other attribute of God.

Issues with claiming that God has these attributes

If God is the most perfect possible being, then each of the perfections attributed to God must be possible, and the combination of the perfections must also be possible. Both of these requirements lead to difficulties. For example, it is unclear what it means to say that 'God knows everything it is possible to know'. Or again, can God will evil? Omnipotence suggests 'yes', perfect goodness suggests 'no'. In the light of this, some philosophers say that God has the perfections he does to the greatest possible *degree* that is *compatible* with his having all perfections.

Omnipotence and the paradox of the stone

MAVRODES, 'SOME PUZZLES CONCERNING OMNIPOTENCE'

Can God create a stone that he can't lift? If the answer is 'no', then God cannot create the stone. If the answer is 'yes', then God cannot lift the stone. So either way, it seems, there is something God cannot do. If there is something God can't do, then God isn't omnipotent.

George Mavrodes argues that this famous paradox makes a faulty assumption: it presupposes the possibility of something logically impossible. The claim that someone, *x*, can make

> Outline and explain the paradox of the stone.

Explain the claim that 'the power to create a stone an omnipotent being can't lift' is logically impossible.

something that is too heavy for x to lift is not normally self-contradictory. However, it becomes self-contradictory – logically impossible – when x is an omnipotent being. 'A stone an omnipotent being can't lift' is not a possible thing; as a self-contradiction, it describes nothing. So 'the power to create a stone an omnipotent being can't lift' is not a possible power. If God lacks it, God still doesn't lack any possible power.

Alternatively, here's a slightly different solution. Suppose we allow that God can lift any stone, but cannot create a stone that he can't lift. But given that there is no limit on God's power of lifting stones, there is, in fact, no limit on God's power of creating stones. So God lacks no power related to lifting or creating stones.

On either solution, the paradox does not show that God lacks any possible power. So it is no objection to God being omnipotent.

SAVAGE, 'THE PARADOX OF THE STONE'

Wade Savage raises the following objection to Mavrodes' argument. Mavrodes uses the concept of an omnipotent being to argue that 'a stone that an omnipotent being cannot lift' is a self-contradiction. But the paradox is trying to show that the concept of an omnipotent being is *self-contradictory*. To bring this out, we should phrase the argument like this (p. 76):

1. Either x can create a stone which x cannot lift, or x cannot create a stone which x cannot lift.
2. If x can create a stone which x cannot lift, then, necessarily, there is at least one task which x cannot perform (namely, lift the stone in question).
3. If x cannot create a stone which x cannot lift, then, necessarily, there is at least one task which x cannot perform (namely, create the stone in question).
4. Hence, there is at least one task which x cannot perform.

5. If *x* is an omnipotent being, then *x* can perform any task.
6. Therefore, *x* is not omnipotent.

If the concept of an omnipotent being is self-contradictory, then an omnipotent being cannot exist. If we assume that an omnipotent being can exist, then we beg the question against the paradox.

    However, Savage argues that there is a solution to the paradox. Although he doesn't notice it, it is the same solution as Mavrodes' second solution. (3) is false. For clarity, let's substitute God for '*x*'. 'God cannot create a stone which God cannot lift' only means that 'if God can create a stone, then God can lift it'. This does *not* entail that there is something that God cannot do. God can create a stone of any size and can then lift that stone. There is no limitation of God's power here.

> Outline and explain Savage's objection to Mavrodes.

> What is the best solution, if any, to the stone paradox?

Omnipotence and supreme goodness

The next issue concerns the coherence of saying that God is both omnipotent and perfectly, or supremely, good.

1. To commit evil is to fail to be supremely good.
2. If God is supremely good, then God cannot commit evil.
3. Therefore, if God is supremely good, there is something that God cannot do.
4. Therefore, God cannot be both supremely good and omnipotent.

> Explain the objection that if God is supremely good, he cannot be omnipotent.

Here are three possible solutions:

1. God has the power to commit evil, and he can will it, so he is omnipotent. However, he always chooses not to, so he is supremely good.
2. There is no distinct 'power to commit evil', because 'evil' doesn't name a distinct act. To commit evil, God would have to do something, e.g. hurt someone unjustifiably. God has all the

powers to bring this about – there is no power he lacks to do whatever the evil act would be – but chooses not to act in that way.

3. Aquinas argues that there is no distinct 'power to commit evil', because evil is not a 'something', but an absence of good. Asking whether God can commit evil is like asking whether God can fail. Being 'able' to fail is not a power; failing demonstrates the lack of power to succeed. There is no 'power to commit evil' as committing evil is the result of the lack of power to do good. As God does not lack the power to do good, God cannot commit evil.

Summa Theologica, Pt 1, Q. 25, Art. 3

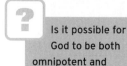
Is it possible for God to be both omnipotent and perfectly good?

The Euthyphro *dilemma*

The previous puzzle discussed good and evil as though they are independent of God. But can God make right be wrong, or good bad? Is morality whatever God wills it to be or is morality something independent of God?

Explain the difference between claiming that what is morally right is right because God wills it and claiming that God wills what is morally right because it is right.

1. If morality is whatever God wills, then if God wills what is (now) morally wrong, then what is wrong will become right – if God commands us to murder babies, then murdering babies would be morally right. What is morally right is right because God wills it.
2. If morality is independent of what God wills, then God cannot make what is wrong be right – murdering babies is wrong whatever God commands. But then, to be good, God's will must conform to something independent of God. God wills what is morally right because it is right.

The answer must be one or the other, but both alternatives can seem unsatisfactory, which creates a dilemma.

To (2), we can object that this places a *constraint* on God. For instance, if God is supremely good, but morality is independent of God, then God cannot will anything, only what is right. This would mean that God is not omnipotent. Or again, God cannot change what is morally right – so God is not omnipotent. Since God is omnipotent, morality is not a restriction on God's will, but dependent on it. Or again, if God exists and is good, then everything that is morally good must relate back to God as the ultimate reality. Given the nature of God, morality must depend on God.

This argument leads us back to (1). But as we will see below, this also faces strong objections.

PLATO, *EUTHYPHRO*

In his dialogue *Euthyphro*, Plato considered the question 'what is piety?' Is piety doing whatever the gods want or do the gods want what is pious? Plato argued that both answers seem unsatisfactory, creating a dilemma. (Our version substitutes 'morality' for 'piety'.)

In response to Socrates' questioning, Euthyphro's first formal definition of piety is 'that which is dear to the gods' or again 'what the gods love'. Socrates then asks whether what is pious is pious because it is loved by the gods, or whether the gods love what is pious because it is pious. Euthyphro answers that the gods love it because it is pious. This makes piety independent of the gods' love – it would count as piety whether or not the gods loved it.

Socrates objects that this can't be right. What 'is dear to the gods is dear to them because it is loved by them, not loved by them because it is dear to them'. Piety, Euthyphro has said, is what is dear to the gods. So piety must be dear to them *because* they love it. Curiously, Plato doesn't support this objection with any arguments. The thought is that what the gods value, they value because they love that thing. To accept this means accepting that there aren't any further *reasons* for the gods loving what they do.

But suppose we agree that piety is independent of what the gods love. So what is it? Euthyphro suggests it is justice in relation to the gods. This requires that we learn how to please them in prayers and sacrifices. This doesn't bring them any benefit; it simply pleases them. But then, objects Socrates, piety once more becomes whatever pleases the gods – what is pious is pious because the gods love it. Euthyphro has found it impossible to say what piety is, independent of what the gods love.

> Outline and explain Euthyphro's struggle to define piety.

Is 'God is good' a tautology?

The discussion so far supports the view that morality is whatever God wills. However, this faces two powerful objections.

The first is this: if good is whatever God wills, then 'God is good' doesn't say anything substantial about God. *Whatever* God wills is by definition good. 'God is good' means no more than 'God wills whatever God wills'. It states a tautology.

Here are two possible replies (a third appears in the 'Going Further' box below):

1. *Reply*: 'God is good' means 'God is good to us', i.e. God loves us and wants what is best for us. And what is best for us can be understood in a way that is not dependent on whatever God wills.
   Objection: But then, there is some standard of what is good, namely what is best for us, which is independent of what God wills.
2. *Reply*: 'God is good' should be understood *metaphysically*, not morally: 'God is good' just means that God has all perfections.
   Objection: But then what is the connection between the metaphysical sense of 'good' and the moral sense of 'good'? Does God being perfect entail that God is *morally* good? If so, then 'God is (morally) good' is still a tautology. If not, then is morality independent of metaphysical perfection?

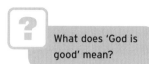

What does 'God is good' mean?

Morality is arbitrary

The second objection to saying that what is good is whatever God wills is that it makes morality arbitrary. *Why* does God will what he wills? On this view, there is no moral reason guiding what God wills because God *invents* morality. But if God has no reasons to will what he does, this means that there is no rational structure to morality. The view also entails that it would be right to murder babies if God willed it. This doesn't seem right! For both these reasons, there must be some independent standard we are implicitly relying on to say that what God wills is, in fact, morally good.

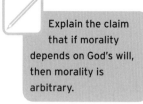

Explain the claim that if morality depends on God's will, then morality is arbitrary.

We may reply that although God's will does not respond to anything independent of it, it is not arbitrary. For example, we can appeal to God's other attributes, such as love. But then aren't we judging God's will by the standard of love? If so, morality is still independent of God. But this is a misunderstanding: the claim is not that the basis of morality is love, but that the basis of morality is *God's* love.

Does this answer make morality arbitrary? Not obviously. God's will is structured by God's love, and it is this that creates morality. God wills what he does because he loves. Yet we may still ask: why does God love what he does? Is this arbitrary? If God loved something else, then morality would be different.

> Outline and explain the *Euthyphro* dilemma, giving one objection to each horn of the dilemma.

Going further: good is the same property as what God wills

A third solution to the *Euthyphro* dilemma is to say that morality *is* the same thing as what God wills, but 'God is good' is *not* a tautology. How is this possible?

The answer depends on a distinction between *concepts* and *properties*. 'God' and 'morally good' are different concepts. It is not an analytic truth that God is good. However, goodness is the same property as what God wills.

> On analytic truth, see ANALYTIC/SYNTHETIC, p. 97.

A different example will help. 'Water' and 'H$_2$O' are different concepts, and before the discovery of hydrogen and oxygen, people knew about water. They had the concept of water, but not the concept of H$_2$O. And they didn't know that water is H$_2$O. So 'water is H$_2$O' is not analytically true. However, water and H$_2$O are one and the same thing – the two concepts refer to just one thing in the world. Water is *identical* to H$_2$O.

The same account can be given of 'good' and 'what God wills' – they are different concepts, and people can have and understand one concept without the other. So 'God is good' is not an analytic truth. However, what is good is the same thing as what God wills. It is not something separate which provides a standard for God's will. Morality is dependent on God. This is a metaphysical truth (about what exists) but not a conceptual truth.

> Explain the claim that what is good is identical with what God wills, yet 'God is good' is not a tautology.

We can object that unless we have an *independent* standard of goodness, we cannot claim that God's will and what is good are the same thing. This is true, but it only applies to how we *know* what is good, not what goodness turns out to *be*. We can only judge that water is H_2O if we have some independent idea of what water is. But that doesn't mean water is not H_2O. Likewise, to judge that what is good is what God wills, we need, *at least initially*, independent concepts of what is good and of what God wills. Which is fine, since we do form these concepts in distinct ways. But once we think that water is H_2O, we will say that whatever is H_2O is water. Likewise, once we come to believe that what is good is what God wills, we may use what we believe God's will to be to start judging what is good. God's will, we may argue, is our best source of knowledge about what is good.

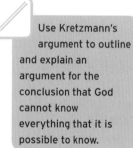

? Can the *Euthyphro* dilemma be solved? If so, how?

KRETZMANN, 'OMNISCIENCE AND IMMUTABILITY'

Is omniscience possible? Is it possible for God to know *everything*, or at least everything that it is possible to know? Norman Kretzmann argues that, as long as we think that God cannot change – that God is 'immutable' – then God cannot be omniscient. The thought that God cannot change comes from the thought that God is perfect. Kretzmann argues:

1. A perfect being is not subject to change.
2. A perfect being knows everything.
3. A being that knows everything always knows what time it is.
4. A being that always knows what time it is is subject to change.
5. Therefore, a perfect being is subject to change.
6. Therefore, a perfect being is not a perfect being.
7. Therefore, there is no perfect being.

This argument is a *reductio ad absurdum*, which is a form of argument that shows that some claim leads to a contradiction.

Use Kretzmann's argument to outline and explain an argument for the conclusion that God cannot know everything that it is possible to know.

The contradiction is (6). If (1)-(5) are true, then the concept of a perfect being is incoherent.

The most obvious premise to attack is (4). Kretzmann starts there.

a. *Objection*: Just because what time it is changes doesn't mean that knowing what time it is counts as a change in knowledge.

Reply: Yes it does. If you know first that it is 1.30 and then you know that it is not 1.30 (because it is 1.40), you know one thing and then another. So what you know changes.

b. *Objection*: A change in your beliefs like this doesn't count as a change in you.

Reply: It's true that you haven't *changed your mind* or decided that you were wrong. And it's true that the change in your beliefs isn't very significant. But it is still true that your beliefs have changed, and so your mind has changed.

Two more objections attack premises (3) and (4) together:

c. *Objection*: God knows everything about the universe 'simultaneously', not 'successively'. In other words, God knows everything 'all at once'; his knowledge doesn't change as the universe changes. (For example, God might know everything 'all at once' because God is transcendent.)

Reply: But this means that God cannot know what time it is *now*, and so is not omniscient. Perhaps God knows the time at which each thing happens - past, present or future. But that doesn't mean that God knows *when* in time we are. To know *that* involves knowing something that changes. If God doesn't change, then God doesn't know where we are in time, so God is not omniscient.

d. *Objection*: God is transcendent, outside time. So God cannot change.

    Reply: God's transcendence is usually understood as there being no time from God's point of view. But that would mean that time is an *illusion* that we suffer from. In turn, that means that it is never true to say 'It is now 1.30 (or any other time)'. If time doesn't exist, then *nothing* changes. This is implausible, so we should reject the idea of God's transcendence.

Perhaps the difficulty is with our interpretation of omniscience (2).

e. *Objection*: Omniscience is not knowing everything, or everything that it is possible to know. Omniscience is knowing what it is logically possible for a perfect being to know. A perfect being transcends time. Therefore, it is logically impossible for a perfect being to know what time it is. But not knowing what it is logically impossible for a perfect being to know is no limitation.

    Reply: This form of argument is unsatisfactory. For instance, 'I am a mortal being, and so it is logically impossible that I should not die. Therefore, dying is no limitation on me'. Obviously, dying is a limitation! The correct conclusion is that a perfect being – one that both transcends time and is omniscient – is logically impossible.

f. *Objection*: Omniscience is knowing everything that it is possible for a perfect being to know without ceasing to be perfect. Knowing what time it is is only possible if one changes, and to change is to be imperfect. Therefore, a perfect being is omniscient without knowing what time it is. (One might argue that a perfect being *could* know what time it is, but chooses not to because to know that would mean becoming changeable.)

    Reply: This is highly counter-intuitive. Knowing what time it is is knowing what is happening *now*. To not know *that* is to lack significant knowledge. And it won't work

Can God know everything that it is possible to know?

to say that God chooses not to know everything: omniscience isn't merely the power to know everything; it is knowing everything.

See OMNIPOTENCE AND SUPREME GOODNESS, p. 167, for a parallel argument regarding omnipotence.

Perhaps the problem, then, is thinking that in order to be perfect, God must be unchangeable (1).

g.   *Objection*: Knowing what time it is from one moment to the next is not a change that affects God's perfection. So God's knowledge does change, in this one small respect.
Reply: Being perfect has also meant being 'complete', never in a state of potential. If God knows what time it is, God's knowledge is - in this respect - not complete; God is yet to know what time it is next.

Suppose nothing ever changed, including time. In such a world, God could know everything and be unchangeable. So what makes omniscience and immutability incompatible is a contingent fact, the fact that things change. So if God exists, God isn't the most perfect *possible* being - the most perfect possible being only exists in a world in which nothing changes. At best, God is the most perfect *actual* being - but that being can't be absolutely perfect, because God either must change or can't be omniscient.

Is the concept of a perfect being logically coherent?

Omniscience and human freedom

If we were able to solve Kretzmann's challenge to God's omniscience, we would still face another puzzle about the relation between God's knowledge and time. Can God know what I will do in the future? If God is eternal, existing outside time, the problem doesn't seem to arise. God already knows what happens in that period of time which we call 'future'. Being outside time, God's knowledge of all events is 'simultaneous'. Past, present and future are all the same to God.

This response defends God's omniscience (although it leads to some of the problems above – see Objections (c) and (d)). But a new problem then arises. If God knows what I will do in the future, are my actions *free*?

1. For me to do an action freely, I must be able to do it or refrain from doing it.
2. If God knows what I will do before I do it, then it must be true that I do that action.
3. Therefore, it cannot be true that God knows what I will do before I do it and be true that I *don't* do that action.
4. If it is true that I do that action, then nothing I can do can prevent it from coming true that I am doing that action.
5. Therefore, if God knows what I will do before I do it, then I cannot refrain from doing that action.
6. Therefore, if God knows what I will do before I do it, then that action is not free.
7. (Therefore, conversely, if my actions are free, God does not know what I will do before I do it.)

If I am free, then this argument entails that God does not know what I will do before I do it. So there is something God does not know, and so God is not omniscient. (For God not to have knowledge of the future, all time cannot be the same for God, so God cannot be eternal, but in some way, must exist within time.) Furthermore, as the future unfolds, God would gain new knowledge. Again, if God gains knowledge, he wasn't previously omniscient.

We could simply conclude that God is omniscient and we are not free. However, this raises another conflict for the concept of God. Freedom – free will – is a great good that allows us to do good or evil and to enter willingly into a relationship with God or not. Without free will, we couldn't choose how to live or what kind of person to be, so our lives would not be meaningful or morally significant. As supremely good, God would want our lives to be morally significant and meaningful, so he would wish us to have free will. If we are not free, God is not supremely good.

Can I be free and God be omniscient? We may argue that God's not knowing what I will do before I do it is not a *restriction* on God's

> (2) also follows from the claim that knowledge is always of true propositions. See TRUTH IS NOT A NECESSARY CONDITION OF KNOWLEDGE, **p. 77.**

> Outline and explain the argument that if God knows my future actions, then my actions are not free.

knowledge. It is *impossible* to know the future, because of the existence of free will. So God still knows everything it is possible to know *at any given time*. And God's gaining knowledge as time passes is consistent with God being omniscient: God always knows everything it is possible to know. It is just that *what* it is possible to know changes over time.

This reply accepts the argument (1)–(7) above, but claims that the argument does not show that God isn't omniscient. But is this a satisfactory view of omniscience?

> Can God be omniscient and not know what I will do in the future?

KENNY, 'DIVINE FOREKNOWLEDGE AND HUMAN FREEDOM'

Anthony Kenny defends a different solution which rejects the argument (1)-(7). He argues that it is possible both for God to know what I will do before I do it and for me to do that action freely. He begins (p. 258) by objecting to premise (2). Generalised, the claim is 'If God knows that *p*, *p* must be true'. This can be understood in two ways, one true and one false:

1. False: 'If God knows that *p*, it is necessarily true that *p*'.
2. True: 'The proposition "whatever God knows is true" is necessarily true'.

> See NECESSARY AND CONTINGENT TRUTH, p. 105.

The false reading misleads us into denying that our actions are free. We said that if God knows what I will do tomorrow, then it must be true that I do that and nothing else. So I *must* do it, I *cannot* not do it, and so I am not free. But the claim is false – there is no reason to think that whatever God knows is a necessary truth. God can know all sorts of contingent truths.

The true reading simply follows from the definition of knowledge. No one can know what is false. But this reading doesn't obviously cause a problem for freedom. Knowing that something *will* happen doesn't mean that it *has* to happen. So for God to know what I will do tomorrow, it only needs to be the case that I *don't* do something else. It doesn't mean that I *can't*.

But we may object that this doesn't solve the problem (p. 264).

1. To do something different from what God knows I will do would mean changing God's knowledge – either changing what God knows (I will do) or making it that God doesn't know what I will do, because I do something else.
2. If God *already* knows what I will do, then changing what God knows would mean changing the past.
3. I can't change the past, so I can't change what God knows.
4. So I can't change what I will do.
5. So there is nothing I *can* do except what God already knows that I *will* do.

Kenny's response is technical and difficult: we don't *change* the future (p. 266) – the future is what happens when all the 'changes' (decisions, choices, etc.) are done. The future is what *will* happen. The past is what *has* happened. There are truths about both. By acting, I don't change the future. Instead, I can change a truth about the future into a truth about the past: 'I will write this book' (future tense) turns into 'I have written this book' (past tense). But, says Kenny, I can equally change a truth about the past: 'I have not written this book' (past tense) becomes 'I have written this book' (past tense).

We are supposing that God's belief about what I will do is true; when I do what God believes I will do, that makes his belief true. That doesn't show that I can't choose or decide what to do; it doesn't show that I cannot act freely.

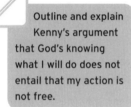

Explain the claim that if God knows what I will do, I can no more change the future than I can change the past.

Outline and explain Kenny's argument that God's knowing what I will do does not entail that my action is not free.

Discussion

Kenny's solution is perplexing. Technically, he may be right that the argument given does not show that God's knowledge of what I will do rules out freedom. However, as soon as we ask *how* it is that God knows what I will do, the puzzle arises again.

Clearly, simply having a true belief that someone will do something doesn't mean that they are not free. For instance, perhaps you can accurately predict that a friend of yours will help this old lady across the street, because he is a kind person, in a good mood, and has just said that this is what he will do. In this instance, your belief is not only true, but justified as well, so we are happy to say that you know what your friend will do. Or again, if your beliefs about what your friend does are generally reliable, then you know what he will do.

But we cannot suppose that God's knowledge of what I will do is like this. Because God is omniscient, his beliefs are not merely reliable, but *complete and infallible*. How can there be complete and infallible knowledge of what someone will choose to do if that choice is not already determined in some way? The justifications we offered above, e.g. knowing someone's character, might give you knowledge of the general shape of their choices and actions, but not every minute detail. And it certainly won't be enough for knowledge of what they will be doing in the distant future. If God knows now what I will be doing on 23 May 2026, this can't simply be because he knows my character well! For a start, God must know whether I will be alive then, and could only know that if the future is fixed in some way. But if the future is fixed, can we act freely?

See THE TRIPARTITE VIEW, p. 75.

See RELIABILISM, p. 89.

?

Is God's omniscience compatible with human freedom?

Key points: the divine attributes

- Traditional monotheistic conceptions of God stem from the idea that God is the most perfect possible being.
- Personal: God has traits similar to those of a person, in particular intellect and will.
- Omniscience: God knows everything it is possible to know. At least much of what God knows, he knows directly, without inference or linguistic representation.
- Omnipotence: God has the power to do anything it is possible to do.
- Supreme goodness: God is the most perfect possible being, and because moral goodness is a perfection, God's will is in accordance with moral values.
- Eternal and everlasting: God's existence has no beginning or end. If God exists in time, then God is everlasting; if God exists outside time, then God is eternal.

- Transcendence and immanence: God is more than the universe, being outside space and perhaps also outside time. Yet God also exists throughout everything that exists.
- We face difficulties in saying coherently what God's individual attributes are, and in attempts to combine them.
- Can God create a stone that he can't lift? One solution may be to say that 'a stone that an omnipotent being can't lift' is a contradiction in terms. Another is to say that God cannot create a stone that he cannot lift, because God can lift any stone. But because there is no limit on God's power to lift stones, there is no limit on God's power to create stones.
- Can God commit evil? If not, is God omnipotent? One can argue that God can commit evil but chooses not to; or that there is no distinct 'power to commit evil'; or that evil is a form of failure, and God cannot fail.
- Is morality independent of God or created by God's will? If the former, is God omnipotent? If the latter, is morality arbitrary? One possible reply is to say that morality is whatever God wills, but God's will is guided by love, so morality is not arbitrary. Another is to say 'good' and 'God's will' are distinct concepts that refer to the same thing.
- Can God know everything, even what time it is, and not change? One solution is to say that God is transcendent, but we can object that this will make time an illusion. Another is to redefine omniscience as knowing everything it is possible for a perfect being to know, but we can object that the concept becomes incoherent as it turns out that there are important things that a perfect being doesn't know.
- Is God's omniscience compatible with human freedom? One response is to define omniscience as what it is possible to know, and then argue that the future is impossible to know because we have freedom.
- Kenny argues that God's knowing what I will do doesn't mean that I *must* do what I do. By doing what I will do, I make God's belief true. We can object that it is difficult to understand *how* God could know the future unless, in some sense, the future is already fixed.

Summary: the concept of God

In this section, we have considered what the concept of God is a concept of, i.e. what the attributes of God are. We have looked at the following issues:

1. How should we best understand the attributes of omniscience, omnipotence, supreme goodness, and God's existing without beginning or end?
2. Do these attributes make sense, e.g. can God know everything it is possible to know? Can God do everything it is possible to do?
3. Can these attributes be combined without incoherence, e.g. can God be omnipotent (e.g. God can will anything) and supremely good (God only wills what is morally right)?
4. Does the nature of God raise puzzles for our understanding of morality and human freedom?

II. Arguments relating to the existence of God

Philosophers have long been fascinated by the possibility of showing that God exists by rational argument. Almost all the most important philosophers in history have discussed such arguments, either to offer support or criticism. We will look at three main types of argument, discussing variations of each and criticisms. The central question of this section is 'Does any argument show – either deductively or inductively – that God exists?'

See PHILOSOPHICAL ARGUMENT, p. 7.

A. Ontological arguments

Ontological arguments claim that we can deduce the existence of God from the concept of God. Just from thinking about what God is, we can conclude that God must exist. Because it doesn't depend on experience in any way, the ontological argument is a priori.

The word 'ontological' comes from ontology, the study of (Greek,-*ology*) what exists or 'being' (*ont*-).

An a priori argument is one whose premises are all a priori.
See A PRIORI/A POSTERIORI, p. 97.

Ontological arguments have held a fascination for philosophers, and almost every major historical philosopher discussed them. We shall discuss two historical variations, a twentieth-century restatement of a historical form, and a new form that arose from developments in logic in the twentieth century. While the overall shape of the argument remains the same, the differences in detail can be philosophically important to the success of the argument.

The *Proslogium* is also known as the *Proslogion*.

ANSELM, *PROSLOGIUM*, CHS 2-4

In THE DIVINE ATTRIBUTES (p. 160), we saw that the idea of God as the most perfect possible being has a long history. And perfection has also been connected to reality: what is perfect is more real than what is not. Anselm's argument makes use of both these ideas.

In Ch. 2, Anselm starts from the concept of God as a being 'greater than which cannot be conceived'. Why define God like this? If we could think of something that was greater than the being we call God, then surely this greater thing would in fact be God. But this is nonsense - God being greater than God. The first being isn't God at all. We cannot conceive of anything being greater than God - if we think we can, we're not thinking of God.

Outline and explain the argument for thinking that God is a being 'greater than which cannot be conceived'.

Anselm then argues that if we think of two beings, one that exists and one that doesn't, the one that actually exists is greater - being real is greater than being fictional! So if God didn't exist, we could think of a greater being than God. But we've said that's impossible; so God exists.

1. By definition, God is a being greater than which cannot be conceived.
2. (We can coherently conceive of such a being, i.e. the concept is coherent.)
3. It is greater to exist in reality than to exist only in the mind.
4. Therefore, God must exist.

In Ch. 3, Anselm adds premise (2) and explains premise (3) further. Conceive of two almost identical beings, X and Y.

However, *X* is a being which we can conceive not to exist; *X*'s not existing is conceivable. By contrast, *Y*'s not existing is inconceivable. We can conceive of such a being, a being who must exist. Clearly, *Y* is a greater being than *X*. Therefore, the greatest conceivable being is a being who, we conceive, must exist. It is inconceivable that the greatest conceivable being does not exist.

Of course, it can *seem* like we can think 'God does not exist'. In Ch. 4, Anselm notes that we can have this thought, we can think this string of words. But, he argues, in having this thought, we fail to understand the concept of God fully. Once we fully understand the concept, we can no longer affirm the thought, because we recognise that it is incoherent.

> Outline and explain Anselm's version of the ontological argument.

GAUNILO'S *IN BEHALF OF THE FOOL*

Anselm received an immediate reply from a monk named Gaunilo. Gaunilo raises several objections, of which the most famous appears in §§5–7. The essence of the objection is that the conclusion doesn't follow from the premises.

How great *is* the greatest conceivable being? Well, if it doesn't exist, it is not great at all – not as great as any real object (§5)! We can *conceive* how great this being *would be if it existed*, but that doesn't show that it *is* as great as all that and so must exist. Suppose we even grant that the non-existence of God is inconceivable (§7). This still doesn't show that God actually exists. First, we need to establish that God does exist. And then from understanding his nature, we can infer that he must exist.

Gaunilo argues that Anselm's inference must be flawed because you could prove anything which is 'more excellent' must exist by this argument (§6). I can conceive of an island that is greater than any other island. And so such an island must exist, because it would be less great if it didn't. This is ridiculous, so the ontological argument must be flawed.

> Outline and explain Gaunilo's perfect island objection to Anselm's ontological argument.

Anselm, *Apologetic*

Going further: Anselm's reply

Gaunilo slips from talking about the *greatest* conceivable being to talking about conceiving of a being that is *greater* than all other beings. So he talks of an island that is greater than other islands. But this doesn't work. It is possible to conceive of the being which, as it happens, is greater than all other beings as not existing. So let's correct Gaunilo here, and talk of 'the island greater than which is inconceivable'.

Anselm claims that the ontological argument works *only* for God, and so this is not a counterexample. Why? Anselm's reasoning is to show that there is something incoherent in thinking that the greatest conceivable being doesn't exist. By contrast, the thought that the greatest conceivable island doesn't exist *is* coherent. When we have this thought, we are still thinking of an island. There is nothing in the concept of such an island that makes it *essentially* or *necessarily* the greatest conceivable island. Compare: an island *must* be a body of land surrounded by water. An island attached to land is inconceivable. But islands aren't essentially great or not. Instead, the thought of an island that is essentially the greatest conceivable island is itself somewhat incoherent. For example, what would make it the greatest?

By contrast, God, argues Anselm, *must* be the greatest conceivable being – God *wouldn't be God* if there was some being even greater than God. So being the greatest conceivable being is an essential property of God. But then because it is greater to exist in reality than merely in the mind, if we think of God as not existing in reality, we aren't thinking of God at all. So to be the greatest conceivable being, God *must* exist.

We may object, however, that even if Anselm is right about the island, Gaunilo's objection is correct: we must first demonstrate that God exists before we can say that God *is*, rather than is merely conceived to be, the greatest conceivable being.

Does Anselm's ontological argument prove the existence of God?

DESCARTES, *MEDITATION* V

Descartes' ontological argument

Descartes' version of the ontological argument talks about God being supremely perfect, rather than 'a being greater than which cannot be conceived', and it relies on his theory of CLEAR AND DISTINCT IDEAS (p. 107.) The argument itself is very brief:

> The idea of God (that is, of a supremely perfect being) is certainly one that I find within me ...; and I understand from this idea that it belongs to God's nature that *he always exists.*
>
> (p. 24)

Once Descartes adds that existence is a perfection, his argument becomes this:

1. I have the idea of God.
2. The idea of God is the idea of a supremely perfect being.
3. A supremely perfect being does not lack any perfection.
4. Existence is a perfection.
5. Therefore, God exists.

Descartes accepts that it is easy to believe that God can be thought of as not existing. But careful reflection reveals that this is a self-contradiction.

A different case helps clarify the point: you may think that there can be triangles whose internal angles don't add up to 180 degrees, but reflection proves this impossible. Descartes begins *Meditation* V by commenting on this fact: our thought is *constrained* in this way. The ideas we have determine certain truths, at least when our ideas are clear and distinct. Once you make the idea of a triangle clear and distinct, you understand that its internal angles add up to 180 degrees, and this shows that this is, in fact, true.

We can apply this to God. Careful reflection on the concept of God reveals that to think that God does not exist is a contradiction in terms, because it is to think that a supremely

> Descartes never defends premise (4). We discuss this claim in KANT, 'ON THE IMPOSSIBILITY OF AN ONTOLOGICAL PROOF OF THE EXISTENCE OF GOD', p. 188.

> Explain Descartes' claim that we can know that clear and distinct ideas are true.

See NECESSARY AND
CONTINGENT TRUTH, p. 105.

perfect being lacks a perfection (existence). Thus, we can know that it is true that God exists. In fact, it shows that God must exist. A contradiction in terms does not just happen to be false, it *must* be false. So to say 'God does not exist' *must* be false; so 'God exists' must be true.

As in the case of the triangle, it is not *our thinking it* that makes the claim (that God exists) true. Just as the concept of a triangle forces me to acknowledge that its internal angles add up to 180 degrees, so the concept of God forces me to acknowledge that God exists. Furthermore, I cannot simply *change* the concept in either case; I can't decide that triangles will have two sides nor that God is not a supremely perfect being. I haven't invented the concept of God, such that it includes existence. I discover it.

God is the only concept that supports this inference to existence, because only the concept of God (as supremely perfect) includes the concept of existence (as a perfection). We can't infer the existence of anything else this way.

Outline and explain Descartes' ontological argument.

HUME, *DIALOGUES CONCERNING NATURAL RELIGION*, PT 9

Both Anselm and Descartes have argued that it is self-contradictory to say that God does not exist. Hume (p. 39) claims that this is simply not true:

1. Nothing that is distinctly conceivable implies a contradiction.
2. Whatever we conceive as existent, we can also conceive as non-existent.
3. Therefore, there is no being whose non-existence implies a contradiction.

See HUME'S 'FORK',
p. 99.

In this argument, Hume is drawing on his analysis of knowledge. To say that 'God does not exist' is a contradiction entails that 'God exists' is a relation of ideas. But this can't be right, because claims about what exists are matters of fact. Put another way, if 'God does not exist' is a contradiction, then 'God exists' must be analytic. But claims about what exists are synthetic.

Descartes could respond in either of two ways. He could claim that 'God exists' is a synthetic truth, but one that can be known by a priori reflection. Or he could claim that 'God exists' is an analytic truth, though not an obvious one. Because he doesn't have the concepts 'analytic' and 'synthetic', he doesn't, of course, say either. Instead, (in an appendix to the *Meditations*) he argues that Hume's premise (2) is false. Because our minds are finite, we normally think of the divine attributes – omnipotence, omniscience, existence, etc. – separately and so we don't notice that they entail one another. But if we reflect carefully, we shall discover that we cannot conceive of any one of the other attributes while excluding necessary existence. For example, in order for God to be omnipotent, God must not depend on anything else, and so must not depend on anything else to exist.

However, this response faces Gaunilo's objection to Anselm: God's attributes only entail each other *if God actually exists*. Of course, if God doesn't exist, then God isn't omnipotent (or anything else), so God's omnipotence doesn't entail his existence.

> Is God's existence entailed by his other properties?

Going further: Leibniz's supplement

Leibniz admired Descartes' argument, but thought that it was incomplete. Descartes assumes that the concept of God is coherent, that a supremely perfect being is possible. Leibniz is right that, for any ontological argument to be valid, this premise is needed. But is it true? We looked at a number of objections in ISSUES WITH CLAIMING THAT GOD HAS THESE ATTRIBUTES (p. 165).

Leibniz claims that a better understanding of what a 'perfection' is will solve the matter. He defines a perfection as a

> *New Essays on Human Understanding*, Bk 4, Ch. 10, p. 219

> Leibniz, 'That a Most Perfect Being Exists'

'simple quality which is positive and absolute, or, which expresses without any limits whatever it does express'. So, for example, 'power' is a perfection. It is unanalysable, positive, and expresses the idea of power without placing limits on power. (Compare 'horsepower', which originally expressed the idea of the power of a horse, which is limited.) Leibniz then argues, in a very abstract piece of reasoning, that because all perfections are simple and positive, it can't be shown that they are incompatible. Nothing about any one perfection places a restriction on any other perfection. It is possible, therefore, that they are compatible, and so that they can all coexist in one being. So a supremely perfect being is possible.

We can object that Leibniz's concept of a perfection is unclear and possibly false. What makes a quality 'positive' rather than 'negative'? And are any qualities 'simple' in the way Leibniz imagines? Our discussion of the attributes of God shows that the matter is complicated. It is doubtful that there is any *general* proof that the concept of God is coherent; we must take each attribute in turn.

> Explain why the ontological proof requires the concept of God to be coherent.

> Kant, *Critique of Pure Reason*, Second Division (Transcendental Dialectic), Bk 2, Ch. 3, §4

KANT, 'ON THE IMPOSSIBILITY OF AN ONTOLOGICAL PROOF OF THE EXISTENCE OF GOD'

Kant presents what many philosophers consider to be the most powerful objection to any ontological argument. It is a development and explanation of Hume's objection. Ontological arguments misunderstand what existence is, or what it is to say that something exists. Premise (3) of Anselm's argument and premise (4) of Descartes' are both false. Things don't 'have' existence in the same way that they 'have' other properties. So existence can't be a perfection or make something 'greater'.

Consider whether 'God exists' is an analytic or synthetic judgement. In claiming that 'God does not exist' is a contradiction, it seems that Anselm, Descartes and Leibniz take 'God exists' to be an analytic judgement. Now, an analytic judgement unpacks a concept. The concept of the predicate, 'three sides', is part of the concept of the subject, 'triangle'. And so the analytic truth 'A triangle has three sides' unpacks the concept of a triangle and tells you something about what triangles are. However, saying '*x* exists' does *not* add anything to a concept of what *x* is. It doesn't tell you anything more about *x*. 'Dogs exist' doesn't inform you about what dogs are.

Put another way, 'existence' isn't a real predicate. The concept of existence is not a concept that can be added into the concept of something. If I say 'The kite is red', I add the concept of 'red' onto the concept of 'kite', and can create the new concept of a red kite. But if I say 'The kite exists' or 'The kite is', this adds nothing to the concept of the kite. The claim that *x* exists is not a claim about my concept of *x*, but a claim that something exists that corresponds to my concept. So the claim that *x* exists is a synthetic judgement, not an analytic one. But that means that it is not contradictory to deny it.

This applies even in the case of God. 'God exists' is just 'God is'; it doesn't add anything to, or unpack, the concept of God. Even if we allow that God, the greatest conceivable being, is possible, that the existence of God is possible, this remains a claim about the concept, not existence. What we want to show is that we can not only coherently think about God (God is possible a priori), but that it is also possible that we actually experience him (God is possible a posteriori). But this we cannot deduce from the conceptual possibility of his existence. For example, there is no difference between the concepts of 100 real thalers (the money of Kant's day) and 100 possible thalers. Adding the concept of something existing does not make the thalers exist. Likewise with God.

1. If 'God does not exist' is a contradiction, then 'God exists' is an analytic truth.
2. If 'God exists' is an analytic truth, then 'existence' is part of the concept of God.
3. Existence is not a predicate, something that can be added on to another concept.

> **?**
> Why does Kant claim that existence is not a predicate?

4. Therefore, 'God exists' is not an analytic truth.
5. Therefore, 'God does not exist' is not a contradiction.
6. Therefore, we cannot deduce the existence of God from the concept of God.
7. Therefore, ontological arguments cannot prove that God exists.

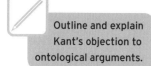

Outline and explain
Kant's objection to
ontological arguments.

MALCOLM, 'ANSELM'S ONTOLOGICAL ARGUMENTS'

Malcolm's argument

Norman Malcolm agrees that the claim that 'existence is a perfection' is false. And so Descartes' ontological argument fails, and so does Anselm's version as he initially presents it. However, in Ch. 3 of the *Proslogium*, when Anselm takes himself to be explaining his argument, in fact he provides a *different* argument, says Malcolm. Anselm says that a being whose non-existence is inconceivable (*Y* in our discussion above: ANSELM, *PROSLOGIUM*, CHS 2-4, p. 182) is greater than a being whose non-existence is conceivable (*X*). It is not *existence* that is a perfection, but the logical impossibility of non-existence. *Necessary existence* is a perfection.

We can show that necessary existence is part of the concept of God. 'God is the greatest possible being' is a logically necessary truth – it is part of our concept of God. Therefore, God's existence cannot depend on anything – because a being that depends on something else for its existence is not as great as a being whose existence is completely independent of anything else. So God cannot depend on anything for coming into existence or staying in existence.

Suppose God exists. Then God cannot cease to exist – nothing can cause God to cease to exist. In that case, God's non-existence is inconceivable. So if God exists, God exists necessarily. Suppose God doesn't exist. Then if God came into existence, God's existence would then be dependent on whatever caused God to exist. This, we said, is impossible. So if God does not exist, then God's existence is impossible.

1. Either God exists or God does not exist.
2. God cannot come into existence or go out of existence.
3. If God exists, God cannot cease to exist.
4. Therefore, if God exists, God's existence is necessary.
5. If God does not exist, God cannot come into existence.
6. Therefore, if God does not exist, God's existence is impossible.
7. Therefore, God's existence is either necessary or impossible.

Malcolm now adds two further premises to complete the form of ontological argument he finds in Anselm's *Proslogium*, Ch. 3:

8. God's existence is impossible only if the concept of God is self-contradictory.
9. The concept of God is not self-contradictory.
10. Therefore, God's existence is not impossible.
11. Therefore (from (7) + (10)), God exists necessarily.

> Outline and explain Malcolm's argument that God's existence is either necessary or impossible.

Malcolm's reply to Kant

Malcolm agrees with Kant that *contingent* existence is not a property, but argues that Kant does not show that *necessary* existence is not a property. Kant discusses the claim 'God exists', but he doesn't satisfactorily distinguish it from the claim 'God exists necessarily'. The two claims are not equivalent. To say that 'God exists necessarily' *is* to unpack the concept of God. It tells us more about what the concept 'God' is a concept of. So it is an analytic judgement, not a synthetic one. Not all claims about what exists have the same kind of meaning.

Kant accepts that it is part of our concept of the greatest possible being that such a being would exist necessarily. But what this means is that 'if God exists, then God exists necessarily'. And this doesn't entail that God exists. In other words, the claim 'if God exists, then God exists necessarily' is compatible with the possibility that God doesn't exist at all.

Malcolm responds that this is confused. If we accept that 'God exists necessarily' is an analytic truth, derived from our concept of God, then this rules out 'it is possible that God doesn't exist'. 'God doesn't exist' is necessarily false.

> Outline and explain Malcolm's ontological argument.

Going further: objections

One objection to Malcolm's argument is that he has not shown that premise (9) is true; is the concept of God coherent? Malcolm admits that he can think of no general proof that it is. But there should be no presupposition that the concept is incoherent, so the argument is sound unless we can *show* that the concept of God is incoherent.

A second objection targets the inference from (3) to (4) (a similar objection can be made for the inference from (5) to (6)). Malcolm may have shown that if God exists, God's existence does not depend on anything, and God cannot cease to exist. But that is *not* the same as saying that God's existence is necessary. There are two confusions here.

First, even allowing that necessary existence is a property, Malcolm's argument only shows that *if* God exists, then God's existence is necessary. If God doesn't exist, then it is false that God's existence is, in fact, independent of anything else, because God doesn't, in fact, exist. Nothing has that property of necessary existence. In his response to Kant, Malcolm rejects this, claiming that 'God exists necessarily' is an a priori truth derived from the concept of God. But we cannot derive this claim from the concept of God; we can only derive the weaker claim that 'if God exists, God exists necessarily'.

Second, the form of words 'God exists necessarily' confuses two distinct claims. The first is that there is a form of existence – necessary existence – which God has. This is why Malcolm says necessary existence is a property. And it is what Malcolm tries to establish by the argument that God's existence can't depend on anything. The second is that it is necessarily true that God exists. This is the conclusion of the ontological argument. Malcolm claims that we can infer that

a.   'God exists' must be true

from

b.   the fact that the concept of God entails that God's existence does not depend on anything.

But this doesn't follow; it confuses two meanings of 'necessarily'. Not depending on anything characterises the nature of God's existence, if God exists; but existence does not characterise God.

   We can argue, therefore, that Kant is not confused. He does not accept the claim that 'God exists necessarily'. He only accepts the claim 'If God exists, then God exists necessarily (i.e. without dependence on anything)'. This conditional claim *is* analytic. But it is compatible with the claim 'It is possible that God does not exist'.

> Explain the difference between God having necessary existence and it being necessarily true that God exists.

Going further: Plantinga, *God, Freedom, and Evil, pp. 34-9, 85-112*

Plantinga provides an overview of the debate between Anselm, Gaunilo and Kant, before offering his own version of the ontological argument starting on p. 98. However, that argument uses the concept of a 'possible world', which he explains earlier in the book. So it is with that explanation that we start.

Possible worlds (pp. 34-9)

A 'possible world' is a way of talking about how things could have been. Propositions describe 'states of affairs'. Propositions can be true or false. A proposition that is true describes the actual world, the way things are, a true state of affairs. A proposition that is false describes the way things are not, a false state of affairs. However,

See NECESSARY AND CONTINGENT TRUTH, p. 105.

false propositions can be necessarily false or just contingently false. A proposition that is necessarily false *cannot* be true - it is impossible for it to be true. A proposition that is only contingently false describes a state of affairs that is possible, but false, given how the world actually is. For example, 'I was born in Kenya' is false, but could have been true. A contingently false proposition describes a way things could have been. We can say that in some other 'possible world', this proposition is true, the state of affairs it describes is part of the way that world is. In some other possible world, I was born in Kenya.

We can also talk about the actual world, the way things are, as a possible world. Everything that occurs in the world is possible - so this is a possible world. But it is a very special possible world, because it is actual. We can also say that 'some proposition *p* is true in some possible world *W*' = '*p* would be true if *W* were the actual world'.

Possible worlds are distinct from one another depending on what we are supposing to be true in that world. So the possible world in which I was born in Kenya is different from the possible world in which I was born in Argentina which is different from the possible world in which I don't exist at all. In different possible worlds, different things exist and the things that exist can have different properties from the properties they have in the actual world.

A proposition that is necessarily false, we said, is impossible. We can say that it is false in every possible world. Similarly, a proposition that is necessarily true is true in every possible world. Importantly, what is necessarily true and necessarily false doesn't change from one possible world to another. The proposition '2 + 2 = 5' is false in every possible world, and there is no world in which it is *possible*. So 'it is possible that 2 + 2 = 5' is

Explain what it means to talk of 'possible worlds'.

also false in every world. Likewise, '2 + 2 = 4' is necessarily true. It is not only true in every possible world, it is necessarily true in every possible world. 'It is impossible that 2 + 2 ≠ 4' is true in every possible world.

Plantinga's ontological argument (pp. 98-112)

We can use talk of possible worlds to interpret key ideas in the ontological argument:

1.   'It is possible that God exists' = 'There is some possible world in which God exists'.
2.   'It is necessarily true that God exists' = 'God exists in all possible worlds'.

Now, we noted that there are possible worlds in which some being, x, exists and ones in which it doesn't, and in different worlds, x has different properties. So

3.   'It is greater to exist in reality than to exist only in the mind' = 'If x exists in some possible world W_1 but doesn't exist in another possible world W_2', then x's greatness in W_1 exceeds x's greatness in W_2.
4.   'God is a being greater than which cannot be conceived' = 'God is the greatest possible being' = 'There is a possible world in which a being (God) exists which has the maximum possible degree of greatness – no other being, in any possible world, has more greatness' (p. 105).

Plantinga uses this framework to understand and criticise previous versions of the ontological argument. We will focus just on the new version that he argues is successful.
     We first need to understand (4). It says that there is some *possible* world in which God exists and is the

greatest possible being. Now, we said that a being can have different properties in different possible worlds. So perhaps God is the greatest possible being in one possible world, but not in another possible world. But that's not right – it isn't *contingent* that God is the greatest possible being. For God to be God at all, then God is the greatest possible being. So in any possible world in which God exists at all, God is the greatest possible being. It is necessarily true that if God exists, God is the greatest possible being.

Let's call a being that has the properties of omniscience, omnipotence, supreme goodness, etc., in *one* possible world 'maximally excellent'. Now, a being that has maximal excellence in *every* possible world is greater than a being that is maximallyexcellent in *one* possible world. On this view, greatness depends not just on the properties a being has in one possible world, but what properties it has in other possible worlds as well. A *maximally* great being will be a being that is maximally excellent in *every* possible world.

Our accounts of maximal excellence and maximal greatness are definitions, so they are necessarily true. So we get these premises:

1.   Necessarily, a being has maximal excellence in a given possible world only it if has omniscience, omnipotence, supreme goodness, etc., in that possible world.
2.   Necessarily, a being is maximally great only if it is has maximal excellence in every possible world.

Now we add

3.   A maximally great being is possible, i.e. there is a possible world in which there is a being that has maximal greatness.

Explain Plantinga's definition of 'maximal greatness'.

This is enough to conclude

4. Therefore, a maximally great being exists (in the actual world).

This is Plantinga's argument in its concise form. But it is worth going more slowly to make the inference clearer. If we put (2) and (3) together, we get the claim that

5. Therefore, there is a possible world in which a being exists such that it has maximal excellence in every possible world.

Now, a being can't have maximal excellence unless it exists. So if it has maximal excellence in every possible world, it must exist in every possible world.

6. Therefore, there is a possible world in which a being exists such that it exists and has maximal excellence in every possible world.

We said above that if 'x exists' is true in every possible world, then 'x exists' is necessarily true. In other words, it is impossible that x doesn't exist. And what is necessarily true doesn't change from one possible world to another. (6) says that it is possible that it is necessarily true that a maximally great being exists. But that means it is necessarily true that a maximally great being exists. From (3), (5) and (6), we get

7. Therefore, a maximally great being exists in every possible world.
4. (Again) Therefore, a maximally great being exists (in the actual world).
8. By definition, God is a maximally great being.
9. Therefore, God exists.

Outline and explain Plantinga's ontological argument.

Discussion

For the argument to work, (3) must be true. Plantinga accepts that he hasn't argued that a maximally great being is possible, it is a premise. But like Malcolm, he claims that there is no reason to reject the claim. God's existence has not been *proven*, until we prove this premise is true; but, claims Plantinga, we have shown that believing in God's existence is reasonable.

See Going further: objections, p. 192.

However, because Plantinga's definition of maximal greatness is new, his concept of a being that is maximally great faces new objections. When previously thinking about the coherence of the concept of God, we were – in Plantinga's terms – thinking about whether a maximally *excellent* being, a being with omnipotence, omniscience, supreme goodness, etc., could exist. Plantinga requires not only that such a maximally excellent being could exist, but also that it is possible that such a being exists *in every possible world*.

So, first, we may accuse Plantinga of begging the question. To think that it is possible that a being that is maximally excellent exists in every possible world is already to accept that it is possible that it is necessarily true that this being exists.

Second, we can object that (2) – Plantinga's definition of maximal greatness – is unsatisfactory. The definition presupposes that x's greatness in a world in which x exists exceeds x's greatness in a world in which x doesn't exist. We can object that this type of comparison doesn't make sense. In a world in which x doesn't exist, x doesn't have zero degree of greatness. Instead, we can't talk of x's degree of greatness at all. If there is no x, then x has *no* degree of greatness, not even zero. So we can't compare x's greatness where x does exist with x's greatness where x doesn't exist. It is not greater to exist than not to exist.

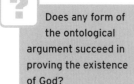

Does any form of the ontological argument succeed in proving the existence of God?

If this objection is right, then we should redefine a maximally great being as a being that is maximally excellent in every world *in which it exists*. So in every possible world in which God exists, God is the greatest possible being. But because the greatest possible being need not exist in every possible world, it is still possible that God does not exist. So we cannot conclude that God exists.

Key points: ontological arguments

- Ontological arguments are a priori. They move from the concept of God to the claim that God exists. More precisely, they conclude that God exists necessarily.
- Anselm's version states that God is the greatest conceivable being and that it is greater to exist in reality than to exist only in the mind. He concludes that God's non-existence is inconceivable, so God exists.
- Gaunilo objects that the greatest conceivable being is not as great as anything real if it doesn't exist. Its being the 'greatest conceivable' doesn't show that it does exist. He also objects that you could show that the greatest conceivable island must exist using this argument.
- Aquinas replies that the ontological argument only works for God. Nothing else exists in such a way that its non-existence is inconceivable.
- Descartes' version claims that it is impossible to think of God, a supremely perfect being, as lacking existence, because existence is a perfection.
- Hume objects that it is not a contradiction to deny that God exists. 'God exists' does not state a relation of ideas, but a matter of fact.
- Descartes can respond that God's attributes entail God's existence. But while they may do so conceptually, they only entail God's existence in fact if God exists.
- Leibniz noted that the ontological argument only works if the concept of God is coherent, i.e. if it is possible that God could exist. He provides a general argument for thinking the concept of God is coherent, but assumes that the attributes of God (as perfections) are positive and simple.
- Kant objects that existence is not a predicate, not a property that something can lack or possess. To say something exists is only to say that something corresponds to a concept we have; it is not to say anything further about that concept. Therefore, 'God exists' is not an analytic judgement, and can be denied without self-contradiction.

- Malcolm objects that while existence is not a perfection, necessary existence is. Because God's existence cannot depend on anything else, God's existence is either impossible or necessary. Since God's existence is not impossible, it is necessary, so God exists.
- We can object that Malcolm is wrong to infer from 'if God exists, God's existence does not depend on anything else' to 'God exists necessarily'. *How* God exists is a property of God's existence, if God exists. But existence – even necessary existence – isn't a property of God.
- A possible world is a way things could be. A contingently false proposition describes a state of affairs that is true in some possible world, i.e. that would be true if that world were the actual world.
- A proposition that is necessarily true is true in all possible worlds. What is necessarily true and what is impossible stays the same across all possible worlds.
- Plantinga argues that the greatest possible being has maximal excellence – omnipotence, omniscience, supreme goodness, etc. – in all possible worlds. Such a being is possible. It is therefore possible that such a being exists in every possible world, i.e. it is possible that it is necessarily true that such a being exists. Therefore, such a being – God – exists.
- We may object that Plantinga hasn't shown that a maximally great being is possible. We may also object that his definition of 'maximally great' is mistaken. If it is, then the argument does not prove that God exists.

B. The argument from design

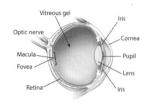

Figure 3.1
Diagram of an eye

It is common to feel wonder and amazement at the complexity and intricacy of living creatures. The way in which living things work requires a huge coordination of lots of tiny bits, each doing their specific job. The eye provides a common example. The eye is for seeing, and its parts work together to make this possible. For example, the muscles attached to the lens change its thickness so that it can focus light from different distances onto the retina.

Without the lens, the muscles, and the retina, the eye wouldn't work properly. The parts serve the purpose of the whole.

The whole of life has this structure, with parts of cells working together to serve the purposes of cells, and cells working together as tissues, and tissues working together as organs, and organs working together to support the life of the organism. What we find is order, 'regularity', throughout nature. But it could have been very different – the universe could have had no order, no regularity. So what explains the order that we find?

The coordination and intricacy of interrelations between parts in living things working together for a purpose suggests that living things have been *designed*. If they are designed, then we can infer that there is a designer. The argument from design argues from the order and regularity that we see in the universe to the existence of a God that designed the universe.

While life has been an important example of possible design in the debate, we will see that the order inherent in the laws of nature may provide more compelling evidence.

PALEY, *NATURAL THEOLOGY*, CHS 1-5, 23

William Paley compares our responses to finding a stone lying in a field and finding a watch lying in a field. If I wondered how the stone came to be there, I might rightly think that, for all I knew, it had always been there. But if I found a watch, I wouldn't feel that the same answer is satisfactory. Why not?

Because, says Paley, the watch has parts that are organised and put together for a purpose, and without the parts being organised as they are, the purpose would not be fulfilled. This property – having parts that are organised for a purpose – is the mark of design. We therefore conclude that the watch must have been designed and made according to that design.

Suppose now that after a while the watch, on its own, produces another watch (Ch. 2). It contains within itself all the robotic parts and tools for constructing a new watch. The second watch has been made by the first watch. Does this explain the *design* of the second watch? No, says Paley. The first watch

I have used the 1843 edition of Paley's *Natural Theology* available at https://ia700409.us.archive.org/1/items/naturaltheology00pale/naturaltheology00pale.pdf

The anthology sets only CHS 1, 2 and 5.

What is 'design', according to Paley?

simply mechanically constructs the parts of the second watch according to a design that it follows, but it doesn't come up with that design. The design of the watch is only explained by its being designed by a designer (Ch. 2, §3).

In Ch. 3, Paley argues that 'the works of nature' have the *same* property as the watch, namely parts organised for a purpose (he discusses the examples of the eye and the ear). In Ch. 4, he notes that living things create new living things (reproduction). But as with the watch, this doesn't explain the organisation of living things, including their ability to produce new living things. Plants don't design their seeds, and hens don't design their eggs. Rather, plants and hens simply mechanically produce seeds and eggs. Now, we rightly infer from the fact that the watch has parts organised for a purpose, that the watch is designed. Thus, in Ch. 5, Paley argues that we are right to infer from the fact that the works of nature have parts organised for a purpose, that they also have a designer.

Paley calls the designer 'God' but so far, he has said *nothing* about the nature of 'God'. In fact, he doesn't turn to this question until Ch. 23, where he argues for two conclusions. First, the designer must be a 'person'. To design requires a mind – consciousness and thought – because design requires that one perceives the purpose and how to organise parts to serve this purpose. So the designer is a mind. Second, the designer must be distinct from the universe, because everything in the universe bears the marks of design. To explain the design of things in the universe, we must appeal to something distinct from the universe.

So, Paley argues:

We shall discuss later the question Is THE DESIGNER GOD?, p. 215. Until then, I will speak of 'the designer'.

1. Anything that has parts organised to serve a purpose is designed.
2. Nature contains things which have parts that are organised to serve a purpose.
3. Therefore, nature contains things which are designed.
4. Design can only be explained in terms of a designer.
5. A designer must be or have a mind and be distinct from what is designed.
6. Therefore, nature was designed by a mind that is distinct from nature.
7. Therefore, such a mind ('God') exists.

Outline and explain Paley's argument from design.

Hume's objections to the argument from design

HUME, *DIALOGUES CONCERNING NATURAL RELIGION*, PTS 2, 8; *AN ENQUIRY CONCERNING HUMAN UNDERSTANDING*, §11

The most famous critic of the argument from design is David Hume. His discussion occurs in the context of a dialogue between three friends – Demea, Cleanthes and Philo. Demea holds that you can only prove the existence of God a priori (i.e. using ONTOLOGICAL ARGUMENTS, p. 181). Cleanthes argues that you can only prove the existence of God using the argument from design. Philo holds that the existence of God is not established by reasoning of either kind.

Hume wrote before Paley, and expresses the argument somewhat differently:

> The intricate fitting of means to ends throughout all nature is just like (though more wonderful than) the fitting of means to ends in things that have been produced by us – products of human designs, thought, wisdom, and intelligence. Since the effects resemble each other, we are led to infer by all the rules of analogy that the causes are also alike, and that the author of nature is somewhat similar to the mind of man, though he has much larger faculties to go with the grandeur of the work he has carried out.
>
> (p. 10)

This is an argument from analogy.

1. In the organisation of parts for a purpose ('the fitting of means to ends'), nature resembles the products of human design.
2. Similar effects have similar causes.
3. The cause of the products of human design is an intelligent mind that intended the design.
4. Therefore, the cause of nature is an intelligent mind that intended the design.

Outline and explain Hume's version of the argument from design.

In Pt 2, Hume, as the character Philo, offers a series of objections attacking the analogy and its use.

Draw up a list of analogies and disanalogies between human inventions and natural objects *without* referring to what causes them.

1. The analogy is not very strong (p. 11). The products of human design, such as a house or a watch, are not much like nature or the universe as a whole. The 'great disproportion' between a part of the universe and the whole universe also undermines the inference that something similar to human intelligence caused the universe (p. 13). We cannot, therefore, reasonably infer that the cause of nature is anything like a human mind.

2. Even if we could infer from part to whole, there is no good reason to choose design by an intelligent mind as the explanation of the whole universe: 'why would we select as our basis such a tiny, weak, limited cause as the reason and design of animals on this planet seems to be?' (p. 13). Thought moves the bodies of animals - why take it to be the original cause of everything?

3. The arrangement of parts for a purpose does not, *on its own*, show that the cause is a designer (p. 12). We can only know this in cases in which we have experience of a designer bringing about such order. We have this experience with the products of human design, but we don't have any such experience in the case of nature. So we can't know the cause of order in nature.

4. Hume's fourth objection assumes his theory of causation. The idea of causation is the idea of a relation between two objects or events - the cause and the effect: whenever you have the cause, you get the effect. Hume calls this 'constant conjunction'. Because causation involves *constant* conjunction, we cannot tell, from a *single* instance of some object or event, what its cause is. Think of one billiard ball hitting another and the second moving away. The second ball's movement could follow many, many events - your breathing, someone walking about the room, a light going on ... How do you know which is the cause? We need

repeated experience of the cause and effect occurring together in order to infer that one thing causes another. Therefore, we can only infer the cause of some effect when we have many examples of the effect and cause (p. 15). But the origin of the universe is unique. To make *any* inference about the cause of the universe, we would need experience of the origins of many worlds.

In Pt 8, Philo argues that we haven't yet shown that the existence of a designer is the *best* explanation.

5.   In order to infer that there is a designer of nature, we have to rule out other possible explanations of the organisation of parts for a purpose. On p. 12, Philo entertains the possibility that matter has 'a source of order within it'. But then he accepts that experience shows us that minds have an inbuilt principle of order but matter does not. On p. 34, he proposes another explanation. Suppose that matter is finite but that time is infinite. Given that there are only a finite number of possible arrangements of matter, over infinite time, all the arrangements of matter – including those we experience as design – would occur. (For this, matter would need to be in motion, but there is no a priori reason to suppose that this isn't possible.)

Of course, there are problems with this proposal, such as why the arrangement of parts should *benefit* organisms. But there are problems with the proposal of a designer as well. For example, in all our experience, mind is joined to matter so that matter can affect mind (e.g. bodily processes can cause mental states, such as pain) just as much as mind can affect matter. Are we to suppose that the designer has a body? Or again, we have no clear concept of a mind that is eternal.

The right conclusion, then, is that neither explanation is clearly better. So the argument from design doesn't show that there is a designer. Instead, we should suspend judgement (p. 37).

In the *Enquiry* §11, Hume repeats many of these points in different ways. But he adds one more that isn't in the *Dialogues*:

See Matters of fact, p. 100.

See Hypothetical reasoning, p. 9.

Outline and explain Hume's argument that we cannot show that the best explanation of order in nature is the existence of a designer.

6. The inference of a designer is 'useless' (pp. 75-6). When we infer from a cause to an effect, we should only attribute properties to the cause that we need in order to explain the effect. Anything else is mere speculation. Now, in most cases, we learn more about a cause through other means. This allows us to make informative predictions about both the cause and its effects. With human inventions, we can find out lots about human beings, so we can make predictions about their inventions, including ones we haven't encountered. But with the designer of nature, *all* we have to go on is what we already know - nature. We can't find out about other designers or other worlds to draw any useful conclusions about nature or the designer. So the hypothesis of a designer adds nothing to our knowledge.

Discussion

Hume's objections all target (1) and (4) of Paley's argument (p. 202 above). Paley claims that the organisation of parts for a purpose is evidence of design and that design can only be explained in terms of a designer. But, Hume argues, we cannot argue this in *all* cases. In particular, we can't know it to be true of nature.

PALEY, *NATURAL THEOLOGY*, CHS 1, 5

Paley rejects Hume's claim, in objections (3) and (4), that we don't know enough to infer a designer (p. 55). *All* we need to know is the organisation of parts for a purpose. This is sufficient to infer that something is designed, and hence a designer exists. Surely we would say this in the case of the watch (p. 13). And the case of nature is no different. If Hume were correct, then if we found a watch in a field, we *could not* reasonably infer that it was designed. But Paley claims (p. 10), even if we had never seen a watch being made, even if we couldn't understand how it was possible, even if we couldn't tell if it could be done by a human being or not, we would still be perfectly correct to conclude, by examining the watch, that it was designed by some designer. We should say exactly the same in the case of nature. (Paley also claims that the inference is correct even if the watch sometimes went wrong or if some of the parts don't contribute to its purpose. Likewise, evidence of some imperfections and irregularities in nature does not undermine the inference that it, too, is designed.)

Paley also defends the hypothesis of an intelligent mind over alternative explanations of design (Hume's objections (2) and (5)). It is *possible* that finite matter has taken all possible combinations of an infinite time (p. 49). But this is clearly a *worse* explanation than the proposal of the existence of a designer, because we have no evidence that matter constantly pushes into new forms or that all possible combinations of matter (plants, animals) have been tried in the past. (We may add that we now know that the universe began around 13.8 billion years ago, so time isn't infinite, and we know that matter doesn't organise itself randomly, but follows very particular laws of nature.) And, Paley claims, minds supply the only explanation of design we know of. Thus, the existence of a designer is the best explanation of the organisation of parts for a purpose.

However, Paley is wrong to say that the organisation of parts for a purpose *can only* be the effect of a mind. If some other explanation (such as evolution – see below) is as good as or better than invoking the existence of a designer, then Paley's argument will fail.

> Outline and explain Paley's defence of the claim that the best explanation of order in nature is a mind.

Going further: Paley and analogy

What of Hume's objection (1)? *Strictly speaking*, Paley doesn't offer an argument from analogy. He does not argue that natural things are *like* watches, so their causes are *like* the causes of watches. He is arguing that watches have a property – the organisation of parts for a purpose – which supports the inference of a designer. Everything that has this property has this cause. Natural things have *exactly this property* as well and so have *exactly that cause*. Thus, he says 'Every observation which was made in our first chapter concerning the watch, may be repeated with strict propriety … concerning … all the organized parts of the works of nature' (p. 45). 'With strict propriety', not 'by analogy'. Natural things have the same property, so they too have a designer.

According to Paley's argument, Hume's objections should apply just as much to our inference regarding the watch – if we found one in a field and had never previously experienced a watch. But perhaps Hume's objections *do* apply. If we have never experienced a watch *or anything relevantly similar*, then we cannot reasonably infer that it is designed. We can only make the inference from the organisation of parts for a purpose to a designer in those cases in which we have the relevant experience (objection (3)). With watches, in fact, we do; but in Paley's thought experiment, *we should assume that we don't*. If we don't, then we can't infer a designer. And that is the situation we are in regarding the natural world.

Compare and contrast Paley's argument from design with Hume's version from analogy.

If you found a watch in a field, and knew nothing about watches, would you be justified in thinking that the watch was designed by someone?

Evolution by natural selection

Neither Hume nor Paley knew or anticipated the explanation of the organisation of parts for a purpose that is now very widely accepted. Darwin's theory of evolution by natural selection provides an excellent account of how the *appearance* of design can come about without being the result of a designer.

Millions of alterations randomly take place. Most disappear without a trace. But some trait that *coincidentally* helps a creature to survive and reproduce slowly spreads. That creature and its descendants reproduce more than others without the trait, so more and more creatures end up with it. It's not that the feature is 'selected' *in order for* the creature to live better and so reproduce more. Instead, the feature simply *enables* the creature to reproduce more, so its descendants also have that feature and they reproduce more and so on. One very small change is followed by another. Over time, this can lead to great complexity, such as the eye. In time, creatures appear to be designed when they are in fact the product of coincidence. So we don't need to say that living things are actually designed by a designer.

This is a better explanation because it is simpler: we aren't inferring the existence of something new, but appealing only to what we already know exists.

However, Paley makes one remark that serves as an objection (pp. 12, 54). We still haven't accounted for the order, the regularity, that *enables* matter to become organised into parts serving a purpose. Evolution works by the *laws of nature*. What explains *these* regularities? The laws of nature become the focus of Richard Swinburne's version of the argument from design.

> **?**
>
> Does the organisation of parts for a purpose in living things give us good reason to believe in the existence of a designer?

SWINBURNE, 'THE ARGUMENT FROM DESIGN'

Swinburne's argument

Swinburne distinguishes between *two* types of order or regularity in nature (pp. 200-2). We have so far discussed regularities of 'spatial order', in which different things, e.g. parts of an eye, exist at the same time in an ordered way, e.g. being organised to serve a purpose. But there are also regularities of 'temporal order' – an orderliness in the way one thing follows another. These temporal regularities are laws of nature. The design evident in nature, then, is in the laws of nature themselves. Swinburne argues that the activity of a designer is the best explanation of the operation of the laws of nature (p. 203).

The argument from spatial order to a designer is weak for two reasons. There is lots of disorder in the universe; and science can explain the emergence of order from disorder, e.g. through evolution. By contrast, the laws of nature are (nearly?) universal and, Swinburne argues, there is no scientific explanation for why the laws of nature are as they are. Science can't tell us *why* the laws of nature are the way they are. It can only tell us that this is how it is. For example, science explains why water boils when you heat it in terms of the effect of heat on the properties of molecules. It explains these effects and these properties in terms of other laws and properties, atomic and subatomic ones. Some further explanation of these may be possible, but again, it will presuppose other laws and properties. Laws can be explained in terms of more general laws, but that's all. So the most fundamental laws, whatever they are, can't be explained by science.

Put another way, science must *assume* the fundamental laws of nature in order to provide any explanations at all. It can't say where they come from or why they are the way they are, because all scientific explanations presuppose laws. Therefore, scientific laws have no explanation unless we can find some other kind of explanation for them.

We use another type of explanation all the time, namely 'personal explanation'. We explain the products of human activity – this book, these sentences – in terms of a person, a rational, free agent. I'm writing things I *intend* to write. This sort of explanation explains an object or an event in terms of a person and their purposes. So we know of regularities in succession – things coming about because someone intentionally brings them about – that are caused by the activity of a person. The hypothesis that a designer exists and created the universe to include the laws of nature provides a personal explanation for the laws of nature, and so for the order of the universe.

So Swinburne argues (p. 205):

1. There are some temporal regularities, e.g. related to human actions, that are explained in terms of persons.

Outline and explain Swinburne's argument that science cannot explain the fundamental laws of nature.

Explain and illustrate the difference between scientific and personal explanation.

2. There are other temporal regularities, e.g. related to the laws of nature, that are similar to those explained in terms of persons.

3. We can, by analogy, explain the regularities relating to the laws of nature in terms of persons.

4. There is no scientific explanation of the laws of nature.

5. (As far as we know, there are only two types of explanation – scientific and personal.)

6. Therefore, there is no better explanation of the regularities relating to the laws of nature than the explanation in terms of persons.

7. Therefore, the regularities relating to the laws of nature are produced by a person (a designer).

8. Therefore, a designer exists.

Even if the explanation in terms of a designer is technically the 'best' – because there is no other – we still might not accept it if it isn't a *good* explanation. One important criterion for this is whether it is simple. Ockham's razor says 'Do not multiply entities beyond necessity'. Swinburne's explanation introduces a new entity – the designer. But if a designer is *necessary* to explain the laws of nature, then the explanation respects Ockham's razor. Swinburne concludes that whether the argument succeeds depends on premises (2) and (3) – how strong is the analogy between human action and the designer's producing the laws of nature?

Outline and explain Swinburne's argument from design.

Swinburne's response to Hume

Swinburne therefore grants that Hume's objections to the analogy *may* be successful. But we should ask how persuasive they are in the context of inference to the best explanation.

So, why choose human reason as a model for explaining the laws of nature (objection (2)) rather than, say, chance (objection (5))? Because other causes of order in the universe *rely on* the laws of nature which they don't themselves explain (p. 209).

Even Hume's account of how chance brings about spatial order assumes regular changes over time (p. 210). Could the laws of nature themselves change randomly over time, sometimes producing regularity, sometimes producing chaos? Perhaps, but given the amount of order in the universe, and the universal applicability of laws of nature, this is a poor explanation of our experience. Explaining temporal regularities in personal terms remains the best explanation.

Swinburne also disagrees with Hume's account of inferring causes (objection (4)). Hume objects that we can't reach conclusions about the causes of a unique object, such as the universe. Swinburne replies (p. 209) that cosmologists have drawn all sorts of conclusions about the universe as a whole. Uniqueness is relative to how something is described. For example, many of the processes involved in the universe as a whole, e.g. its expansion, can be identified repeatedly in other contexts. And Swinburne argues that Hume's principle in objection (6) – that we attribute to a cause *no more* than is needed for the effect – is mistaken. He agrees with Hume that if this is all we could do, that would be fairly useless. The cause would *only* be known as 'whatever it is that produces this effect'. But clearly we do more than this in science all the time, e.g. in supposing some cause is another subatomic particle rather than a goblin.

However, Swinburne doesn't say *how* we do this or *why* it is justified. The answer is that we draw on *what else* we already know that is relevant, e.g. that there are subatomic particles but no goblins. An inference to the best explanation is supported by how the explanation (the cause) fits with what else we know. Hume's objection is that in the case of the designer, there is *nothing* else we know about the designer apart from nature. So we cannot draw any informative conclusions.

A better response to Hume's objection (6) is this: just being able to infer that the universe has a designer – even if this knowledge is otherwise 'useless' – is itself important. If we can, in addition, show that the designer has the traditional properties of God, then this is a conclusion that changes our understanding of the whole world.

> **?** How successful is Swinburne's defence of the design argument against Hume's criticisms?

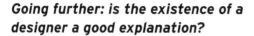

Going further: is the existence of a designer a good explanation?

On p. 208, Swinburne refers to an objection of Hume's in *Dialogues* Pt 4. Hume, as Philo, objects that for the designer to be a satisfactory explanation of design in nature, we would in turn need to explain the designer. A mind is as complex and as ordered as nature, so if the order in nature requires an explanation, so does the order of the designer's mind. If we can't explain the designer, then it would be better to stop our attempts at explanation at the level of nature.

Swinburne replies (just as Cleanthes does in the *Dialogues*) that this misrepresents explanation. Science is full of examples of explanation that don't explain what is assumed in the explanation. Science will introduce an entity – like a subatomic particle – in order to explain something, e.g. explosions in a nuclear accelerator. However, these new entities now need explaining, and scientists don't yet know how to explain them. This is absolutely normal, and has happened repeatedly throughout the history of science.

If we will always have *something* we can't explain, why invoke a designer? Why not just say we can't explain scientific laws? Because invoking a designer explains one more thing, namely scientific laws, and we should explain as much as we can. This is a principle of science and philosophy. If you give up on this, you give up on pursuing these forms of thought. So we can still say that the designer is a good explanation for scientific laws even if we can't explain the designer.

Discuss the claim that it is legitimate to introduce something you can't explain in order to explain something else.

Going further: multiverse theory

There is a recent popular development of Hume's objection (5). Suppose that instead of just this universe, there are or have been millions of universes. Each had randomly different scientific laws, and in most cases, the laws didn't allow the universe to continue to exist – as soon as it began, it ended. Others existed for a time, but the development of order was limited, e.g. there was no life. Given all the possible universes, and all the possible variations in scientific laws, a universe such as ours would come to exist through chance eventually. It doesn't need any special explanation.

This explanation can be compared to winning the lottery. It is very unlikely that *you* will win, but it is highly likely that *someone* will win. For whoever wins, that *they* won is a huge coincidence; but we don't need any special explanation for it (such as 'someone intended them to win, and rigged the lottery'). So, likewise, there is nothing special about this universe, except that it has, by chance, the right laws for order to exist.

We can object that just as the lottery explanation assumes that millions of people are playing, multiverse theory assumes the existence of *huge* numbers of other universes. These other universes are completely inaccessible to us, and we have little evidence for their existence (multiverse theory is also invoked to explain some phenomena in quantum mechanics, but this is theory, not evidence). Is the hypothesis that there are millions of universes better than the hypothesis that there is a designer? Two considerations:

1.   We might think that the existence of a designer is a simpler explanation: just one designer, not millions of universes. On the other hand, the designer is a new *kind* of thing, whereas we already know that universes can exist.
2.   If the designer is God, then God's existence is also supported by other evidence, e.g. religious experience. On the other hand, we also have evidence *against* the existence of God, namely THE PROBLEM OF EVIL (p. 234). At least we don't have evidence against the existence of other universes.

> Explain the argument from multiverse theory that the laws of nature need no special explanation.

> Is the existence of a designer the best explanation for the laws of nature?

Is the designer God?

The argument from design is intended as an argument for the existence of God. However, Paley, Hume and Swinburne all agree that even if we could infer the existence of a designer of the universe, it is an *extra step* to argue that the designer is God. And, because we are relying on analogy, this extra step faces difficulties.

HUME, *DIALOGUES CONCERNING NATURAL RELIGION*, PT 5

If we are arguing for a designer on the basis of a similarity between human inventions and the universe, then shouldn't we think that the designer is *more* similar to human beings than God is traditionally said to be? Here are five objections based on this idea.

1. The scale and quality of the design reflect the power and ability of the designer (p. 24). The universe isn't infinite. So we can't infer that the designer is infinite. And we can't tell whether the universe is perfect; perhaps it contains some mistakes in design. If so, we should say that the designer isn't fully skilled, but made mistakes. So we can't infer that the designer is perfect or infinite in power or knowledge. We also have no reason to think the designer is good. By contrast, God is said to be omnipotent, omniscient and supremely good. So we can't infer that the designer is God.

2. Designers are not always creators (p. 25). Someone who designs a car may not also build it. So we can't infer that the designer of the universe also created the universe. The creator could just be following someone else's designs. But God is said to be the creator of the universe; so we can't infer that the designer is God.

3. The design may have resulted from many small improvements made by many people (p. 25). So we cannot infer that 'the designer' is just one person. More generally, we can't infer that the powers to design and create a universe are all

See *An Enquiry concerning Human Understanding*, §11, p. 73

See THE CONCEPT OF GOD, p. 160.

united in one being, rather than being shared out between lots of different beings. But God is said to be one.

4. We find mind always connected to body (p. 25). There is no reason to think that the designer has no body. But God is thought to be just a mind.

5. Designers can die even as their creations continue (p. 26). So the designer may have designed the universe and then died. God is said to exist eternally, so again, we can't say the designer is God.

In summary, the argument from design doesn't show that the designer is omnipotent, omniscient, the creator of the universe, just one being, non-corporeal, or even still in existence. So it doesn't show that God – as a single omnipotent, omniscient, eternal creator spirit – exists.

Outline and explain Hume's argument that the design argument cannot establish the existence of God.

Kant's critique

Critique of Pure Reason, Second Division (Transcendental Dialectic), Bk 2, Ch. 3, §6

Kant echoes Hume's first two points. The argument from design can only work by analogy, and so, on the basis of order in nature, we can at best infer that there is a designer of nature. We can't draw any conclusions about the designer creating the universe or matter – just as human designers don't literally create the matter they work with, but only shape it. Again, we can only say that this designer must be 'very great', though we don't really understand how great and can't form any 'determinate' ideas of this being.

SWINBURNE, 'THE ARGUMENT FROM DESIGN', PP. 209-10; PALEY, *NATURAL THEOLOGY*, CHS 24-6

Swinburne accepts Hume's objection (1) - if the designer is God, many of God's traditional qualities will need to be established by some other argument. Paley, by contrast, argues that the argument from design *can* establish that the designer has all the features of God (Ch. 24). He accepts that the argument shows only that the designer has the power and knowledge necessary to create this universe, but he says that such power and knowledge is 'beyond comparison and there is no reason ... to assign limits to it' (p. 287). So, considered in terms of our ability to conceive of such power and knowledge, they are unlimited, and so infinite. 'Infinite' power is a 'superlative', like 'best' and 'greatest'. We are expressing our conception of such power in the strongest terms we have.

In Ch. 26, Paley adds that the designer is good. The design of nature *benefits* natural organisms and also gives rise to more pleasure than is strictly necessary for the design to work. Furthermore, where there is evil, we have no evidence to think that it is by design. However, to assess this last point will require us to discuss THE PROBLEM OF EVIL (p. 234).

In reply to (2) and (3), Swinburne invokes Ockham's razor. Simplicity requires that we shouldn't suppose that two possible causes exist when only one will do. If we can explain the design and creation of the universe by supposing that there is just one being capable of this, then we shouldn't suppose that there is more than one being unless we have positive evidence that there is. If, for instance, different parts of the universe operated according to different laws, then that could be evidence for more than one designer being involved. But, as Paley also argues (Ch. 25), the uniformity of nature gives us good reason to suppose that there is just one designer and creator.

In reply to (4), the explanation requires that the designer *doesn't* have a body. Having a body means that one has a particular location in space and can only act on a certain area of space. If God's effects are the laws of nature, and these hold throughout the universe, then God can act everywhere in space simultaneously. So it is better to say that God has no body.

In reply to (5), Swinburne asserts that the objection only works if we are thinking about things in spatial order, such as inventions. But temporal order – regularities in 'what happens next' – requires that the agent is acting *at that time*. To bring

> Compare Paley's conception of omnipotence and omniscience with those discussed in OMNIPOTENCE and OMNISCIENCE, p. 162. Are his definitions plausible?

> Outline and explain the claim that the laws of nature provide evidence that there is only one designer, who has no body.

about order in what happens next, I must act. If I don't act, then the laws of nature take over. But these laws of nature are exactly what we are explaining in terms of God's activity. So God acts wherever the laws of nature hold. So God must continue to exist.

Paley adds (Ch. 24) that this also establishes that God's existence has no beginning or end. It has no beginning, because at such a time, there would have been nothing – and out of nothing, nothing can come into existence. So the designer, God, must always have existed. This does not establish that the designer, God, cannot – at some point in the future – cease to exist; but if we reflect on what kind of existence God must have in order to *always* have existed, then we have reason to think that God must continue to exist always as well.

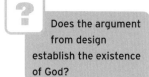

See ARGUMENTS FROM CAUSATION, p. 220.

?

Does the argument from design establish the existence of God?

Key points: the argument from design

- Arguments from design use the order and regularity we find in life and the universe to infer the existence of a divine designer.
- Paley identifies the property of having parts that are organised for a purpose as the property from which we infer that human artefacts are designed. He then claims that natural things have this same property, so the inference that they are also designed is equally valid.
- Hume expresses the argument differently, using analogy: artefacts created by humans exhibit purpose and order, and so do natural things. From purpose and order in artefacts, we infer that the artefact was designed. As natural things are similar, in exhibiting design, we may infer that a similar cause, an intelligent mind, explains their design.
- Hume objects that the analogy is weak – natural things aren't very like human artefacts. So we cannot infer that they have a similar cause.
- Hume argues that there is no reason to think that human thought provides a good model for explaining natural things, and we have not shown that the cause of order and regularity

could not simply be the chance arrangement of matter over infinite time. Paley responds that the existence of a designer is the best explanation.

- However, Darwin's theory of evolution by natural selection explains how living things can have parts organised for a purpose without being designed by a designer.
- Hume also objects that having parts organised for a purpose doesn't show that the cause is a designer in all cases. To make any causal inference, we need repeated experience of the relation between cause and effect, but we don't have it regarding the origin of universe or life. Paley can respond that if Hume were right, we could not infer that human artefacts of which we have no experience nevertheless have a designer.
- We can ask *why* nature is capable of producing apparently designed things, i.e. what explains the laws of nature that enable this. Swinburne argues that science cannot provide a satisfactory explanation of fundamental laws, since scientific explanations always presuppose laws. So we need a personal explanation. Therefore, God is the only explanation of design, and so the best.
- Swinburne responds to Hume by arguing that the human mind provides the best (only) model of explaining the regularity of the laws of nature. He also criticises Hume's theory of causation for being too limited.
- Swinburne argues that the fact that we can't explain God is no objection. Science is always postulating things that it cannot explain in order to explain other things.
- Multiverse theory argues that if there are or have been huge numbers of universes, the chance that *one* would have laws that enabled order is high. So we shouldn't infer that there is a designer.
- We can object that this requires that many such other universes do or have existed, a claim for which we have little independent evidence.
- Hume objects, and Kant agrees, that even if there is a designer, we can't infer that the designer is God. If similar effects have similar causes, then the designer is imperfect and finite, because natural things appear to be imperfect and finite. The designer

may not be the creator, the design might be the collaboration of many people, and the designer might have died.

- Swinburne accepts the first objection, but Paley responds that to be so great as to design the universe is equivalent, from our point of view, to being omnipotent and omniscient.
- Swinburne argues that the claim that there is just one designer who is also the creator is simpler, and so better than the other hypotheses. Finally, if the laws of nature are the effects of God's action, God must continue to exist as long as the laws of nature hold.

C. The cosmological argument

The question at the heart of the cosmological argument is 'why does anything exist?' The argument is that unless God exists, this question is unanswerable. There are different forms of the argument. We will look at six – one from motion, four from causation, and two from existence. St Thomas Aquinas gives one of each kind, and we will start with his version in each instance.

Arguments from causation

AQUINAS, *SUMMA THEOLOGICA*, PT 1, Q. 2, ART. 3

The argument from motion

We can summarise Aquinas's argument from motion like this:

1. Some things in the world are in motion.
2. Whatever is in motion is put into motion by something else. Nothing can move itself.
3. If *A* is put into motion by *B*, and *B* is also in motion, then *B* must have been put into motion by something else again.
4. If this goes on to infinity, then there is no first mover.
5. If there is no first mover, then there is no other mover, and so nothing is in motion.

6. Therefore, there must be a first mover.
7. The first mover is God.

We can raise questions about (2) and (5) and the move from (6) to (7). It turns out, however, that the argument from motion is - on one interpretation at least - just a special case of Aquinas' argument from causation. Premise (2) of the argument from motion states that things are always put in motion by something else. We can understand this as a claim that the motion of *A* is an *effect* of some action of *B*, for instance *B*'s motion, which *causes* *A*'s motion. The first mover will, therefore, also be the first cause of movement. If the argument from causation fails, the argument from motion will fail as well. So we shall discuss objections to both versions together.

The argument from causation

1. We find, in the world, causes and effects.
2. Nothing can be the cause of itself. (If it were, it would have to exist before itself, which is impossible.)
3. Causes follow in order: the first causes the second which causes the third, etc.
4. If you remove a cause, you remove its effect.
5. Therefore, if there is no first cause, there will be no later causes.
6. Therefore, given that there are causes, there cannot be an infinite regress of causes.
7. Therefore, there must be a first cause, which is not itself caused.
8. God is the first cause.

Compare Aquinas' arguments from motion and causation.

Discussion

The argument from causation is relatively straightforward. Premise (6) may cause some confusion, however. The idea of an infinite regress of causes is difficult to understand. The important point is this: infinity is not a very large number. If there is literally an infinite chain of causes, that chain of causes *never* has a starting point. We never reach an account, therefore, of how the process gets started – it never gets started, it has always been.

We know more about the universe now than people did when Aquinas was writing. Our best scientific theory suggests that the universe began just under 14 billion years ago as a Big Bang. But the Big Bang doesn't necessarily mark the beginning of the chain of causation – what caused the Big Bang?

If we can infer the existence of a first cause, why think that first cause is God? Aquinas is here assuming a number of things about our concepts of God and of natural things. It is part of our concept of God that God is uncaused; it follows, for example, from his omnipotence. By contrast, our concept of natural things is that they are part of a causal chain, each thing being caused by something before it. So God obviously fits the bill as a first cause; nothing else does.

See e.g. MALCOLM'S ARGUMENT, p. 190.

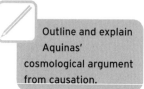

Outline and explain Aquinas' cosmological argument from causation.

The Kalam argument

'*Kalam*' was medieval Islamic theoretical theology.

The Kalam argument is also an argument from causation, but it differs from Aquinas' version by focusing specifically on things being caused *to exist*.

1. Of anything that begins to exist, something causes it to exist.
2. The universe began to exist.
3. Therefore, there is a cause of the existence of the universe.

To get to the conclusion that God is the cause of the universe, we have to add further premises to the Kalam argument.

Premise (1) assumes that something can't come out of nothing. Premise (2) is based on the claim that the universe cannot have always existed. If the universe has always existed, it is infinite in time. This is impossible, so the universe must have a beginning. Why?

Going further: infinity

Infinite time is not a 'very long time'. It means, quite literally, that there was no beginning, ever. Because the universe exists, to claim that the universe has always existed is to claim that an *actual* infinity – something that is in fact infinite – exists. This is quite different from talking about the *idea* of infinity. The idea of infinity makes sense; but does it make sense to think that something infinite actually exists?

The universe gets older as time passes, we naturally think. But this couldn't happen if the universe were infinitely old, because you cannot add any number to infinity and get a bigger number: $\infty + 1 = \infty$. So if the universe is infinitely old, it is not getting any older as time passes! Or again, to have reached the present, an infinite amount of time would need to have passed. But it is not possible for an *infinite* amount of time to have passed, since infinity is not an *amount*. So if the universe was infinitely old, it could never have reached the present.

The same point applies to an infinite series of causes (in support of Aquinas' argument from causation). Each new cause doesn't add one more cause to the series, since $\infty + 1 = \infty$. And we would never have reached the point in the series of causes at which we are now if it were an infinite series.

> Outline and explain the argument that it is impossible for the universe to have always existed.

> Outline and explain the Kalam argument.

DESCARTES, *MEDITATION* III, PP. 15-16

In the *Meditations*, Descartes tries to bring into doubt all his beliefs. He doubts whether an external, physical world exists, but is certain that he exists. In *Meditation* III, he offers two proofs that God exists. The first is DESCARTES' TRADEMARK ARGUMENT (p. 144). The second is a cosmological argument. It is unusual because the only thing that Descartes knows to exist, at this point in the *Meditations*, is himself. So Descartes asks what causes *his* existence, rather than the existence of the universe. As the argument is long and complicated, I have divided it into sections.

> See DESCARTES ON THE EXISTENCE (AND NATURE) OF THE SELF, p. 106.

1. If I cause my own existence, I would give myself all perfections (omnipotence, omniscience, etc.).
2. I do not have all perfections.
3. Therefore, I am not the cause of my existence.

4. A lifespan is composed of independent parts, such that my existing at one time does not entail or cause my existing later.
5. Therefore, some cause is needed to keep me in existence. My existence is not uncaused.
6. I do not have the power to cause my continued existence through time.
7. Therefore, I depend on something else to exist.

8. I am a thinking thing and I have the idea of God.
9. There must be as much reality in the cause as in the effect.
10. Therefore, what caused me must be a thinking thing and have the idea of God.

See GOING FURTHER: DEGREES OF REALITY, p. 146, for discussion of premise (9).

11. Either what caused me is the cause of its own existence or its existence is caused by another cause.
12. If its existence is caused by another cause, then its cause is in turn either the cause of its own existence or its existence is caused by another cause.
13. There cannot be an infinite sequence of causes.
14. Therefore, some cause must be the cause of its own existence.
15. What is the cause of its own existence (and so, directly or indirectly, the cause of my existence) is God.

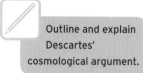

Outline and explain Descartes' cosmological argument.

Descartes adds a further argument, picking up premise (5).

16. Some cause is needed to keep me in existence.
17. There cannot be an infinite chain of causes because what caused me also causes my continued existence in the present.
18. My parents, or any other supposed cause of my existence, do not keep me in existence.
19. The only cause that could keep me in existence is God.

DISCUSSION

We will, in the next section, discuss objections that apply to all three versions of the cosmological argument. However, it is worth briefly evaluating Descartes' unique addition of the claim that his continued existence through time also needs to be caused. There are two misunderstandings that need to be countered to make the claim clear.

One might object that my continued existence doesn't require a cause, because *nothing changes* – I simply continue to exist. If I cease to exist, *that* requires a cause. But this misunderstands both causation and continued existence. I am sitting on a chair – nothing is changing. But there is a cause of this continued state of affairs, namely gravity and the rigidity of the chair. Should either of those *standing conditions* change, then I would no longer be sitting on the chair. I'd either be floating (no gravity) or sitting on the ground (collapsed chair). That people don't die at any given instant is the result of whatever it is that keeps them alive. Therefore, we should accept that my continued existence does require a cause. It is worth noting that what causes my continued existence must itself continue to exist – it can't be a cause in the past, since my continued existence must be caused from moment to moment.

We might object, however, that my continued existence is simply dependent on the immediately preceding state of affairs, and so we don't need to say that what caused me to exist in the first place also keeps me in existence. For instance, my bodily processes keep me alive at any moment, but they didn't give me life. But this forgets that Descartes is talking about his *self*, which is his mind, not his body. Descartes has argued that he, his mind, is an entirely separate substance from the body. So what keeps a mind in existence through time? If it was something in his mind itself, he would know, he claims. And it can't be his parents – they only gave existence to his body (if he has one). The only explanation he can think of is God.

It is worth noting, then, that we could argue that Descartes is wrong to think that minds are separate substances from bodies. If we are bodies, then our continued existence could be caused by the ever-changing physical conditions of our bodies and environment.

Explain why Descartes claims that his continued existence requires a cause.

See DESCARTES ON THE EXISTENCE (AND NATURE) OF THE SELF, p. 106.

What role does Descartes' view of the self play in his cosmological argument?

Issues concerning arguments from causation

Hume raises three objections to cosmological arguments from causation. The first attacks the assumption that everything (apart from the first cause) has a cause. The second attacks the claim that there must be a first cause. And the third attacks the claim that the first cause is God.

The causal principle

A Treatise of Human Nature, Bk 1, Pt 3, Ch. 3

See HUME'S 'FORK', p. 99.

Must everything have a cause? Hume argues that this claim is not analytic; we can deny it without contradicting ourselves. (Every *effect* has a cause is analytic. But is everything an effect?) Likewise, 'Something cannot come out of nothing' is also not analytic. That means that these claims are not *certain*. Now, our experience supports these claims, but experience cannot establish that a claim holds *universally*. And in particular, we may argue, we have no experience of such things as the beginnings of the universe (nor perhaps, the cause of the continued existence of a mind as a separate substance). Furthermore, the beginning of the universe is not an event like events that happen within the universe. For instance, it doesn't take place in space or time, since both come into existence with the universe. We cannot apply principles we have developed for events *within* the universe, such as 'everything has a cause', to the universe as a whole.

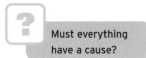

Must everything have a cause?

Is a first cause necessary?

Cosmological arguments reject the possibility of an infinity of causes to infer the existence of a first cause. But do we know that an infinity of causes is impossible? Again, it is not an analytic truth, nor can we have experience of this matter. It seems conceivable, therefore, that something has always existed, and each thing has in turn caused the next. This universe – what exists as we know it now – came into existence just less than 14 billion years ago. But even if *this* universe has a beginning, perhaps it was caused by a previous (or another) universe, and so on, infinitely.

However, we saw above (GOING FURTHER: INFINITY, p. 223) that an actual infinity of causes leads to paradoxes. If these paradoxes cannot be resolved, then they are genuine self-contradictions (e.g. that each new cause adds to the number of causes and that it does not). Anything that entails a contradiction must be false. So, if he cannot solve the paradoxes, Hume is wrong: we can deduce that there cannot be an infinite series of causes.

> Can the claim that there is an infinite series of causes avoid paradox?

To this response, we can add another. Science tells us that time came into existence with the universe. Time itself 'began' with the beginning of the universe just under 14 billion years ago. That means that whatever caused the universe (if it has a cause) cannot exist 'before' the universe – there is no 'before' the universe! Instead, the cause of the universe must exist outside time (which is fine if the cause is God). We think incorrectly then if we think that another universe, one that existed *before* this universe, caused this universe. If there is an infinite series of causes, this cannot be how it takes place. Hume might respond that we simply *can't know* the answer here. So we should draw no conclusions.

A third response claims that if there is not a first cause, we cannot explain the *whole series* of causes. We can explain one cause in terms of the one before, but not why there is a series of causes at all. Hume dismisses this – 'uniting' the individual causes into a series is 'an arbitrary act of the mind'. The series doesn't have any separate existence that needs explanation.

> *Dialogues concerning Natural Religion*, Pt 9, p. 39

> Is there a first cause of all that exists?

Is the first cause God?

The causal arguments from Aquinas and the Kalam say little to defend the claim that the first cause is God. Descartes, however, argues that the cause of his existence must be a mind which itself has the idea of God (10). This depends on premise (9), that a cause must have as much 'reality' as its effect. Hume argues that this is neither an analytic truth nor is it established by experience. Rather, 'anything may produce anything'. There is no a priori reason to think that matter cannot produce thought, and experience would indicate

> *A Treatise of Human Nature*, Bk 1, Pt 3, Ch. 15, §1. For Hume's theory of causation, see HUME, *DIALOGUES CONCERNING NATURAL RELIGION*, PTS 2, 8, p. 203.

that matter does indeed produce thought. So we cannot infer that either the first cause or what sustains Descartes' continued existence as a mind must itself be a mind, let alone one that has the perfections attributed to God.

An inductive argument

Swinburne, *The Coherence of Theism*

On the differences between these types of argument, see Deductive argument, p. 8 and Hypothetical reasoning p. 9.

The three versions of the cosmological argument above are intended to be deductive. However, Richard Swinburne claims that the cosmological argument is better understood as an inference to the best explanation. If we look over the three cosmological arguments above, it is apparent that we can't deduce God's existence. But – at least for the versions from Aquinas and the Kalam – the premises are plausible, and the inferences are intuitive. God's existence isn't logically proven, but it is probable, given the premises, because God's existence is the best explanation for why the universe exists.

For example, although it is not an analytic truth that everything that begins to exist has a cause, Hume agrees that it is probable – our experience supports it. And the theory of the Big Bang and the problems with actual infinities make it more plausible that the universe (or matter/energy) has not existed without beginning, but came into existence. If we reject God as an explanation for the existence of the universe, we need another explanation that is better.

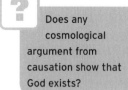

Outline and explain Swinburne's inductive cosmological argument.

See Going further: multiverse theory, p. 214.

As discussed in Swinburne, 'The Argument from Design' (p. 209), Swinburne argues that there is no better explanation for the laws of nature. We can apply this to what exists as well. Just as science can't explain the fundamental laws of nature, according to Swinburne, we can also argue that scientific explanation must always assume that something exists. If we explain this universe in terms of another universe, we then have to explain the existence of that universe. And the same questions about appealing to other universes arise here as with the argument from design.

Does any cosmological argument from causation show that God exists?

We can object, as we did in the case of the argument from design, that introducing God is not the best explanation, e.g. because it is not the simplest. We can also object that even this version of the cosmological argument doesn't show that the cause of the universe has the traditional attributes of God.

Arguments from contingency

AQUINAS, *SUMMA THEOLOGICA*, PT 1, Q. 2, ART. 3

Aquinas offers a third cosmological argument, from 'possibility' or 'contingency'. He distinguishes between contingent existence and necessary existence. Something exists contingently if it is possible for it to exist and for it not to exist. Something exists necessarily if it must exist, i.e. if it is impossible for it not to exist.

1. Things in the universe exist contingently.
2. If it is possible for something not to exist, then at some time, it does not exist.
3. If everything exists contingently, then it is possible that at some time, there was nothing in existence.
4. If at some time, nothing was in existence, nothing could begin to exist.
5. Since things did begin to exist, there was never nothing in existence.
6. Therefore, there is something that does not exist contingently, but must exist.
7. This necessary being is God.

See also NECESSARY AND CONTINGENT TRUTH, p. 105.

Outline and explain Aquinas' cosmological argument from contingency.

OBJECTIONS

1. We can object to premise (2). Just because it is *possible* for something not to exist doesn't mean that it *actually* does not exist at some time. We have no reason to think that everything that is possible actually occurs. Aquinas might reply that if something *always* existed, then we need a very peculiar explanation for how this could be so given that its existence is not necessary.
2. We can object to premise (4), which states THE CAUSAL PRINCIPLE (p. 226). As Hume argued, it is not a self-contradiction to deny this, although experience does support it.
3. The inference in (6) doesn't follow. We should agree that it is *possible* that, if everything exists contingently, then at some point, nothing exists. But from the fact that it is possible, it

Is Aquinas right to claim that everything contingent does not exist at some point?

doesn't follow that there *actually* was or will be nothing in existence. It is equally possible that there has always been, and always will be, some contingent thing in existence.

Aquinas could reply that because each contingent thing exists contingently, then all contingent things (e.g. the universe) *as a whole* exist contingently. Therefore, according to premise (2), all contingent things did not exist at some point. But we can object that this applies a property of a part of the universe to the whole universe. Just because each thing exists contingently, it doesn't follow that the collection of all things exists contingently. We will return to this objection below.

Copleston's argument from contingency

In a radio debate with Bertrand Russell, Frederick Copleston presented a version of the cosmological argument from contingency that emphasises the need to *explain* what exists.

1. Things in the universe exist contingently.
2. Something that exists contingently has (and needs) an explanation of why it exists; after all, its existence is not inevitable.
3. This explanation may be provided by the existence of some other contingent being. But then we must explain these other contingent beings.
4. To repeat this ad infinitum is no explanation of why anything exists at all.
5. Therefore, what explains why contingent beings exist at all can only be a non-contingent being.
6. A non-contingent being is one that exists necessarily, and doesn't need some further explanation for why it exists.
7. This necessary being is God.

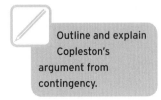

Outline and explain Copleston's argument from contingency.

OBJECTIONS TO THE ARGUMENT FROM CONTINGENCY
1. Russell accepts that of any particular thing in the universe, we need an explanation of why it exists, which science can give us. But it is a mistake to think that we can apply this idea to the

universe itself (5). Just because everything in the universe is contingent (and so needs an explanation), it doesn't follow that the universe is also contingent or needs an explanation. The universe is 'just there, and that's all'.

Russell is arguing that the argument commits the fallacy of composition. This fallacy is an inference that because the parts have some property, the whole has the property, too. For instance, each tissue is thin, so the box of tissues is thin. Not true.

See FALLACIES, p. 14.

However, we can reply that inferring from parts to whole does not always commit the fallacy of composition. For instance, each part of my desk is wooden, so my desk is wooden. We can argue that the same applies in the cosmological argument. For instance, if every part of the universe ceased to exist, so would the universe. This shows that just as everything in the universe is contingent, so is the universe. As a contingent being, the universe requires an explanation.

If the argument doesn't commit the fallacy of composition, Russell needs to find some other objection to the principle that *all* contingent beings, including the universe, require an explanation for their existence.

?

Does Copleston's argument from contingency commit the fallacy of composition?

2. We could develop such an objection from Hume. It is not an analytic truth that all contingent beings *have* an explanation (2), any more than it is an analytic truth that everything has a cause. And so Russell remarks that while scientists will look for causes, that doesn't imply that they can find them everywhere. Likewise, we should leave open the possibility that the universe has no explanation.

This and the objections below are from *Dialogues concerning Natural Religion*, Pt 9, p. 39.

This objection can be avoided by giving up the deductive form of the cosmological argument, and following Swinburne (above) to claim that it is an inference to the best explanation instead. God's existence is certainly a better explanation than no explanation at all!

3. Another closely related objection is this. We noted in IS A FIRST CAUSE NECESSARY? (p. 226) that Hume objects that uniting everything into a single whole is 'an arbitrary act of the mind'.

We can apply that here to say that once we explain each thing in turn, we don't need a further explanation for the whole thing.

We can reply that the explanations of each part are in terms of other contingent things. So this will lead to an infinite regress of explanation, which is unsatisfactory (4).

4. Hume also objects to the conclusion (7). Let us suppose that (6) is correct, there is some necessary being. It need not be God but could be matter/energy (in some form) that is a necessary being. We can't show that it is incompatible with the nature of matter, Hume claims, that it necessarily exists. For example, a fundamental law of physics is the conservation of energy: the total amount of matter/energy in the universe remains constant, it cannot be increased or decreased. If a version of this law applied even at the beginning and end of this universe and others, then matter/energy is a necessary being.

We can respond that we have no reason to believe that this law does apply at the beginning (and possibly the end) of the universe. The Big Bang theory suggests that matter/energy was created, along with time and space, i.e. the universe came into existence – so it is contingent.

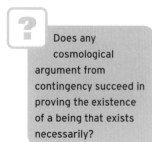
Does any cosmological argument from contingency succeed in proving the existence of a being that exists necessarily?

5. A final objection, to (6), comes from Russell. The concept of a being that necessarily exists is problematic. It would need to be self-contradictory to deny its existence, and it isn't clear how this is possible. This issue was discussed at length in ONTOLOGICAL ARGUMENTS (p. 181). If we can't make sense of the concept of a being that necessarily exists, then we have reason to reject the cosmological argument from contingency.

Key points: the cosmological argument

- Aquinas' argument from motion argues that everything derives its motion from something else, so there must be a first mover. The argument is a special case of the argument from causation.

- Aquinas' argument from causation argues that each thing is caused by something else, so there must be a first cause. An infinite regress of causes is impossible.
- The Kalam argument claims that everything that begins to exist has a cause, the universe began to exist, and so it has a cause. It rests on the claims that something can't come out of nothing (the causal principle) and that an actual infinity (such as the universe existing for an infinite time) is impossible.
- Descartes argues that he depends on something else to exist, and as a thinking thing with the idea of God, his cause must also be a thinking thing with the idea of God. He also rejects the possibility of an infinite series of causes, and concludes that there must be something whose existence is not caused by anything else – God.
- Hume objects that the claim that everything, or everything that begins to exist, has a cause is not an analytic truth. We cannot establish that it holds without exception.
- Hume also objects that the claim that there cannot be an infinite series of causes is not analytic. However, we can reply that allowing that there can be an infinite series of causes leads to paradoxes.
- We can also object that the argument doesn't establish that the first cause is God.
- The arguments from causation try to *deduce* that God exists. Swinburne argues that God's existence is the *best explanation*. This avoids many of the objections.
- Aquinas argues that contingent things do not exist at all times. Because this would lead to nothing existing, and so nothing ever existing, there must be something that exists necessarily.
- We can object that while this is possible, it is also possible that some contingent thing or other has always existed.
- Copleston argues that anything that exists contingently requires an explanation of its existence. An infinite series of explanations of contingent things in terms of other contingent things is unsatisfactory. So what explains why contingent things exist must itself exist necessarily.
- Russell objects that the argument commits the fallacy of composition. The universe doesn't require an explanation. We

can reply that if everything in the universe ceased to exist, so would the universe. So the universe exists contingently and requires an explanation.

- We can object that while we may search for such explanations, it is not an analytic truth that everything has an explanation of its existence. We can reply that the argument nevertheless works as an inference to the best explanation.
- Hume objects that once we have explained each thing, we don't need an additional explanation of the whole universe. We can reply that only explaining each thing in turn will lead to an infinite regress of explanations.
- Hume also objects that matter/energy could be what exists necessarily, so we can't conclude that God exists.
- Russell objects that the concept of a being that exists necessarily is incoherent, so the conclusion that such a being exists must be false.

D. The problem of evil

The problem of evil is widely considered to be the most powerful argument against the existence of God. We shall consider two versions of the argument. The central issue is whether evil, as it occurs in this world, either proves that God, as traditionally conceived, does not exist or at least makes the belief in such a God unreasonable.

An outline of the problem

Throughout the discussion, I shall take 'God' to refer to a being that is supremely good, omnipotent and omniscient.

In THE DIVINE ATTRIBUTES (p. 160), we saw that God is traditionally understood to be supremely good, omnipotent and omniscient. The existence of evil causes problems for believing that such a being exists. Here's the argument:

1. If God is supremely good, then he has the desire to eliminate evil.
2. If God is omnipotent, then he is able to eliminate evil.

3. If God is omniscient, then he knows that evil exists and knows how to eliminate it.
4. Therefore, if God exists, and is supremely good, omnipotent and omniscient, then evil does not exist.
5. Evil exists.
6. Therefore, a supremely good, omnipotent and omniscient God does not exist.

> What is the problem of evil?

Two versions of the argument

There are two versions of this argument.

The *logical problem of evil* claims that the mere existence of evil is logically incompatible with the existence of God. In other words, the following claims cannot all be true:

1. God is supremely good.
2. God is omnipotent.
3. God is omniscient.
4. Evil exists.

If any three of the claims are true, the fourth *must* be false. On this version, the argument above is deductive.

The *evidential problem of evil* makes a weaker claim. It claims that the *amount and distribution* of evil that exists is *good evidence* that God does not exist. On this version, the argument above is inductive.

> Explain the differences between the evidential and logical problems of evil.

Two types of evil

To understand the argument, we need to be clear on what 'evil' means in this context. 'Evil' usually refers to the morally wrong actions or motives of human beings. So we say that Hitler was evil in trying to eradicate the Jews from Europe or that ethnic cleansing is an evil policy. This is *moral evil*.

But this isn't the only kind of evil the problem of evil is talking about. There is also *natural evil*, also known as 'physical evil', which refers to *suffering* caused by natural events and processes, e.g. the suffering caused by earthquakes, diseases, the predation of animals on each other, and so on.

In the first instance, the two types of evil are distinct. What people choose to do to each other is not usually the result of natural events. Sometimes it is: famine may drive people to stealing and killing; but this is the exception. And natural events are not usually the result of what people choose to do. Again, sometimes they are – the results of global warming could be an example.

We need to keep both types of evil in mind when we look at responses to the problem of evil. In particular, some responses may solve the problem of moral evil, but don't answer the problem of natural evil.

> Explain the differences between moral and natural evil.

The logical problem of evil

MACKIE, 'EVIL AND OMNIPOTENCE'

Mackie outlines the logical problem of evil as above, that (1)-(4) are inconsistent, although he (mistakenly) omits the claim that God is omniscient. He argues that that we need to add two additional claims before we get inconsistency:

5.   Good is opposed to evil, such that a good thing eliminates evil as far as it can.
6.   There are no limits to what an omnipotent thing can do.

One way out of the inconsistency is to give up one of the claims. For example, someone might deny (4), arguing that evil doesn't exist. What we call evil isn't really evil. An alternative is to deny (6): there are limits to what an omnipotent God can do. We'll consider this claim at length in the discussion below. Mackie accepts that such moves - if they can be defended - solve the problem.

He then considers a series of common responses which, he argues, do not solve the problem. We will look at three: the claims that good can't exist without evil, that the world is better with some evil in it than it could be if there were no evil, and that evil is the result of free will.

Good can't exist without evil

This is a very general claim. It claims that there can be *no* good without *some* evil. (We will look at the more specific claim that *some* goods that exist can't exist without evil below.) As such, it denies either (5) or (6) or both. Being omnipotent, God can presumably do anything that is logically possible. But if it is *logically impossible* for good to exist without evil, then God can't create a world in which good can exist without evil. And evil does not oppose good, but in some sense is necessary for it.

See OMNIPOTENCE, p. 162.

In what sense? By analogy, someone might argue that one colour requires the existence of other colours, e.g. to generate a contrast. But, Mackie argues, there is no reason why everything couldn't be red. Of course, if everything was red, then we probably wouldn't notice this (it would just be 'how things are') and we wouldn't have a word for red. But that is a claim about *how we think and talk*. It doesn't show that things wouldn't *be* red. Likewise, if there was no evil, we wouldn't *know* that things were good; but that doesn't show that God can't create a world in which there is good but no evil. What God can do isn't restricted by human language or thought.

An alternative is to argue that evil doesn't 'exist' in any positive sense – it is simply the absence of good. This would show that good and evil are logically opposed, like red and 'not-red'. But that still doesn't show why God couldn't create a world which has no absence of good, a 'fully good' world.

See OMNIPOTENCE AND SUPREME GOODNESS, p. 167.

Finally, suppose we allow that good can't exist without evil. That only shows that the world, to contain any good at all, must contain *some* evil. In that case, the existence of God isn't logically incompatible with the existence of evil. But surely God would not allow *so much* evil. We will return to this point in THE EVIDENTIAL PROBLEM OF EVIL (p. 243).

Is there any good reason to think that good *cannot* exist without evil?

The world is better with some evil in it than it could be if there were no evil

We can develop the previous point by focusing on specific kinds of good and evil. While it may or may not be true that *any* good requires evil, there are some goods that clearly require some evil. The logical problem of evil assumes that God has the desire to eliminate *all* evil. But this isn't true if some evil is *necessary for a greater good*. In particular, there are virtues, such as sympathy, benevolence and courage, that require suffering to exist. A universe without suffering would be a universe without these virtues; and a universe without either suffering or virtue would be a worse universe than one in which there is both suffering and virtue. The evil of suffering makes the good of virtue possible.

Mackie puts the point like this: call suffering a 'first-order' evil and pleasure a first-order good. 'Second-order' goods, such as virtues, aim at maximising first-order goods (pleasure) and minimising first-order evils (suffering). But second-order goods are impossible without first-order evils. We can now argue that these second-order goods are more important or more valuable than first-order goods, so a universe that contains them is significantly better than a universe with only first-order goods, so much so that the existence of first-order evils does not outweigh second-order goods. So God brings about a universe with second-order goods and first-order evils.

Mackie objects, however, that we have left *second-order evils*, such as malevolence, cruelty and cowardice, out of consideration. We have only explained how a universe with first-order evils (and second-order goods) could be better than one without first-order evils. But we haven't explained how a universe, such as ours, that has both first- and second-order evils is better than one without both. We haven't shown how the existence of God is compatible with the existence of second-order evils.

> Outline and explain the argument that the existence of God is compatible with the existence of first-order evils.

Evil is due to human free will

Perhaps we can solve this challenge by supplementing the previous answer by an appeal to free will. Second-order evils are the result of free will. Being morally imperfect, we do not always use our free will for good, but sometimes bring about evil. However, this is compatible with the existence of God because being free is such a significant good that it outweighs the evil that we bring about. The universe is better with free will and second-order evils than it would be without either.

Why doesn't God just make us choose what is good? Because, we can reply, this isn't logically possible. To be free is for one's choices not to be determined. If God *made* us choose good, then our choices would be determined, so we wouldn't be free.

However, Mackie objects, second-order evils are not logically necessary for free will, in the way first-order evils are necessary for second-order goods.

1. It is possible to freely choose what is good on one occasion.
2. If it is possible to freely choose what is good on one occasion, then it is logically possible to freely choose what is good on every occasion.
3. God can create any logically possible world.
4. Therefore, it is possible for God to create a world in which creatures are free and freely choose only what is good.
5. God would eliminate evil that is not necessary for a greater good.
6. Second-order evil is not necessary for a greater good.
7. Second-order evil exists.
8. Therefore, God does not exist.

> Outline and explain Mackie's argument that second-order evil is inconsistent with the existence of (an omniscient, omnipotent, supremely good) God.

PLANTINGA, *GOD, FREEDOM, AND EVIL*, PP. 7-59

On the logical problem of evil

Why does God allow evil? If we try to answer this question, to give a reason why God allows evil, we offer a *theodicy*. The three

Explain Plantinga's distinction between a theodicy and a defence. Why is a defence enough to defeat the logical problem of evil?

Pp. 34-9 are discussed in POSSIBLE WORLDS, p. 193. Pp. 39-54 present a very complex defence of Plantinga's premise (6) below.

See DISCUSSION, p. 178.

responses that Mackie discusses are theodicies. Plantinga takes a different approach. Suppose we don't, or even can't, know why, in fact, God allows evil. This isn't enough to show that God's existence is *inconsistent* with the existence of evil. We don't need to discover and defend *the true explanation* for why evil exists. All we need to do, to defeat the logical problem of evil, is show that the existence of God *is consistent* with evil. Two (or more) claims are consistent if they *can* both (or all) be true together. To show this, we don't need to show that the claims *are* true. Plantinga calls this approach a 'defence' rather than a theodicy.

Our discussion of Mackie showed that God's existence is not inconsistent with *some* evil. For example, first-order evils are necessary for second-order goods. The difficulty that remained was whether second-order evil is consistent with the existence of God. Plantinga develops the argument from free will, not as a theodicy, but as a defence.

The free will defence

On pp. 29-34, Plantinga presents the heart of the argument. He first presents these definitions:

1. To be *free* is to be able to do or refrain from some action, not to be causally determined to act in one way or another. (One can be free and still be predictable.)
2. A *morally significant action* is one which it is either right or wrong to perform. (An action that is permissible to do or omit, e.g. have a banana for breakfast, is not morally significant.)
3. A creature is *significantly free* if it is free to do or refrain from morally significant actions.
4. Moral evil is evil resulting from the actions of significantly free creatures. (This contrasts with natural evil.)

Plantinga then offers the following argument (p. 30):

1. A world containing creatures that are significantly free is better than a world containing no free creatures.

2. God can create significantly free creatures.
3. To be significantly free is to be capable of both moral good and moral evil.
4. If significantly free creatures were caused to do only what is right, they would not be free.
5. Therefore, God cannot cause significantly free creatures to do only what is right.
6. Therefore, God can only eliminate the moral evil done by significantly free creatures by eliminating the greater good of significantly free creatures.

If the conclusion, (6), is asserted as a true claim, this argument is a form of the free will theodicy. The free will defence, however, only claims that (6) is *possible*. If this is possible, then the existence of evil, including second-order evil, is logically consistent with the existence of God.

Natural evil

The free will defence only tackles moral evil. So how do we make the existence of natural evil consistent with the existence of God? We discussed one response in THE WORLD IS BETTER WITH SOME EVIL IN IT THAN IT COULD BE IF THERE WERE NO EVIL (p. 238). Plantinga provides a distinct argument (p. 57), derived from Augustine. Augustine argues that natural evil is the result of the free actions of *non-human* creatures, namely Satan and his fallen angels. The traditional story goes that the Devil was an angel, created by God, endowed with free will. But he rebelled against God, and since then has sought to bring evil into the world. Natural evil is one of the effects of his actions, so natural evil is a form or consequence of moral evil. While Augustine argued that this was a *true explanation* of natural evil, Plantinga's free will defence only needs to claim that this is *possible*.

> Outline and explain Plantinga's free will defence.

Going further: how good is free will?

Plantinga's claim (1) compares a world with creatures that are free with a world without such creatures. We can object that this leaves out other possibilities. Even if free will is a great good, that doesn't mean we should never interfere with it. For example, if we see someone about to commit murder and do nothing about it, it is no defence to appeal to how wonderful it is that the murderer has free will. To eliminate some evils, one has to eliminate certain instances of free will. But this type of selective interference is compatible with the existence and goodness of free will; it doesn't eliminate a greater good. So God would interfere in this way.

We can challenge this. If God always interfered to prevent us from causing evil, then this is equivalent to his causing us to do good. In that case, we don't have free will at all.

We can refine the objection. God could interfere just on those occasions on which we would bring about terrible evil. Or again, God could have given us free will without giving us the power to commit terrible evil. The point is that free will doesn't seem *such* a good thing that each occasion of choosing freely is a good thing. *Some* choices are better eliminated. Wouldn't a limited kind of free will have been better?

One response, from John Hick, is that the value of free will depends on what one can do with it. A world in which we couldn't harm each other – either because we didn't have the power to do so or because God always interfered to stop us – would also be one in which we would have very little responsibility for each other's well-being.

Whether or not this justifies the moral evil that human beings do, we can raise the objection again regarding Satan. Is the free will of Satan so good that it outweighs all the natural evil that he has caused? Surely a world without Satan would be a better world, and a world that God could have created. If Satan exists, then this is logically inconsistent with the existence of God and the free will defence fails to justify natural evil.

Hick, *Evil and the God of Love*, Ch. 16, §3

? Is the existence of evil logically inconsistent with the existence of God?

The evidential problem of evil

The evidential problem of evil does not challenge the claim that the existence of evil is *consistent* with the existence of God. Rather, it claims that the amount of evil, the kinds of evil, and the distribution of evil are good evidence for thinking that God does not exist. Put another way, we can grant that evil as we know it does not make it *impossible* that God exists. But the fact that it is possible doesn't show that it is *reasonable* to believe that God exists. Planets made of green cheese are logically possible; but it isn't reasonable to think they exist. The evidential problem of evil tries to show that belief in an omnipotent, omniscient, supremely good God is unreasonable, given our experience of evil.

The discussion of the logical argument has been very abstract. But the problem of evil more naturally arises, as a challenge to belief in God, when we consider specific examples of evil. Innocent children suffer agonising deaths. Animals are eaten alive or develop chronic debilitating illnesses. Natural disasters, such as the tsunami of December 2004, kill hundreds of thousands of people. In wars and ethnic cleansing, people kill each other in the millions, the worst example being the Holocaust of World War II. People who have already suffered terribly may suffer more, without reprieve. Who suffers and how much is very unfair.

The examples are intended as illustrations of the kind, amount or distribution of evil that an omniscient, omnipotent, supremely good God would eliminate. Even if certain evils are necessary for certain goods, are all these evils necessary? It seems that a better world is possible, one that contains free will and second-order goods and some evil, but less – and less terrible – evil than exists. This is a good reason to believe that God does not exist.

> Outline and explain the evidential problem of evil.

PLANTINGA, *GOD, FREEDOM, AND EVIL*, PP. 59-64

Plantinga argues that the free will defence can deal with the evidential problem. To recap, according to Plantinga, the free will defence shows that it is *possible* that most of the evil in this world is moral evil (because it is possible that natural evil is the result of the moral evil of Satan). It also shows that it is *possible* that God could not create a world with less evil without reducing the good, i.e. it is *possible* that there is no better balance of moral good and moral evil than the one that exists.

Turning to the evidential problem, how are we to assess how *probable* this is? Do we have any evidence *against* these claims? Plantinga argues that we don't. In particular, the amount of evil that exists, on its own, neither supports nor opposes the claim that a better balance of good and evil is possible. Therefore, it does not make it less likely that God exists.

> Outline and explain Plantinga's response to the evidential problem of evil.

OBJECTION

Plantinga's argument only considers the *amount* of evil, and in a very abstract way – the total amount in the universe. But the evidential problem also appeals to the kinds and distribution of evil. These are more difficult to dismiss as not providing evidence that a better balance of good and evil *is* possible.

Going further: appeals to ignorance

The evidential problem of evil appeals to an intuition, that there is *no good reason* that *could* justify the amount and distribution of evil in the world. However, we may reply that we don't know this. It may be that all evil serves some higher purpose, but we simply don't, and perhaps can't, know what that purpose is or how evil serves it.

However, this is not a satisfactory answer as it stands.

1. There is no good *that we know of* that could justify the evil that we see. Any good that we can think of (such as free will or second-order goods) could be obtained without God *having* to allow the evil that exists.
2. *Whatever* good evil is supposed to be necessary for, if it's anything we can think of already, it won't justify evil.

3. Therefore, evil can only be justified by a good that we are simply not familiar with.
4. It is *probable* that we know most goods.
5. Therefore, it is *probable* that there is no such good.

We often infer from what we know to what we don't know in this way. For example, we constantly form beliefs about the future: the sun will rise tomorrow, chairs won't suddenly sprout wings, and so on. We do this because we think the future will be like the past. Inferring from 'nothing we know of will justify evil' to 'nothing will justify evil' is just the same. When reasoning about what is *probable*, we don't usually allow the appeal to ignorance on its own. To defeat the objection, what we need is a *good reason* for thinking that *there is* some good that we don't know about.

We can also apply the objection to Plantinga's free will defence. He argues that we have no evidence *against* the claim that there is no better balance of good and evil. But this is not enough. Given the objection above, to make belief in God reasonable, we need a good reason *for* the claim that no better balance between good and evil is possible.

> Can the evidential problem of evil be answered by appealing to our ignorance?

HICK, *EVIL AND THE GOD OF LOVE*, CHS 13-17

In The world is better with some evil in it than it could be if there were no evil (p. 238), we encountered the argument that evil is necessary for virtue. It is therefore necessary for us to become good people, for us to grow morally and spiritually. John Hick develops the argument further.

The vale of soul-making theodicy

In Ch. 13, Hick argues that we shouldn't think that God has finished creating human beings. We are unfinished. The first stage of our creation is given by evolutionary history, which brings into existence creatures - us - who are capable of conscious fellowship with God. The second stage of our creation is both individual and more difficult. It involves bringing each person freely towards personal, ethical, and spiritual virtues and a relationship with God. This work of perfection is individual, rather than collective. It does not entail that the world as a whole is getting better, morally speaking.

The response to the problem of evil – in both logical and evidential forms – is that such virtuous development is impossible unless there is evil to respond to and correct. For example, we can't be courageous unless there is danger, we can't be benevolent unless people have needs, we can't learn forgiveness unless people treat us wrongly, and so on. Through struggles and suffering, not only with natural disasters and illness (first-order evil), but also with our own motives and the actions of other people (second-order evil), we mature and develop spiritually. Both natural and moral evil are necessary. Defenders of the problem of evil often assume that God would seek to maximise pleasure and minimise pain. Such an environment *may* be suitable for perfected creatures, but it is no good for helping unperfected creatures like us develop. We can understand this world, then, as a place of 'soul-making'.

As Mackie points out, on this view God is not benevolent, if that means seeking to reduce suffering. Instead, God seeks our development of virtues, and this requires suffering. We can note, however, that God is still benevolent in another sense, namely intending our greatest good. Because God is good, he wants us to become good, and so he wants a world in which this is possible. It turns out that such a world must contain evil. And so the existence of evil is compatible with the existence of God.

God could have created creatures that had some version of the virtues immediately. But the virtues we achieve that result from challenges, discipline, and overcoming temptation, are 'good in a richer and more valuable sense' than the qualities of someone simply created good. In addition, Hick argues (Ch. 14, §4), there are some attitudes that God *could* not create, but must come through freedom. It is impossible to create free human beings that can be guaranteed to respond to God in authentic faith and love. Setting up human nature in this way would be tantamount to a form of manipulation, and so the attitudes would be inauthentic.

Challenges from the evidential problem

We may object that the argument addresses the logical problem, but hasn't yet offered a response to the amount, kind or distribution of evil. In essence, the theodicy only justifies *all* evil if *all* evil leads to spiritual growth. So we can object:

1. What about animal suffering? Animals don't grow spiritually, so how is the natural evil that they suffer justified?
2. Is it plausible that terrible evils are really necessary for our moral and spiritual growth?
3. A great deal of evil doesn't (appear to) contribute to spiritual growth. Many people suffer terribly in a way that breaks their spirit, e.g. children who never recover from being abused; others suffer at the end of their lives when there is little time to develop further; people die prematurely, before they have a chance of spiritual growth; people who need to grow spiritually don't suffer much at all; others who are already leading good and mature lives suffer a great deal.

Hick discusses each objection in turn. But we first need to understand the value of pain and its distinction from suffering. Physical pain is valuable not primarily in the information it provides when we are ill, but in the lessons we learn about how to preserve ourselves, about risks and dangers (Ch. 15, §3). Life without pain would not be better – it would not be life as we know it at all, and it certainly would not be a life in which we were able to develop morally and spiritually. We should also distinguish between pain and suffering. Much of our suffering – in its self-centredness, self-pity, desire to avoid weakness and mortality – is a result of our response to pain. It needn't be like

> Outline and explain the soul-making theodicy.

this (which is not to say it is easy!), and these aspects can be understood as a result of our going wrong morally (Ch. 16, §1). We endure pain without suffering in experiences of adventure, triumph over obstacles, etc.

Animals: We shouldn't misrepresent the experience of animals (Ch. 15, §5). They live in the present without fear of death or of future pains or dangers. And, as just argued, to be alive is to be subject to pain. But why, if they don't have souls to be perfected, should they exist (and so feel pain) at all? Wouldn't a world without animals and their pain be better? Hick's reply is that if we were the only living things or so clearly set apart from the rest of nature, we would lose some of our *cognitive freedom* (Ch. 15, §5). If God proved that he exists, we would not really be free to choose whether or not to develop a relationship with him. For us to develop the best form of faith and love, there must be 'epistemic distance' between us and God. So the world needs to be one which we can understand as though God did not exist. The existence of animals and our close relationship to them serves that purpose. We have an account of our origin and place in nature independent of God. This provides the justification of animals and their pain – it is a necessary part of a world in which our souls may be perfected.

Terrible evils: Terrible evils are terrible in contrast to more 'ordinary' evils (Ch. 16, §4). If we remove the terrible ones, the next-to-terrible ones will seem exceptional and we will wonder why those are permitted. If we continue to remove the worst evils, eventually we arrive at a world in which there is little evil but also very little human freedom, moral responsibility, or the development of moral and spiritual virtues.

Pointless evil: What about the distribution of evil, evil that seems to fail to contribute to the purpose of soul-making? We cannot rationalise such evils, says Hick. They must remain a challenge and a mystery (Ch. 16, §6). However, we can understand that the existence of such irrational evils is part of the process of soul-making. Imagine a world in which we knew, on every occasion when someone suffered, that it was for the best. This

Explain Hick's argument that animal pain is not something that God would eliminate.

would leave us without deep sympathy, the kind that is evoked precisely in response to suffering that is unjust and excessive. We may add that we would need neither faith nor hope, both of which depend on uncertainty and unpredictability. But faith and hope are two central virtues, two ways in which souls grow spiritually. So for our souls to grow spiritually, it *must* look like the distribution and amount of evil are unfair or unjustified.

None of Hick's theodicy succeeds as a response to the problem of evil unless our souls *are* perfected. But we can object that this is frequently not the case. People die undeveloped, morally and spiritually immature or corrupt. Hick accepts the point. The theodicy only works if we also believe in a life after death (Ch. 17, §1). Indeed, we must believe in universal salvation as well: if there are wasted lives or unredeemed sufferings, he claims, then either God is not supremely good or not all-powerful.

> **?** Must evil appear unjustified for us to grow spiritually?

> **?** In light of the existence of evil, can the belief in an omniscient, omnipotent, supremely good God be reasonable?

Key points: the problem of evil

- The problem of evil is this: if God is supremely good, then he has the desire to eliminate evil. If God is omnipotent, then God is able to eliminate evil. If God is omniscient, then he knows that evil exists and knows how to eliminate it. Evil exists, so an omniscient, omnipotent, supremely good God does not.
- The logical problem: the existence of evil is logically incompatible with the existence of God.
- The evidential problem: the amount and distribution of evil makes the existence of God very unlikely.
- 'Evil' means moral and natural evil. Moral evil is that caused by beings with free will. Natural evil is suffering caused by natural processes, e.g. drought and predation.
- Mackie argues that the logical problem needs two additional premises: a good thing eliminates evil as far as it can; and there are no limits to what an omnipotent thing can do. One way to solve the logical problem is to give up one of the claims involved.

- Mackie rejects the proposal that good can't exist without evil. Unless we can show that it is logically impossible for good to exist without evil, God's omnipotence is restricted.
- We can argue that the world is better with some evil in it than if there were no evil. In particular, some evils are necessary for greater goods. Mackie discusses how second-order goods require first-order evil. However, this does not justify second-order evil.
- We can argue that second-order evil (and much first-order evil) is the result of human free will. Mackie objects that God could have created a world in which we freely choose the good all the time.
- Plantinga distinguishes between a theodicy – an account of why God allows evil – and a defence, which only tries to show that the existence of both God and evil is consistent.
- Plantinga's free will defence argues that the world is better with free creatures, but free creatures cannot be caused to do what is right. It is therefore *possible* that God can only eliminate the moral evil done by significantly free creatures by eliminating the greater good of significantly free creatures. So the logical problem does not show that the existence of God and evil is logically inconsistent.
- We can object that this doesn't cover natural evil. Plantinga follows Augustine in claiming that it is possible that natural evil is the result of moral evil by Satan.
- Even if free will is a great good, this does not mean it should not be interfered with. We can argue that God would prevent some, or the worst, evil actions, including those of Satan.
- We can object that the free will defence doesn't answer the evidential problem of evil. Plantinga responds that we don't have any evidence against the claims that God can only eliminate evil by eliminating free will, and that natural evil is the result of moral evil caused by Satan.
- We can respond that we cannot appeal to ignorance to solve the evidential problem of evil. We need some reason to think that evil *is* justified, not just that it could be.
- Hick presents the soul-making theodicy, which says that evil is necessary for moral and spiritual growth. This world is not

intended to achieve the greatest balance of pleasure over pain, but to provide an environment in which our souls can develop.

- We can object that this doesn't deal with animal suffering. Hick responds that pain is necessary for life, and animals are alive so that we have cognitive freedom, i.e. the existence of God is not forced on us.
- Terrible evils are justified by understanding that they are 'terrible' in comparison – however much or little evil there was, whatever is worst will look terrible.
- To the objection that not all evil contributes to spiritual growth, Hick responds that unless it appeared this way, we would not develop deep sympathy for each other (and, we can add, faith and hope).
- To the objection that people's souls are not developed, Hick argues that the theodicy only succeeds if there is an afterlife in which we are perfected.

Going further: assumptions made by arguments relating to the existence of God

Although what follows does not appear explicitly on the syllabus, it is worth reflecting on the underlying assumptions made by the ontological, design, and cosmological arguments regarding what it is for God to exist, at least if we understand these arguments at face value.

First, they assume that God is a being that exists independently of (and prior to) human beings and religious beliefs. For example, to be the cause of the existence of the universe *in a literal sense*, God must exist independently of the universe. Second, they assume that the statement 'God exists' is, in some sense, a statement of fact. If they establish their conclusion, then 'God' refers to a being that exists, and 'God exists' is a belief that is objectively true. Third, they assume that the belief – or knowledge – that God exists is something that *could* be supported, or established, by reasoning. In other words, the existence of God can be deduced or inferred as the best explanation from premises that are more certain or plausible than God's existence. These assumptions are also shared by discussions of the problem of evil.

However, these are not assumptions that all philosophers of religion – or all people who believe in God – accept. We will discuss some alternative interpretations of what 'God exists' means in Religious language (next). And if you study philosophy of religion after A Level, you will probably find that there are yet more ways of understanding what we are talking about when we are talking about God.

> **?**
> Why is it important to identify and discuss the assumptions made by arguments for and against the existence of God?

Summary: arguments relating to the existence of God

In this section, we have looked at three forms of argument for the existence of God:

1. ontological arguments, from the concept of God alone;
2. arguments from design, from the order and regularity in the universe;
3. cosmological arguments, from the existence of things.

We have also discussed how the existence of evil raises a challenge to the existence of an omniscient, omnipotent, supremely good God. In our discussion, we have looked at the following questions and issues:

1. How do Anselm, Descartes, Malcolm and Plantinga try to prove the existence of God from the concept of God alone?
2. What are the differences between different forms of the ontological argument?
3. What does it mean to say that God is the greatest possible or conceivable being?

4. What does it mean to say that something exists or exists necessarily? Is existence or necessary existence a predicate?

5. Does the concept of possible worlds help us understand or establish the ontological argument?

6. Is the apparent purpose found in living creatures and the organisation of their parts evidence of design?

7. Does an analogy between human inventions and the natural world support the claim that there is a designer of the natural world?

8. What is the best explanation of the regularity that we find in the laws of nature?

9. If there is a designer of the natural world, is that designer God?

10. Must the universe have a first cause?

11. Is an actual infinity possible?

12. What are the differences between deductive and inductive forms of the cosmological argument?

13. Does anything that exists contingently need an explanation for its existence?

14. What assumptions do arguments for the existence of God make about religious belief and language?

In this section, we have discussed how the existence of evil raises a challenge to the existence of an omniscient, omnipotent, supremely good God. We have looked at the following issues and questions:

15. What is the logical problem of evil? How does it differ from the evidential problem of evil?

16. What is the difference between a theodicy and a defence?

17. What is the free will defence and does it solve the logical problem of evil?

18. Does the fact that we need to face evil in order to grow spiritually justify the amount and distribution of evil in the world?

III. Religious language

Because religious
language is based on
talk about God, I shall
use the phrases to
mean the same thing.

What are we doing when we are talking about God? Are we stating truths, facts, how things are, in a way that is similar to how science describes the world? One problem with thinking that talk about God makes statements about the world is that we cannot establish the truth of such claims via sense experience. Can we meaningfully talk about what is 'true' unless we can somehow establish that truth? Is religious language meaningful in some other way, e.g. expressing an attitude or commitment toward the world, rather than trying to describe it? Is talk about God meaningful at all? To discuss these questions, we'll need to think not just about religious language, but about what makes language meaningful in general.

Verificationism

AYER, *LANGUAGE, TRUTH AND LOGIC*, CHS 1, 6; AYER, *THE CENTRAL QUESTIONS OF PHILOSOPHY*, PP. 22-7

In the 1930s, a school of philosophy arose called logical positivism, concerned with the foundations of knowledge. It developed a criterion for when a statement is meaningful, called the principle of verifiability, also known as the verification principle. On A. J. Ayer's version, the verification principle says that a statement only has meaning if it is either analytic or empirically verifiable. He explains and defends the principle in *Language, Truth and Logic*, Ch. 1, and discusses it further in *The Central Questions of Philosophy*, pp. 22-7.

What it is for a statement to be analytic was discussed in ANALYTIC/SYNTHETIC (p. 97). A statement is empirically verifiable if empirical evidence would go towards establishing that the statement is true or false. For example, if I say 'The moon is made of green cheese', we can check this by scientific investigation. If I say 'The universe has 600 trillion planets', we can't check this by scientific investigation in practice, but we can do so *in principle*. We know how to show whether it is true or false, so it is 'verifiable' even though we can't actually verify it. Furthermore, we don't need to be able to *prove* that an empirical claim is true or false. For empirical verification, it is enough for empirical evidence to raise or reduce the probability that a statement is true.

The principle can be understood as a development of HUME'S 'FORK' (p. 99). However, while Hume's 'fork' provides an account of what we can *know*, the verification principle is an account of what statements have *meaning*. But because we cannot know what doesn't have meaning, the verification principle also places limits on what we can know. Like Hume's 'fork', it defends a form of KNOWLEDGE EMPIRICISM (p. 96), arguing that a priori propositions must be analytic or meaningless. On Ayer's view, philosophy doesn't give us knowledge of a reality that transcends the investigations of science or common sense. It is not a source of speculative or metaphysical truth.

So what can we say about the proposition 'God exists' and other claims about God? Despite the best attempts of the ONTOLOGICAL ARGUMENTS (p. 181), Ayer argues in Ch. 6, we cannot prove 'God exists' from a priori premises using deduction alone. So 'God exists' is not analytically true. On the other hand, if 'God exists' is an empirical claim, then it must be possible to imagine the conditions under which we would say that it was or was not a fact. But we cannot empirically test whether God exists or not. If a statement is an empirical hypothesis, it predicts that our experience will be different depending on whether it is true or false. The claim 'God exists' makes no predictions about our experience. So it is not empirically verifiable.

1. The verification principle: all meaningful claims are either analytic or empirically verifiable.
2. 'God exists' is not analytic.
3. 'God exists' is not empirically verifiable.
4. Therefore, 'God exists' is not meaningful.

Because most religious language depends on 'God exists' being meaningful, we can argue that most religious language is also meaningless.

> What is the verification principle?

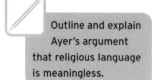

Outline and explain Ayer's argument that religious language is meaningless.

Some philosophers argue that religious language attempts to capture something of religious experience, although it is 'inexpressible' in literal terms. Ayer responds that whatever religious experiences reveal, they cannot be said to reveal any facts. Facts are the content of statements that purport to be intelligible and can be expressed literally. If talk of God is non-empirical, it is *literally* unintelligible, hence meaningless.

Objections

WIDENING EMPIRICAL VERIFICATION

We can question whether the idea of 'empirical verification' is understood too narrowly by Ayer. He assumes that for 'God exists' to be empirically verifiable, we have to know how to test the claim against sense experience. But we could argue that the meaning of 'God exists' is related to and secured by *making sense* of empirical experience, e.g. in using HYPOTHETICAL REASONING (p. 9). For example, we could use THE ARGUMENT FROM DESIGN (p. 200) to infer that God's existence is the best explanation for the nature of the universe. Or again, THE PROBLEM OF EVIL (p. 234) takes the existence and extent of suffering to be evidence against the existence of God. Both arguments treat 'God exists' as a meaningful, factual claim to which empirical evidence is relevant. However, we use philosophy, not science, to test the claim. What we mean by 'God exists' will be shown by these arguments.

HICK, 'THEOLOGY AND VERIFICATION'

Hick understands verification to involve removing rational doubt, ignorance or uncertainty about the truth of some proposition through experience. An empirically verifiable claim makes some prediction about how our experience would be under certain conditions, e.g. 'There is a table next door' can be verified by sight or touch, but it requires us to go next door. Hick agrees with Ayer that 'God exists' is not a claim that we verify through our current experience. The disagreement between theist and atheist is not about what to expect in life.

However, this isn't enough to show that religious language is meaningless. Hick develops the idea of 'eschatological verification', verification in the afterlife or at the end of time. In believing that God exists, the (traditional Christian) theist believes that there will be unambiguous experiences of God in life after death. The atheist denies this.

Does this show that 'God exists' is meaningful? First, it must be meaningful to speak of an afterlife. All empirically verifiable statements are conditional – they predict what we will experience under certain conditions of observation. However, for this to apply to the afterlife, the concept of personal existence after death must be logically possible. Second, we must be able to form some conception of what an experience of God could be. Hick argues that we already have *some* sense of this, since we are aware that our experience in this life is ambiguous – it doesn't establish or disprove God's existence. He suggests that an experience of our personal fulfilment and relation to God could serve as verification.

> Eschatology is the study (*-ology*) of the 'last things' (Greek *eskhatos*) – death, the final judgement, and the ultimate destiny of human beings.

> Outline and explain Hick's concept of eschatological verification, and his argument that it establishes the meaningfulness of religious language.

REJECTING THE VERIFICATION PRINCIPLE

The previous responses accept the verification principle in some amended form. But a more common response is to reject it. According to the verification principle, the principle itself is meaningless. The claim that 'a statement only has meaning if it is analytic or can be verified empirically' is not analytic and cannot be verified empirically. But if the principle of verification is meaningless, then what it claims cannot be true. So if the principle is true, it is meaningless, and so not true. Obviously, if it is false, it is false. Either way it is not true. Therefore, it does not give us any reason to believe that religious language is meaningless.

Ayer claims that the principle is intended as *a definition*, not an empirical hypothesis about meaning. In other words, it is intended to reflect and clarify our understanding of 'meaningful' uses of

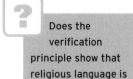

? Does the
verification
principle show that
religious language is
meaningless?

words. Ayer accepts that the principle isn't obviously an accurate criterion of 'literal meaning', but that is why he provides arguments in specific cases, such as religious language, which support it.

But in that case, the verification principle is only as convincing as the arguments that are intended to show that it is the right definition of 'meaningful'. If we do not find the arguments convincing, the principle provides no independent support.

Going further: verification and falsification

One response to the difficulties facing the verification principle is to replace it with a 'falsification' principle. A claim is falsifiable if it is logically incompatible with some (set of) empirical observations. We can suggest, then, that a claim is meaningful only if it rules out some possible experience. For example, 'There is a fork there' is incompatible with – rules out – the experience of reaching out and grasping nothing but thin air where we see the fork.

One apparent advantage of falsification is how it deals with generalisations. A claim such as 'All swans are white' threatens to be meaningless according to the verification principle, because no experience will prove it true – there might always be a swan out there somewhere which isn't white. However, it is easy to prove false – observing a single non-white (black) swan will do it!

However, this advantage is balanced by distinct disadvantages. Hick notes that there are particular claims that are easy to verify but impossible to falsify, such as 'There are three successive 7s in the decimal determination of π', 3.141592 …. As soon as we find three 7s in a row, we have verified the claim. But because the decimal determination of π is infinitely long, we can never show that it is false (if it is false), because there may always be three 7s together later in the series. Or again, as Ayer notes, existence claims are very difficult to falsify. 'There is a yeti' is easier to know how to prove true than false, since we can't search everywhere at the same time. So are claims about the future, e.g. 'The sea will one day encroach on

'Theology and
Verification', §2

*The Central Questions
of Philosophy*, p. 29

this land'. And so are probability claims. 'There is a one-in-six chance the rolled die will show a six' is not falsified by 20 sixes in a row, since the probability of one-in-six may be restored over a larger number of throws. And this is always true, no matter how many times you roll the die.

So a falsification principle that requires a meaningful statement to entail some decisive, refuting empirical experience is unacceptable. Many meaningful statements do not clearly entail an observation with which they are logically incompatible. If, on the other hand, we weaken falsification to talk about evidence which would 'count against' the truth of some claim, then this is not different from Ayer's version of the verification principle. As explained above, for a statement to be 'verifiable', we know what experiences will support *or reduce* the probability of a claim. It is already part of Ayer's theory that we need to know what empirical experiences would lead us to reject a claim as well as what experiences support it.

> **?**
>
> Does the falsification principle for meaning improve on the verification principle?

Cognitivist and non-cognitivist accounts of religious language

A cognitivist account of religious language argues that religious claims aim to describe how the world is, and so can be true or false. Religious claims express beliefs that such-and-such is the case. To believe that God exists is to believe that 'God exists' is true. The verification principle is a cognitivist view of language generally. It says that language is only meaningful if it is cognitive.

However, a number of philosophers have offered non-cognitivist accounts of religious language. A non-cognitivist account argues that religious claims do not try to describe the world and cannot be true or false, at least in the sense of stating facts. They express an attitude toward the world, a way of understanding or relating to the world, rather than a belief that is true or false. (We may still want to talk of religious 'beliefs' but this is better understood as 'faith' or 'belief in God' than as 'belief that God exists'.) Non-cognitivist theories will need to find some alternative criterion for how religious language is meaningful, one that does not depend on stating factual claims.

> **Outline and explain three differences between cognitive and non-cognitive accounts of religious language.**

FLEW, HARE AND MITCHELL, 'THEOLOGY AND FALSIFICATION'

In a debate published in the journal *University*, Anthony Flew, Richard Hare and Basil Mitchell discussed the meaning of religious language.

Flew's challenge

Flew opened the debate with a story from John Wisdom's article 'Gods'. Two explorers come across a clearing in the jungle in which both flowers and weeds grow. One claims that the clearing is the work of a gardener; the other disagrees. They try to detect the gardener by various means – first keeping watch, then an electric fence, then dogs – but never discover him or her. At each stage, the 'believer', however, rejects the claim that their failure is evidence that the gardener doesn't exist, saying first that the gardener must be invisible, then intangible, then leaves no scent and makes no sound. The 'sceptic' finally asks how the claim that there is such a gardener differs from the claim that the gardener is imaginary or doesn't exist at all.

Flew's point is that for a claim to be meaningful, for it to be asserting something, there must be something it is denying. In other words, there must be some way of establishing that it is false, something that leads us to withdraw the claim. If we know what the claim rules out, we can understand what the claim means. But if there is nothing it rules out, then the claim is not a genuine attempt to say something true. For example, the theory of evolution by natural selection rules out aliens coming to Earth and demonstrating that they had planted 'fossils' (which they had made) for us to find. If this happened, we would give up the theory of evolution.

> **Flew is arguing that empirical assertions must be cognitive to be meaningful. He doesn't present a *general* theory of meaning.**

Likewise, if 'God exists' is a real claim, then there should be some possible experience that would lead us to accept that it is false. Something should be able to 'count against it', e.g. the existence of evil. If you are not prepared to accept that anything could show that God doesn't exist, then saying 'God exists' states nothing at all. Flew objects that many religious believers refuse to accept that anything could show that God doesn't exist. Instead, they keep *qualifying* what it means to think that 'God exists'. For example, they might argue that the existence of evil only shows that we don't understand God's plans.

See THE PROBLEM OF EVIL, p. 234.

Outline and explain Flew's argument that religious language loses its meaning if we cannot falsify religious claims.

Hare's 'bliks'

Hare rejects Flew's form of cognitivism. Religious beliefs are not like assertions that can be shown to be true or false. Instead, they are part of someone's attitude toward or view of the world (or some aspect of it), which Hare calls a 'blik'. For example, someone may be paranoid that university lecturers want to murder him. He doesn't count anything as evidence against this view (this is a normal feature of delusions). But the difference between his view and the view of the rest of us is meaningful, important and makes a difference to how we live. Another example is someone who trusts the properties of steel or the continued ability of a road to support cars v. someone who doesn't; or someone who thinks everything happens by chance v. someone who believes in laws of nature. A disagreement in bliks can't be decided by empirical experience, and two people who disagree may not assert anything different about what to expect from experience. Yet the disagreement is meaningful. To hold that God exists is a blik, as is the view that God does not exist.

It is unclear whether Hare thinks religious language is cognitive or not. On the one hand, there is a truth of the matter (whatever one believes) whether university lecturers are trying to kill you or not or whether everything happens by chance or not. So it seems bliks can be true or false, which suggests that they are cognitive. On the other hand, because bliks can't be

What, according to Hare, is a 'blik'?

falsified, Hare claims that they work more like attitudes or commitments than beliefs. This would suggest that they are non-cognitive. But notice that *any* empirical claim which would normally be held as a (cognitive) belief (about the motives of university lecturers, the properties of steel, the explanations of science) could be held as a (non-cognitive) blik. The difference is how the person thinks about it.

When someone holds a blik about some claim, while the rest of us just hold falsifiable beliefs, we tend to think that the person is *irrational* in some way. Does Hare's analysis entail that religious believers are irrational? If not, why not? Hare doesn't say. As Flew objects, Hare's theory that religious belief is a blik is very unorthodox and fails to make sense of what religious believers actually say. If religious claims aren't assertions, then a claim such as 'You ought to do it because it is God's will' becomes 'You ought to do it' (since 'it is God's will' is not an assertion, but the expression of a blik). But this is not what religious believers mean.

Is religious belief a blik?

Mitchell's response

Mitchell accepts Flew's cognitivism and his argument that for an empirical claim to be meaningful, we must allow something to count against it. But he disagrees with Flew's claim that an assertion is only meaningful if we are willing to *withdraw* it in light of certain experiences. Suppose there is a war in which someone's country has been occupied, and he joins the resistance movement. One day, this partisan meets a stranger who tells him that he is the leader of the resistance. The partisan is very impressed by the stranger and trusts him deeply. However, the stranger later acts in ambiguous ways, sometimes seeming to help the resistance and other times apparently helping the enemy. But the partisan, because he trusts the stranger, continues to believe that the stranger is on the side of the resistance, and so must have some good reason for his ambiguous behaviour.

If the partisan refused to count the ambiguous actions of the stranger as *evidence* against the claim that the stranger is on the side of the resistance (as in the case of Hare's bliks), this would be merely irrational. Such a view would empty religious language of its meaning. But on the other hand, the partisan is not rationally required to simply relinquish his view. His trust sustains his belief in the stranger, and we cannot say, in the abstract, just how much evidence against his belief is needed before his belief becomes irrational.

Likewise, religious language makes assertions, but these claims are not simply provisional hypotheses, to be discarded in the face of contrary experiences. They involve a certain commitment as well. A claim can be meaningful without us being able to say what experiences would lead us to relinquish it, as long as we recognise that experiences can count against it.

Flew accepts Mitchell's response. However, he argues, in essence, that THE LOGICAL PROBLEM OF EVIL (p. 236) is insoluble. We are unable to find any justification of evil that is compatible with an omniscient, omnipotent, supremely good God, and the only way out for religious believers is to qualify what they mean by God or his purpose for us. We can object, however, that this is now no longer an argument about whether religious claims are meaningful, but about whether they are either true or coherent.

> Outline and explain Mitchell's theory of religious language.

> If no experience could falsify the claim 'God exists', does this claim state anything meaningful?

Non-cognitivism

People don't normally acquire religious beliefs by argument or testing evidence. Instead, they come to an understanding of the world that is expressed in values and a way of living. When someone converts to a religion, what changes isn't so much intellectual beliefs, but their *will*, what they value and how they choose to live. We can argue that this supports non-cognitivism. 'God exists' is not a statement of fact, but has meaning as an expression of a non-cognitive attitude or commitment. These attitudes – which include attitudes towards other people, nature, oneself and human history

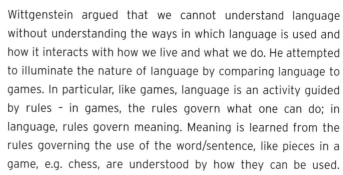

Explain the claim that religious language expresses an attitude.

– present the world in a certain light and support commitments to act in certain ways and to mature as a spiritual being.

How does language have meaning if it doesn't state facts? Probably the most influential theory of language that non-cognitivism appeals to is that of Ludwig Wittgenstein.

Going further: Wittgenstein on religious language

Wittgenstein, *Philosophical Investigations*

Wittgenstein argued that we cannot understand language without understanding the ways in which language is used and how it interacts with how we live and what we do. He attempted to illuminate the nature of language by comparing language to games. In particular, like games, language is an activity guided by rules – in games, the rules govern what one can do; in language, rules govern meaning. Meaning is learned from the rules governing the use of the word/sentence, like pieces in a game, e.g. chess, are understood by how they can be used.

Meaning, then, is often a matter of how words are *used*. Appreciating this requires a distinction between *surface grammar* and *depth grammar*: words or sentences in one context describing *objects* or an *event* may be similar on the surface to ones that in another context do nothing of the sort, e.g. 'The bus passes the bus stop', 'The peace of the Lord passes under-standing'. To understand a particular 'piece' of language, one must look at how the language is used, as meaning is not given by the form of words alone.

When looking at how words are used, we need to look at the 'language game' – that bit of language and the rules it follows – which gives the words their meaning. (Wittgenstein lists as examples of language games asking, thanking, cursing, praying, greeting and so on.)

The idea of 'language games' emphasises the foundation of language in activity. Wittgenstein says that a language game is the speaking part of a 'form of life'. A form of life is far broader than any specific language game; it is the foundation out of

Explain Wittgenstein's claim that the meaning of a word is its use.

which language games grow, the collection of cultural practices which embed language games. The very foundation is biology, and Wittgenstein often emphasises how our natural reactions form the basis for language games. (Think of talking about pain or colour or even responses to music.) But the biology is always taken up in a particular culture, and what is 'natural' is often only natural within a particular way of living as a human being. 'Human nature' involves both biology and culture.

So religious language must be understood as part of a religious life. Religious language contains the many different language games of praise and worship, prayer, miracles and so on; but it can also be understood as forming a game in its own right, governed by particular rules – those displayed in theanalysis of its depth grammar. Wittgenstein argued that religious language has a depth grammar quite distinct from its surface grammar. Its surface grammar can look empirical, as though, like science, religious language is talking about things and events. This is misleading.

A central part of Wittgenstein's analysis is that 'God exists' is not a statement of fact. It is not about a *thing*, an *object* that exists as part of the world like natural objects do. It is not a claim about an entity at all. Of course, if it is not an empirical statement, then believing it is not an empirical belief: 'a religious belief could only be something like a passionate commitment to a system of reference. Hence, although it's a *belief*, it's really a way of living, or a way of assessing life. It's passionately seizing hold of *this* interpretation'. He argued that if we look at how the statement is *used*, what it *expresses* for people who believe it, we see that it is used not as a description, but to express a form of commitment.

Wittgenstein, *Culture and Value*, 64

This can be illustrated by talk of the Last Judgement. This is not a hypothesis about a possible future event; if it was, it would be utterly bizarre. (What's the evidence? How is such a belief formed?) The Last Judgement is a 'picture', an understanding of life by which the believer is guided through life. Religious language expresses an emotional attitude and understanding

Outline and explain Wittgenstein's account of religious language.

of life and a commitment to living life according to that understanding. To understand religious language is to understand the place of certain statements in the life of the believer and religious community. And the nature of religious belief shows that these statements are not factual.

So Wittgenstein agrees with Ayer that religious language is not empirical. But Wittgenstein disagrees with Ayer's inference that religious language is not meaningful, because he rejects the verification principle in favour of a theory of meaning as use.

Discussion

An important implication of non-cognitivist views of religious language is that we can't criticise or support religious beliefs by using *evidence*. Religious beliefs cannot be criticised on the grounds that they are *not true* or highly *improbable*, because this presupposes that religious language makes factual claims, and it does not. So, for example, both THE ARGUMENT FROM DESIGN (p. 200) and THE PROBLEM OF EVIL (p. 234) are irrelevant as attempts to prove or disprove the existence of God. This, we can object, cuts religious belief off from reason too severely.

A non-cognitivist can respond that, as part of human life, religious belief still needs to *make sense* of our experiences. The problem of evil could be relevant here. Not any set of attitudes and commitments makes sense in light of our experience. The difficulty now, however, is to know what it is for a non-cognitive attitude to 'make sense', given that it doesn't make any claims about what is true and what is not. ·

A second objection, already made against HARE'S 'BLIKS' (p. 261), is that non-cognitivism conflicts with how many believers think of God and their faith. Wittgenstein's account looks like a *reinterpretation* of religious belief, not an analysis of it. It also makes *what you believe* much less important, as religious faith is about how we live. Yet many religious believers who act in similar ways and hold similar values argue that there is something distinctive and important about the different beliefs they hold. Furthermore, within the history of any religion, there have been heated arguments about how to interpret a particular doctrine (e.g. in Christianity, the Incarnation), when it is very difficult to see how the different interpretations could make any impact on different ways of living. All this suggests that religious language is intended to be true, i.e. fact-stating, and not just expressive.

We can argue that Wittgenstein was right to point to the expressive use of religious language. But he was wrong to think that because religious beliefs express attitudes, they cannot *also* be cognitive. There is no reason to think that they cannot be *both*, as Mitchell's theory suggests. After all, religious believers *do* think they are saying something factual when they say 'God exists'. It has this use.

> Can the view that religious language is non-cognitive make sense of religious belief?

> Is religious language meaningful? If so, how? If not, why not?

Key points: religious language

- The verification principle claims that only statements that are analytic or empirically verifiable are meaningful. Empirical verification does not require proof, but being able, in principle, to provide evidence that makes an empirical claim more or less probable.
- Ayer argues that 'God exists' is neither analytic nor empirically verifiable, and is therefore meaningless.
- We can object that religious language takes its meaning from attempting to make sense of experience in general, even though it cannot be directly verified by sense experience.
- Hick argues that eschatological verification – provided by experiences after death – are relevant to showing whether God exists. Therefore, religious language is not meaningless.
- We can object that the verification principle is self-defeating: it is neither analytically true nor empirically verifiable. By its own standard, it is meaningless. It therefore cannot show that religious language is meaningless. Ayer argues it is a definition. But it will only be convincing as a definition if his arguments for its implications are convincing.
- The falsification principle claims that a statement is meaningful only if it is logically incompatible with some empirical experience. This faces difficulties, as some meaningful claims, such as existence and probability claims, cannot be falsified.

- A cognitivist account of religious language argues that religious claims describe how the world is, can be true or false, and express factual beliefs.
- A non-cognitivist account of religious language argues that religious claims do not describe the world, cannot be true or false, and express an attitude toward the world.
- Flew argues that for a claim to be meaningful, it must rule out some possible experience. 'God exists' is meaningless because religious believers do not accept any experience shows that they are mistaken.
- Hare argues that religious beliefs are part of a 'blik', an attitude to or view of the world that is not held or withdrawn on the basis of empirical experience. Disagreements in bliks are, nevertheless, meaningful.
- We can object that Hare's analysis cannot help us distinguish between rational and irrational bliks and fails to make sense of how religious believers actually use religious language.
- Mitchell argues that religious language is cognitive, but religious belief also involves commitment. Therefore, experiences can count against religious claims without the believer withdrawing the claim.
- Wittgenstein argues that to understand what a word means, we must understand its use in the particular 'language game' in which it is employed. The surface grammar of sentences can be very different from their depth grammar. The foundations of language lie in our practices.
- He argues that religious belief is part of a distinctive language game. The depth grammar of religious language shows that God is not a thing that exists. Instead, talk of God is used to express a commitment to a particular way of living and to a framework for understanding and guiding life.
- We can object that if religious language is not cognitive, religious beliefs can't be criticised or supported by reasoning.
- We may also object that many religious believers think religious language is partly cognitive. Religious language can both express attitudes and describe the world.

Summary: religious language

In this section, we have looked at the meaning of religious language, and looked at challenges to the view that it is meaningful at all. In our discussion and evaluation of these claims, we have looked at the following questions:

1. What is the verification principle? Does it show that 'God exists' is a meaningless statement?
2. What is the difference between a cognitivist and non-cognitivist account of religious language?
3. Must a religious claim, such as 'God exists', rule out certain possible experiences in order to be meaningful?
4. Does religious language express an attitude toward life?

4   PREPARING FOR THE EXAM

To get good exam results, you need to have a good sense of what the exam will be like and what the examiners are looking for, and to revise in a way that will help you prepare to answer the questions well. This probably sounds obvious, but in fact, many students do not think about the exam itself, only about what questions might come up. There is a big difference. This chapter will provide you with some guidance on how to approach your exams in a way that will help get you the best results you can.

It is divided into four sections: the examination, understanding the question, revision, and exam technique. In the last two sections, I highlight revision points and exam tips. These are collected together at the end of the chapter.

The examination

The structure of the exam

There is one exam, lasting three hours and covering the whole AS. It has two sections: Section A Epistemology and Section B Philosophy of Religion. All the questions are compulsory – there is no choice in what you can answer.

Each section has three types of question. First, there are questions that ask you to define or explain an important philosophical idea. On the specimen exam papers, these take the form of one 2-mark and one 5-mark question, but they may take a different form in the future (always adding up to 7 marks). Second, there are two 9-mark questions that ask you to explain a more complex theory or argument. Third, there is one 15-mark open-ended essay question that asks you to evaluate a philosophical claim.

Here are the questions from the specimen exam paper:

Section A Epistemology
1. What is empiricism? (2 marks)
2. Explain why, for Locke, extension is a primary quality. (5 marks)
3. Outline and explain the key differences between *idealism* and *indirect realism*. (9 marks)
4. Outline and explain the tripartite view of knowledge ('Justified True Belief'). (9 marks)
5. Are there innate ideas? (15 marks)

Section B Philosophy of Religion
1. In his ontological argument, how does Anselm define God? (2 marks)
2. Outline the problem of evil. (5 marks)
3. Outline the *Euthyphro* dilemma. (9 marks)
4. Outline Aquinas' First Way (the argument from motion). (9 marks)
5. Is religious language meaningless? (15 marks)

If you've been doing the questions in the margin of this textbook, these kinds of questions should be very familiar.

Assessment objectives

The examiners mark your answers according to two principles, known as 'Assessment Objectives' (AOs). They are:

AO1: Demonstrate understanding of the core concepts and methods of philosophy.
AO2: Analyse and evaluate philosophical argument to form reasoned judgements.

So AO1 requires you to understand how philosophers have argued, and AO2 requires you to be able to argue – to construct and evaluate arguments – yourself. Except for the 15-mark questions, all the marks available are for AO1. For the 15-mark questions, 7 marks are for AO1 and 8 marks are for AO2. How well you write also makes a contribution, so it is important to write clearly and grammatically, so that the examiner can understand what you mean. Don't try to impress using big words or long sentences – it just gets in the way of clarity and precision.

Understanding the question: giving the examiners what they are looking for

More information on this is available in the Mark Schemes that the AQA publish online.

The key to doing well in an exam is understanding the question. I don't just mean understanding the *topic* of the question, like 'idealism' or 'religious language'. Of course, this is very important. But you also need to understand what the question is asking you to *do*. Each type of question tests different kinds of philosophical knowledge and skill.

Short-answer questions

The first questions of each section test the *accuracy* and *precision* of your understanding.

Taken from Anselm, *Proslogium*, Chs 2-4, p. 182.

One- or 2-mark questions ask you to define a concept. The examiners want you to be *concise*. State the definition as clearly and precisely as you can and then move on. Don't waffle or talk around the concept. So my answer to 'In his ontological argument, how does Anselm define God?' is this:

> Anselm defines God as a being greater than which cannot be conceived.

Five-mark questions ask you to outline and/or explain an important philosophical concept or claim. Explaining involves not just describing the idea, but giving a sense of the reasoning or thought behind it. Say enough to give a full explanation, but again, stay concise and don't waffle. So, my answer to 'Explain why, for Locke, extension is a primary quality' is this:

Taken from THE DISTINCTION BETWEEN PRIMARY AND SECONDARY QUALITIES, p. 44.

> For Locke, the primary qualities of a physical object are qualities that are 'utterly inseparable' from the object, whatever changes it goes through, even if it is divided into smaller and smaller pieces. The object has these properties 'in and of itself'. Extension is a primary quality, according to Locke, because physical objects must always have *some* extension or other.

I might explain this further by saying

> This is because physical objects exist in space, and so they must take up a certain amount of space. The amount of space they take up in any dimension is their extension.

It is important not only to state the essential claims but to *order* them and *link* them logically. Without these links ('so', 'because', 'therefore'), you haven't got an explanation.

It's fine to use numbered arguments, as I have throughout this book. For example, my answer to 'Outline the problem of evil' is this:

Taken from AN OUTLINE OF THE PROBLEM, p. 234.

> The problem of evil argues that the existence of evil causes difficulties for believing in an omniscient, omnipotent, supremely good God.

1. If God is supremely good, then he has the desire to eliminate evil.
2. If God is omnipotent, then he is able to eliminate evil.
3. If God is omniscient, then he knows that evil exists and knows how to eliminate it.
4. Therefore, if God exists, and is supremely good, omnipotent and omniscient, then evil does not exist.
5. Evil exists.
6. Therefore, a supremely good, omnipotent and omniscient God does not exist.

It's only a 5-mark question, so I wouldn't go into the distinction between the logical and evidential problems, or if I did, it would be very brief:

> The logical problem of evil claims that the mere existence of evil is logically incompatible with the existence of God. The evidential problem of evil claims that the amount and distribution of evil that exists is good evidence that God does not exist.

Nine-mark questions

Nine-mark questions generally ask you to explain a more complex argument or theory. The marks are still all for AO1, your understanding of the argument or theory, so you should not *evaluate* it. This is very important, because any time spent on evaluation is simply wasted – no marks are available. If you are asked to explain a theory, you should not discuss whether it is convincing or true. If you are asked to explain an argument, this could be an argument supporting a claim or an objection to it. The argument that you are explaining is *itself* an evaluation (a reason to believe or reject a claim). You need to explain the argument or objection and how it works as an argument or objection – but you should not discuss whether it is a *good* argument or objection.

As with the 5-mark questions, the examiners are looking for clarity, precision, and an *explanation* that sets out the central claims in a way that demonstrates the logical links between them. The answer needs to work as a single 'whole', rather than a number of disconnected 'bits'. In addition, you will need to stay focused and relevant and use technical philosophical language appropriately (i.e. with clarity, precision and only when it is needed). So my answer to 'Outline and explain the tripartite view of knowledge ("Justified True Belief")' is this:

> The tripartite view of knowledge claims that knowledge is justified, true belief. It claims that if you know some proposition, *p*, then

On the difference between understanding and evaluation, see Understanding arguments (p. 10), Evaluating arguments (p. 11), and Evaluating claims (p. 12).

Taken from The tripartite definition of knowledge, p. 75.

1. the proposition *p* is true;
2. you believe that *p*;
3. your belief that *p* is justified.

And if you have a justified true belief that *p*, then you know that *p*.

The tripartite definition aims to provide a complete analysis of the concept of propositional knowledge. Its three conditions, taken together, are intended to be 'equivalent' to knowledge. The conditions are 'necessary and sufficient conditions' for knowledge that *p*. First, it says that *if* all the three conditions are satisfied, then you know that *p*. You don't need anything else for knowledge; the three conditions, together, are *sufficient*. Second, it says that *if* you know that *p*, then you have a justified true belief that *p*. There is no other way to know that *p*, no other analysis of knowledge. So, it claims, each of the three conditions is *necessary*.

First, you cannot know a proposition that is false. A false belief is not knowledge, but only a belief. Second, in order to know a proposition you must believe it. Third, a true belief is not knowledge if it is simply likely or believed without reason of evidence. Only a justified true belief is knowledge.

The view claims that because justified true belief is both necessary and sufficient for knowledge, knowledge and justified true belief *are the same thing*.

Fifteen-mark questions

When you are answering a short-answer question or 9-mark questions, what you need to do is straightforward. You don't need to make any choices about *what* concepts or arguments to talk about, since that is specified by the question. By contrast, 15-mark questions are much more open-ended. You are asked to evaluate a claim. To do this, you will need to construct and evaluate arguments for and against the claim. Because there are marks available for AO2, if you do not evaluate the philosophical claims, theories and arguments that

See Evaluating arguments and Evaluating claims, pp. 11–12.

you discuss, then you cannot get a good mark for the question, no matter how clear and accurate you are in explaining them.

In addition to evaluating individual claims and arguments, your answer as a whole needs to work as one long argument. Arguments have a clear conclusion – you need to decide from the very beginning what your conclusion will be. This should never be simply 'there are points against and points in favour'. You need to *weigh up* the pros and cons – this is what evaluation is. For 'Is religious language meaningless?', your conclusion could be:

1. 'yes', e.g. you defend VERIFICATIONISM (p. 255);
2. 'no', e.g. you defend MITCHELL'S RESPONSE (p. 263) or WITTGENSTEIN ON RELIGIOUS LANGUAGE (p. 264);
3. something conditional, 'yes/no if …', e.g. you defend Flew's response to Mitchell;
4. something sceptical, 'we cannot know because …' (for this particular question, the last option is quite hard to defend!).

With your conclusion in mind, you need to select which arguments and theories you will discuss. Make sure that you look at arguments both for and against your conclusion. The examiners are more interested in the *quality* of what you write than the quantity. Three points are relevant here:

1. Don't aim for a comprehensive discussion of the question, covering all the angles. Perhaps just discuss two arguments – ones that you think are really strong or important – but discuss them with depth and rigour. One good discussion is worth more than many weak or superficial points.
2. The examiners don't expect you to try to provide a 'balanced' account. They are testing your skill at arguing. So your answer can take the form of a very strong argument in favour of your conclusion and then strong replies to objections that can be raised.
3. To make your answer coherent, what you argue at each point in the answer should make some contribution to your conclusion. It fits into a logical structure.

There is no single right way to do all this (which is one reason I don't give a sample answer here). So you will need to plan your approach and answer to the question carefully. How to do this, and much more on answering essay questions, was discussed in WRITING PHILOSOPHY (p. 17). Once again, it's fine to use numbered arguments. It's also fine to use bullet points, particularly if you are running out of time.

Revision: it's more than memory

There are lots of memory tricks for learning information for exams. This section isn't about those. Revision isn't just about learning information, but also about learning how to use that information well in the exam. If you've been answering the questions throughout this book, then you have been putting into practice the advice I give below.

    In revising for the exam, you need to bear in mind the structure of the exam and the Assessment Objectives. First, the five questions in each section are all compulsory, and cover different areas of the syllabus, so you'll need to revise the whole syllabus. Second, thinking about the 15-mark questions, structure your revision around the central questions or topics that the syllabus covers. In Epistemology, these are perception, knowledge, rationalism v. empiricism on knowledge, and the debate over innate ideas. In Philosophy of Religion, they are the concept of God, the three arguments for the existence of God, the problem of evil and religious language.

See THE EXAMINATION, p. 270.

    AO1 tests your understanding of central concepts and claims in these areas and how arguments are constructed for or against claims. We can break this down further. For the short-answer questions,

> R1: Learn the concepts and definitions that are central to the philosophical theories studied.

The glossary (p. 287) can help with this. For the 5- and 9-mark questions,

R2: Learn who said what. What are the most important claims they made? What arguments did they use to defend their claims?

However, AO1 tests your *understanding*, not just your knowledge, of these claims and arguments. So you will need to show how the arguments are supposed to work. What are the premises and conclusion, and how is the conclusion supposed to follow from the premises?

R3: Spend time identifying the main claims and arguments involved in each issue you have studied, putting arguments in your own words, stating clearly what the conclusion is and what the premises are. Explain how the reasoning is supposed to work.

This is difficult, because philosophical ideas and arguments are abstract and complicated, so it can be hard to know just what they mean. But the examiners also want precision. So it is worth thinking further about whatever you find hardest to understand.

R4: Revise those concepts, claims and arguments that are hard to understand. Try to identify the differences between different interpretations. Which interpretation is best and why?

The exam questions do not explicitly ask for examples, but examples can prove very helpful when explaining a claim, objection or theory. If you are going to use examples, you want them to be good – clear, relevant, and supportive of the point you want to make. You can either remember good examples you have read, or create your own. In either case, you should know precisely what point the example is making. An irrelevant example demonstrates that you don't really know what you are talking about.

R5: Prepare examples beforehand, rather than try to invent them in the exam. They must be short and they must make the right point – so try them out on your friends and teachers first.

What about AO2? How do you revise evaluation? Fifteen-mark questions test you on how well you build an argument, deal with objections, and come to a supported conclusion. The best way to prepare for it is to spend time *thinking* about the arguments and issues. You might know and even understand Hume's arguments against rationalism, but you may never have stopped to really work out whether you think they are any good. Get involved!

So think about the different kinds of objection that can be raised to claims and arguments. Relate a particular argument to other arguments and viewpoints on the issue, and reflect on whether the objections to an argument undermine it. Work through the arguments so that you understand for yourself the pros and cons of each viewpoint.

See EVALUATING ARGUMENTS and EVALUATING CLAIMS, pp. 11-12.

R6: Think reflectively about the arguments and issues. Practise arguing for and against a particular view. Think about the place and importance of the arguments for the issue as a whole.

Your answer needs to work as an argument itself, a coherent piece of reasoning. This means that what you write should also take the form of premises and conclusion. The premises will be your judgements as you go along, in response to this view or that objection. These judgements need to add up to a conclusion. You shouldn't end your essay with a totally different point of view than your evaluations in the essay support. In other words, do the judgements you reach reflect the arguments you have presented?

R7: Think about how your judgements on the various arguments you have studied add up. Do they lead to one conclusion, one point of view being right? Or do you think arguments for and against one position are closely balanced?

These first seven revision points relate to taking in and understanding information. There are two more points that will help you organise the information, learn it better, and prepare you for answering exam questions. This is especially important in relation to the 15-mark questions.

Fifteen-mark questions are open-ended, and so you will need to choose to discuss what is *relevant* to the question being asked. Knowing what is relevant is a special kind of knowledge, which involves thinking carefully about what you know about the theories in relation to the question asked. A good way of organising your information is to create answer outlines or web-diagrams for particular issues.

For example, you could create an outline or web-diagram for innate knowledge. Think about the essential points, and organise them, perhaps like this:

1. What is innate knowledge? Is there more than one interpretation?
2. Who argued against innate knowledge? What are the main arguments?
3. Who argued for innate knowledge? What knowledge did they say was innate? What arguments did they use?
4. What are the main arguments for and against the claim that there is innate knowledge?
5. What is your conclusion on the issue, and why?

With an outline structured like this, you should be able to answer any question that comes up on innate knowledge.

R8: Create structured outlines or web-diagrams for particular issues. Try to cover all the main points.

Finally, once you've organised your notes into an outline or web-diagram, time yourself writing exam answers. Start by using your outline, relying on your memory to fill in the details. Then practise by memorising the outline as well, and doing it as though it were an actual exam. You might be surprised at how quickly the time goes by. You'll find that you need to be very focused – but this is what the examiners are looking for, answers that are thoughtful but to the point.

R9: Practise writing timed answers. Use your notes at first, but then practise without them.

Exam technique: getting the best result you can

If you've understood the exam structure, and know what to expect, the exam will seem less daunting. You'll have a good idea about how to proceed, and a sense of how the questions are testing different aspects of your knowledge. This section gives you some tips on how to approach the questions when you are actually in the exam.

Exams are very exciting, whether in a good way or a bad way! It can be helpful, therefore, to take your time at the beginning, not to rush into your answers, but to plan your way. The tips I give below are roughly in the order that you might apply them when taking the exam.

First, how long should you spend on each part? The marks give a rough guide. There are 80 marks available, 40 for Section A and 40 for Section B. You have 3 hours or 180 minutes. That's a little over 2 minutes for each mark. However, this isn't exact – the answer for each 2-mark question will probably take less than 4 minutes, while you should probably leave more than 30 minutes for each 15-mark question, especially because these answers require more planning. And because the exam covers five topics, you'll probably find that you know the answer to some of the questions better than others. Give yourself a little extra time for the questions you find difficult. You don't need to answer the questions in the order in which they are set. You might want to answer the ones you are confident about first, to get the best marks you can, and come back to the others later on. Don't lose marks on the questions that you can do, by not giving yourself enough time to answer them well.

> E1. The number of marks available for each part is a rough guide to how long you spend on it. But allow a little extra time for the 15-mark questions and parts you find difficult. Choose what order to answer the questions in.

Before you start to write your answer to any part, read the question again very closely. There are two things to look out for. First, notice what the question is asking you to do. Remember that you need to display your *understanding*, not just your knowledge, of the philosophical issues. So you'll need to explain claims and arguments, not just state them. Second, notice the *precise* phrasing of the question. For example, the sample question 'Outline and explain the key differences between *idealism* and *indirect realism*' asks you to explain the *differences* not the similarities between these theories. Many students have a tendency to notice only what the question is about, e.g. empiricism or religious language. They don't notice the rest of the words in the question. But the question is never 'So tell me everything you know about *x*'! Make sure your conclusion – and your discussion – answers the actual question set.

See Understanding the question, p. 272.

> E2. Before starting your answer, read the question again very closely. Take note of every word to make sure you answer the actual question set. Remember to explain, and not just state, claims and arguments.

With 15-mark questions, and for many 9-mark questions as well, before you start writing, it is worth organising your thoughts first.

What are you going to say, in what order? Whether you are explaining or evaluating arguments, you need to present ideas in a logical order. Especially for 15-mark answers, if you've memorised an outline or a web-diagram, quickly write it out at the beginning so that you note down all the points. It is very easy to forget something or go off on a tangent once you are stuck into the arguments. Having an outline or web-diagram to work from will help you keep your answer relevant and structured. However, you might discover, as you develop your answer, that parts of the outline or diagram are irrelevant or just don't fit. Don't worry – the outline is only there as a guide. It will also remind you how much you still want to cover, so it can help you pace yourself better. If you do run out of time, you can indicate to the examiners that they should look at your plan – they will give marks for it.

> E3. For longer answers, before you start writing, it can be worth writing out your outline or web-diagram first. This can help remind you of the key points you want to make, and the order in which you want to make them.

Because philosophy is about the logical relationship of ideas, there are a number of rules of thumb about presentation. Here are four important ones.

> E4. Four rules of thumb:
>
> a. Explain 'technical terms', like 'tripartite view' or 'the ontological argument', unless it is clear from the context that you know what they mean.
> b. Keep related ideas together. If you have a thought later on, add a footnote indicating where in the answer you want it to be read.
> c. Explain a theory before evaluating it.
> d. Don't state the conclusion to an argument before you've discussed the argument, especially if you are going to present objections to that conclusion. You can state what the argument hopes to show, but don't state it *as* a conclusion.

If you use examples, you need to keep them short and relevant, and explain why they support your argument. An example is an illustration, not an argument in itself.

> E5. Keep your examples short and make sure they support the point you want to make. Always explain how they support your point.

For 15-mark questions, it is worth noting that evaluation is more than just presenting objections and responses side-by-side. Get the objections and the theory to 'talk' to each other, and come to some conclusion about which side is stronger.

> E6. For 15-mark questions, make sure your discussion is not just reporting a sequence of points of view, but presents objections and replies, weighs up the arguments, and reaches a particular conclusion.

Finally, it is very easy to forget something, or say it in an unclear way. Leave time to check your answer at the end. You might find you can add a sentence here or there to connect two ideas together more clearly, or that some phrase is imprecise. These little things can make a big difference to the mark.

> E7. Leave time to check your answer at the end. You may want to add a helpful sentence here and there.

Revision tips

R1.   Learn the concepts and definitions that are central to the philosophical theories studied.

R2.   Learn who said what. What are the most important claims they made? What arguments did they use to defend their claims?

R3. Spend time identifying the main claims and arguments involved in each issue you have studied, putting arguments in your own words, stating clearly what the conclusion is and what the premises are. Explain how the reasoning is supposed to work.

R4. Revise those concepts, claims and arguments that are hard to understand. Try to identify the differences between different interpretations. Which interpretation is best and why?

R5. Prepare examples beforehand, rather than try to invent them in the exam. They must be short and they must make the right point – so try them out on your friends and teachers first.

R6. Think reflectively about the arguments and issues. Practise arguing for and against a particular view. Think about the place and importance of the arguments for the issue as a whole.

R7. Think about how your judgements on the various arguments you have studied add up. Do they lead to one conclusion, one point of view being right? Or do you think arguments for and against one position are closely balanced?

R8. Create structured outlines or web-diagrams for particular issues. Try to cover all the main points.

R9. Practise writing timed answers. Use your notes at first, but then practise without them.

Exam tips

E1. The number of marks available for each part is a rough guide to how long you spend on it. But allow a little extra time for the 15-mark questions and parts you find difficult. Choose what order to answer the questions in.

E2. Before starting your answer, read the question again very closely. Take note of every word to make sure you answer the actual question set. Remember to explain, and not just state, claims and arguments.

E3. For longer answers, before you start writing, it can be worth writing out your outline or web-diagram first. This can help remind you of the key points you want to make, and the order in which you want to make them.

E4. Four rules of thumb:

    a.   Explain 'technical terms', like 'tripartite view' or 'the ontological argument', unless it is clear from the context that you know what they mean.

    b.   Keep related ideas together. If you have a thought later on, add a footnote indicating where in the answer you want it to be read.

    c.   Explain a theory before evaluating it.

    d.   Don't state the conclusion to an argument before you've discussed the argument, especially if you are going to present objections to that conclusion. You can state what the argument hopes to show, but don't state it *as* a conclusion.

E5. Keep your examples short and make sure they support the point you want to make. Always explain how they support your point.

E6. For 15-mark questions, make sure your discussion is not just reporting a sequence of points of view, but presents objections and replies, weighs up the arguments, and reaches a particular conclusion.

E7. Leave time to check your answer at the end. You may want to add a helpful sentence here and there.

GLOSSARY

(with Joanne Lovesey)

a posteriori – Knowledge of propositions that can only be known to be true or false through sense experience.

a priori – Knowledge of propositions that do not require (sense) experience to be known to be true or false.

ability knowledge – Knowing 'how' to do something, e.g. 'I know how to ride a bike'.

abstract – Theoretical (rather than applied or practical) and removed from any concrete objects or instances.

acquaintance knowledge – Knowing 'of' someone or some place, e.g. 'I know the manager of the restaurant' or 'I know Oxford well'.

actual world – The world as it is. The actual world is a possible world, specifically the one we live in.

ad hoc – A statement or a move in an argument that suits the purpose at hand but has no independent support.

analogy – Similarity in several respects between different things.

analysis – Process of breaking up a complex concept or argument in order to reveal its simpler constituents, thereby elucidating its meaning or structure.

analytic – A proposition that is true (or false) in virtue of the meanings of the words. For instance, 'A bachelor is an unmarried man' is analytically true, while 'A square has three sides' is analytically false.

antecedent – The proposition that forms the first part of a conditional statement, usually the part of the sentence that comes after 'if', e.g. in both 'If it rains then I will get wet' and 'I will get wet if it rains', the antecedent is 'it rains'.

argument – A reasoned inference from one set of claims – the premises – to another claim, the conclusion.

argument map – Visual diagram of how the premises of an argument relate to one another and to the conclusion.

assertion – The claim that a proposition is true.

assumption – A proposition accepted without proof or evidence as the basis for an inference or argument.

atemporal – Not existing in time or subject to the passing of time.

begging the question – The informal fallacy of (explicitly or implicitly) assuming the truth of the conclusion of an argument as one of the premises employed in an effort to demonstrate its truth.

belief – Affirmation of, or conviction regarding, the truth of a proposition, e.g. 'I believe that the grass is green'.

blik – An attitude to or view of the world that is not held or withdrawn on the basis of empirical experience.

Cartesian circle – Refers to the circular reasoning Descartes seems to employ regarding clear and distinct ideas and God: Descartes cannot rely on clear and distinct ideas before proving God exists, but he cannot prove that God exists without relying on clear and distinct ideas.

causal principle – The claim that everything has a cause.

circular – An argument is circular if it employs its own conclusion as a premise.

clear and distinct idea – A clear idea is 'present and accessible to the attentive mind'; a distinct idea is clear and also sharply separated from other ideas so that every part of it is clear.

closure, principle of – If I know that the premises are true, and I validly deduce the conclusion from the premises, then I know the conclusion.

***cogito*, the** – Refers to Descartes' first certain knowledge, 'I think'.

cognitive – Language or thought that can be true or false and aims to express how things are.

cognitivism – A cognitivist account of religious language argues that religious claims aim to describe how the world is, and so can be true or false. They express beliefs that such-and-such is the case. To believe that God exists is to believe that 'God exists' is true.

coherent – A set of statements are coherent if they are consistent and increase each other's probability.

common sense – The basic perceptions or understandings that are shared by many (most) people.

compatible – Two properties are compatible if it is possible for something to have both of them at once. Two claims are compatible if they are consistent.

composition, fallacy of – The informal fallacy of attributing some feature of the members of a collection to the collection itself, or reasoning from part to whole, e.g. sodium and chloride are both dangerous to humans, therefore sodium chloride (salt) is dangerous to humans.

concept – Any abstract notion or idea by virtue of which we apply general terms to things.

conclusion – A proposition whose truth has been inferred from premises.

conditional – A proposition that takes the form of 'if …, then …'. The conditional asserts that if the first statement (the antecedent) is true, then the second statement (the consequent) is also true, e.g. 'If it is raining then the ground is wet' asserts that if it is true that it is raining, it is true that the ground is wet.

consequent – The proposition that forms the second part of a conditional statement, usually the part of the sentence that occurs after 'then', e.g. in both 'If it will rain then I will get wet' and 'I will get wet if it will rain', the consequent is 'I will get wet'.

consistent – Two or more statements are consistent if they can both be true at the same time.

constant conjunction – Two things always happening together, or one after the other.

contingent – A proposition that could be either true or false, a state of affairs that may or may not hold, depending on how the world actually is.

contradiction – Two claims that cannot both be true, and cannot both be false; or one claim that both asserts and denies something, e.g. 'It is raining and it is not raining'.

copy principle, Humean – All simple ideas are copies of impressions.

cosmological argument – An argument for God's existence that claims that unless God exists, the question 'why does anything exist?' is unanswerable. Arguments from causation claim that everything must have a cause, and causal chains cannot be infinite, so there must be a first cause. Arguments from contingency claim that every contingent thing must have an explanation for its existence, and this can ultimately only be provided by something that exists necessarily.

counter-argument – An argument that attempts to establish a conclusion that undermines another argument or the conclusion of another argument.

counterexamples, method of finding – If a theory makes a general claim, such as 'All propositional knowledge is justified true belief', we only need to find a single instance in which this is false (a counterexample) to show that the general claim is false and so something is wrong with the theory.

counter-intuitive – Something that doesn't fit with our intuition.

declarative sentence – A sentence used to convey information or make a statement. To test if something is a declarative sentence, check if it is still grammatically correct if you put it after 'It is the case that ...', e.g. 'It is the case that the grass is green'.

deductive (deduction) – An argument whose conclusion is logically entailed by its premises, i.e. if the premises are true, the conclusion cannot be false.

defence, free will – An attempt to show that there is no inconsistency between the existence of evil and the existence of God, because it is possible that God would allow evils that arise from free will in order that we (or other beings) can have free will.

definition – An explanation of the meaning of a word. Philosophical definitions often attempt to give necessary and sufficient conditions for the application of the term being defined.

design, argument from – There is complexity in the world that is evidence of design, and design requires a designer. This is God. The evidence of design that is appealed to is usually the organisation of parts for a purpose or temporal regularities expressed by the laws of nature.

dilemma – Two mutually exclusive and exhaustive options (horns), both of which face significant objections.

direct realism – Physical objects exist independently of our minds and of our perceptions of them and the immediate objects of perception are mind-independent objects and their properties.

disanalogy – A point of dissimilarity between two things, something that two things don't have in common.

disjunction – An either/or claim, e.g. 'Either it will rain or it will be sunny'.

disjunctive theory of perception – If something looks a certain way, then one of two quite different things is going on: either I directly perceive a mind-independent physical object that is *F* or it appears to me just as if there is something that is *F*, but there is nothing that is *F*.

distinction – A difference or contrast between things.

empirical – Relating to or deriving from experience, especially sense experience, but also including experimental scientific investigation.

empiricism (aka 'knowledge empiricism') – The theory that there can be no a priori knowledge of synthetic propositions about the world (outside my mind), i.e. all a priori knowledge is of analytic propositions, while all knowledge of synthetic propositions must be checked against sense experience.

empiricism, concept – All concepts are derived from experience. There are no innate concepts.

enumerative induction – The method of reasoning that argues from many instances of something to a general statement about that thing, e.g. 'The sun has risen in the morning every day for *x* number of days, therefore the sun rises in the morning'.

epistemology – The study (*-ology*) of knowledge (*episteme*) and related concepts, including belief, justification and certainty. It looks at the possibility and sources of knowledge.

equivocation, fallacy of – The use of an ambiguous word or phrase in different senses within a single argument, e.g. 'All banks are next to rivers, I deposit money in a bank, therefore I deposit money next to a river'.

eschatological – The study (*-ology*) of the 'last things' (Greek *eskhatos*) – death, the final judgement, and the ultimate destiny of human beings.

eternal – Timeless (atemporal).

Euthyphro dilemma – Does God will what is morally good because it is good, or is it good because God wills it? If the former, God is not omnipotent, if the latter, morality is arbitrary.

everlasting – Existing throughout all time, without beginning or end.

evil, moral – Bad things that arise as the result of the actions of free agents, e.g. murder.

evil, natural – Bad things, especially pain and suffering, that arise as the result of natural processes, e.g. people dying in earthquakes.

explanation – An intelligible account, e.g. of why something happens. The thing to be explained (*explanandum*) is usually accepted as a fact, and what is used to explain it (the *explanans*) is usually plausible but less certain.

external world – Everything that exists outside of our minds.

fallacy/fallacious – An error in reasoning. More exactly, a fallacy is an argument in which the premises do not offer rational support to the conclusion. If the argument is deductive, then it is fallacious if it is not valid. If the argument is inductive, it is fallacious if the premises do not make the conclusion more likely to be true.

falsifiable – A claim is falsifiable if it is logically incompatible with some (set of) empirical observations.

falsification principle – A claim is meaningful only if it is falsifiable, i.e. it rules out some possible experience.

form of life – The foundation out of which language games grow, the collection of cultural practices which embed language games.

free will – The capacity of rational agents to choose a course of action from among various alternatives.

Gettier case – A situation in which we have justified true belief, but not knowledge, because the belief is only accidentally true given the evidence that justifies it.

grammar, depth – The way a sentence functions in its use within a specific language, and which determines its meaning.

grammar, surface – The grammatical structure of a sentence as it appears, given by its grammatical parts (nouns, verbs, etc.).

hallucination – A non-veridical perceptual experience that is not coherently connected with the rest of our perceptual experience.

hallucination, argument from – Against direct realism: the possibility of hallucinations that are subjectively indistinguishable from a veridical perception means that we don't immediately perceive physical objects, but sense-data.

Hume's 'fork' – We can have knowledge of just two sorts of claim: the relations between ideas and matters of fact.

hypothesis – A proposal that needs to be confirmed or rejected by reasoning or experience.

hypothetical reasoning – Working out the best hypothesis that would explain or account for some experience or fact.

idea – An object of perception, thought or understanding. Locke uses the term to refer to a complete thought, taking the form of a proposition, e.g. 'Bananas are yellow'; a sensation or sensory experience, e.g. a visual sensation of yellow; or a concept, e.g. 'yellow'.

idea, complex – An idea that is derived from two or more simple ideas.

idea, simple – A single, uniform conception or sensory experience, with nothing distinguishable within it.

idealism, Berkeley's – All that exists are minds and ideas. What we think of as physical objects are, in fact, bundles of ideas. The immediate objects of perception (ordinary objects such as tables, chairs, etc.) are ideas, mind-dependent objects. *Esse est percipi (aut percipere)* – to be is to be perceived (or to perceive).

identical, numerically – One and the same thing. Everything is numerically identical to itself, and nothing else.

identical, qualitatively – Two or more things are qualitatively identical if they share their properties in common, e.g. two separate copies of the same picture.

illusion – A distortion of sense experience that means what we perceive is different from what exists.

illusion, argument from – Against direct realism: illusions can be 'subjectively indistinguishable' from veridical perception (e.g. a crooked stick in water), so we see sense-data, and not physical objects, immediately.

illusion, Cartesian argument from – Throws doubt on always believing what our senses tell us. His argument from dreaming throws doubt on all sense perception, and therefore, on whether physical objects exist. His argument from the evil demon makes these doubts more vivid.

immanent – God exists throughout everything that exists.

immutable – Not subject to change.

impossibility, logical – Self-contradictory, e.g. a round square.

impossibility, physical – Goes against the laws of nature, e.g. it is physically impossible for humans to fly unaided.

impression – Experiences that we are immediately and directly aware of, which can either be impressions of 'sensation' or impressions of 'reflection'. Impressions of sensation derive from our senses; impressions of reflection derive from our experience of our mind, including emotions.

inconceivable – Impossible to imagine, think, or grasp.

inconsistent – Two statements are inconsistent if they can't both be true at the same time.

indirect realism – We perceive physical objects, which exist independently of the mind, indirectly via sense-data which are caused by and represent physical objects.

inductive (induction) – An argument whose conclusion is supported by its premises, but is not logically entailed by them, i.e. if the premises are true, the conclusion may be false, but this is unlikely (relative to the premises).

infallibilism – To be knowledge, a belief must be certain. If we can doubt a belief, then it is not certain, and so it is not knowledge.

inference – Accepting a proposition as true on the basis of reasoning from other propositions taken to be true.

inference to the best explanation – An inductive argument form where the conclusion presents the 'best explanation' for why the premises are true.

infinite – Without any bounds or limits, e.g. the natural numbers form an infinite series, the numbers continue in both directions (positive and negative numbers) without any end point.

innate – Knowledge or ideas that are in some way present 'from birth'.

innatism, concept – The claim that some of our concepts are innate, not derived from experience, but somehow part of the structure of the mind.

innatism, knowledge – The claim that there is at least some innate knowledge, not derived from experience but somehow part of the structure of the mind.

intuition – Direct non-inferential awareness of abstract objects or truths.

intuition, rational – The capacity to discover the truth of a claim just by thinking about it using reason.

invalid – Not valid. A deductive argument is invalid if it is possible for the premises to be true while the conclusion is false.

justification – What is offered as grounds for believing an assertion.

Kalam argument – A form of cosmological argument that claims that everything that begins to exist has a cause, and the universe began to exist, so there is a cause of the universe.

language game – A linguistic practice, constituted by certain 'rules' that determine the meaning of the words used. A speaking part of a 'form of life'. Wittgenstein's examples include asking, thanking, cursing, praying.

law of nature – Fixed regularities that govern the universe; statements that express these regularities.

logical positivism – Twentieth-century philosophical movement that used the verification principle to determine meaningfulness.

matters of fact – States of affairs, how the world is. According to Hume, they are known through experience and induction, especially causal inference.

maximal excellence – An entity possesses maximal excellence if and only if it is omnipotent, omniscient, and supremely good.

maximal greatness – An entity possesses maximal greatness if and only if nothing can be greater than it. Plantinga specifies maximal greatness as maximal excellence in every possible world – that is, an entity is maximally great if and only if it is necessarily existent and necessarily maximally excellent.

meaningful – Having a linguistic meaning.

metaphysics – The branch of philosophy that asks questions about the fundamental nature of reality. *Meta-* means above, beyond, or after; *physics* enquires into the physical structure of reality.

mind-dependent – Depending on a mind for existence or definition, e.g. ideas are mind-dependent.

mind-independent – Not depending on a mind for existence or definition. According to realism, physical objects are mind-independent.

Molyneux's question – Concerns the coordination of information from different senses. Molyneux asked Locke (in a letter) whether a man who has been born blind and who has learnt to distinguish and name a globe and a cube by touch, would be able to distinguish and name these objects simply by sight, once he had been enabled to see.

monotheism – The view that there is only one God.

motion, argument from – A form of cosmological argument that states that there are things in motion, and everything in motion needs to be put into motion, therefore there must have been a first mover.

multiverse theory – The claim that there are or have been (many) other universes. It can be used as an objection to the argument from design, to argue that the chance that some universe with laws that enabled order is high. So we shouldn't infer that there is a designer.

necessary – A proposition that must be true (or if false, it must be false); a state of affairs that must hold.

necessary condition – One proposition is a necessary condition of another when the second cannot be true while the first is false, e.g. being a man is a necessary condition of being a bachelor, because if you are not a man you cannot be a bachelor.

no false lemmas – The 'no false lemmas' condition is sometimes added to the tripartite theory of knowledge and says that for something to count as knowledge it must be the case that you did not infer it from anything false. (A lemma is a claim part way through an argument.)

non-cognitive – Language or thought that cannot be true or false and does not aim to express how things are.

non-cognitivism – The view that religious claims do not try to describe the world and cannot be true or false. Rather, they express an attitude toward the world, a way of understanding or relating to the world.

non-natural – Existing outside of, or not produced by, nature.

normative – Relating to 'norms', rules or reasons.

objection – Something that is given as a reason against either an argument or conclusion.

objective – Independent of what people think or feel. A claim is objectively true if its truth does not depend on people's beliefs.

Ockham's razor – The principle that states that we should not put forward a hypothesis that says many different things exist when a simpler explanation will do as well. 'Do not multiply entities beyond necessity'. A simpler explanation is a better explanation, as long as it is just as successful.

omnipotent – Having perfect power. Often defined as having the ability to do anything it is possible to do.

omnipresent – Being present everywhere at the same time.

omniscient – Having perfect knowledge. Often defined as knowing everything that it is possible to know.

ontological argument – Ontological arguments claim that we can deduce the existence of God from the concept of God. The word 'ontological' comes from ontology.

ontology – The study of (-*ology*) of what exists or 'being' (*ont-*).

pantheism – The view that God and the universe are the same thing.

paradigm – A system or frame of reference which contains the background assumptions we make when looking at new evidence.

paradigm shift, Kuhnian – Changes in the concepts, assumptions and methods that we use to understand and explain reality, e.g. the shift from Newtonian to Einsteinian physics.

paradox of the stone – Can God create a stone that he can't lift? If the answer is 'no', then God cannot create the stone. If the answer is 'yes', then God cannot lift the stone. So either way, it seems, there is something God cannot do. If there is something God can't do, then God isn't omnipotent.

perception – Awareness of apparently external objects through use of the senses.

perception, immediate objects of – What we are directly aware of in perception, which may be physical objects or sensations of these.

perceptual variation, argument from – Against direct realism: different people perceive the same physical object differently. Therefore, what each person perceives is how the object appears to them. This appearance is mind-dependent sense-data. Physical objects are therefore not perceived directly.

physical object – Material objects, including things like tables, books, our own bodies, plants, mountains.

plausible – Fits with what else we already know.

possible – Capable of happening/existing/being the case. If a claim is possible, it could be true.

possible world – A way of talking about how things could be. Necessary truths (falsehoods) are true (false) in all possible worlds, whereas contingent truths are true in some possible worlds and false in others. Saying that something is possible (impossible) is saying that it is true in some (no) possible world.

predicate – The part of a sentence or clause containing a verb or adjective and stating something about the subject, e.g. in 'Jane is happy' the predicate is 'is happy'.

premise – A proposition that, as part of an argument, provides or contributes to a reason to believe that the conclusion is true.

preservation of truth – Valid arguments preserve truth, meaning that when the premises are true, anything that logically follows from them will also be true.

primary quality – Properties that are 'utterly inseparable' from the object, whatever changes it goes through, even if it is divided into smaller and smaller pieces. The object has these properties 'in and of itself'. Locke lists extension (he also talks of size), shape, motion, number and solidity as primary qualities.

problem of evil – The existence of evil either rules out or is evidence against the existence of an omnipotent, omniscient, supremely good being.

property – An attribute or characteristic of an object, e.g. the property of being green, or being tall.

property, relational – A characteristic that something has only in relation to another thing, e.g. 'being taller than Bob', or 'being in love with Jack'.

proposition – A declarative statement (or more accurately, what is claimed by a declarative statement), e.g. 'Mice are mammals'. Propositions can go after 'that' in 'I believe that ...' and 'I know that ...'.

propositional knowledge – Knowing 'that' some claim – a proposition – is true or false, e.g. 'I know that Paris is the capital of France'.

prove – To demonstrate that a proposition is true by giving a sound deductive argument with that proposition as the conclusion.

rationalism – The theory that there can be a priori knowledge of synthetic propositions about the world (outside my mind). This knowledge is innate or gained by reason rather than derived from sense experience.

reason – A statement presented in justification for a claim. A good reason in some way raises the probability that the claim is true.

reasoning – The process of thinking about something in a logical way – in particular, drawing inferences on the basis of reasons.

reductio ad absurdum – A form of argument that shows that some claim leads to a contradiction.

reflection – Locke: our experience of 'the internal operations of our minds', gained through introspection or an awareness of what the mind is doing. More generally, thinking.

relations of ideas – Hume: relations of ideas are established by pure thought or reflection and are 'intuitively and demonstratively certain'. The negation of a relation of ideas is a contradiction.

reliabilism – Reliabilism claims that you know that p if p is true, you believe that p, and your belief is caused by a reliable cognitive process. (More sophisticated versions also claim that for something to count as knowledge you must also be able to discriminate between 'relevant possibilities' in the actual situation.)

represent – A relation of one thing (e.g. sense-data) to another (e.g. physical objects) established by an accurate and systematic correlation of the first to the second.

resemblance – A relation of similarity (in properties or appearance) between two things, e.g. sense-data and physical objects.

sceptical – Not easily convinced, or having doubts or reservations. (Not to be confused with scepticism.)

scepticism – The view that our usual justifications for claiming our beliefs amount to knowledge are inadequate, so we do not in fact have knowledge.

scope – The extent or range over which something applies, e.g. the scope of this textbook is the AQA AS philosophy syllabus.

secondary quality – Properties that physical objects have that are 'nothing but powers to produce various sensations in us'. Locke lists 'colours, sounds, tastes and so on', later adding smells and temperature.

self-evident – A proposition that can be known just by rational reflection on that proposition.

sensation – Our experience of objects outside the mind, perceived through the senses.

sense experience – Experiences given to us by our senses.

sense-data (singular **sense-datum**) – Mental images or representations of what is perceived, the 'content' of perceptual experience. If sense-data exist, they are the immediate objects of perception and are 'private', mind-dependent mental things.

senses – Capacities that give us experience of the external world. They include sight, hearing, smell, taste, touch and bodily awareness.

sensible quality – A property that can be detected by the senses.

signposts – Sentences that indicate what the text is about, what has been, is being, or will be argued, e.g. 'I will now argue that …'.

simultaneous – At the same time.

solipsism – The view that only oneself, one's mind, exists. There are no mind-independent physical objects and there are no other minds either.

sophism – The use of plausible arguments that are actually fallacious, especially when someone dishonestly presents such an argument as if it were legitimate reasoning.

soul – The immortal, non-material part of a person.

sound – A deductive argument is sound if it is valid with true premises.

subjective – That which depends upon the personal or individual, especially where it is supposed to be an arbitrary expression of preference.

sufficient condition – One proposition is a sufficient condition for another when the first cannot be true while the second is false. For example, being a dog is sufficient for being an animal, because something can't be a dog without also being an animal.

synthetic – A proposition that is not analytic, but true or false depending on how the world is.

systematic correlation – A relationship between two things whereby a change in one is always accompanied by a change in the other.

tabula rasa – Latin for 'blank slate'. Locke claims that at birth our mind is a *tabula rasa*, meaning we have no innate knowledge or ideas.

tautology – A statement that repeats the subject in the predicate, that 'says the same thing twice', e.g. 'Green things are green'.

theodicy – An attempt to explain how or why an omnipotent, omniscient, supremely good God would allow the (apparent) presence of evil in the world.

theodicy, soul-making – God allows evil because it is necessary for us to develop virtue.

time-lag argument – Against direct realism: because it takes time for us to perceive physical objects, we don't see them directly, e.g. as light takes 8 minutes to reach the earth from the sun, if you look at the sun you are actually seeing it as it was 8 minutes ago. Therefore, you are not perceiving the sun directly.

timeless – Not in time (atemporal).

trademark argument, Descartes' – An a priori argument, claiming that I have an idea of God and this must have originated from God himself, so God must exist.

transcendent – 'Outside' or 'beyond' the universe.

tripartite theory of knowledge – Justified, true belief is necessary and sufficient for propositional knowledge. (S knows that p if and only if S is justified in believing that p, p is true, and S believes that p.)

true – A proposition is true if things are as it states, e.g. the proposition 'The grass is green' is true if the grass is green, and otherwise it is false.

unanalysable – Not subject to analysis.

universal – A statement that applies to all/every member of a class or domain, e.g. 'All whales are mammals' and 'Every boy likes ice cream'.

unperceived objects – Objects that exist when not perceived by anyone.

unsound – A deductive argument is unsound if it is either invalid or has at least one false premise.

valid – If the premises are true, then the conclusion must be true. In this case, we say that the conclusion is entailed by the premises. Only deductive arguments can be valid.

veridical – A proposition that is true or an experience that represents the world as it actually is.

verifiable, empirically – A statement is empirically verifiable if empirical evidence would go towards establishing that the statement is true or false.

verification, eschatological – Verification of God's existence in the afterlife or at the end of time.

verification principle – All meaningful claims are either analytic or empirically verifiable.

virtue, epistemic – A skill, ability or trait of the mind or person that contributes to gaining knowledge and forming true beliefs.

INDEX BY SYLLABUS CONTENT

SUBJECT INDEX